Prentice Hall LITERATURE

PENGUIN EDITION

Unit Two
Resources

Grade Eight

PEARSON

Upper Saddle River, New Jersey
Boston, Massachusetts
Chandler, Arizona
Glenview, Illinois

BQ Tunes Credits
Keith London, Defined Mind, Inc., Executive Producer
Mike Pandolfo, Wonderful, Producer
All songs mixed and mastered by Mike Pandolfo, Wonderful
Vlad Gutkovich, Wonderful, Assistant Engineer
Recorded November 2007 – February 2008 in SoHo, New York City, at
Wonderful, 594 Broadway

ISBN–13: 978-0-13-366443-0
ISBN–10: 0-13-366443-0
7 8 9 10 11 12 V036 15 14 13 12
CC

CONTENTS

BQ Tunes

But Can We? performed by Fake Gimms

We find ourselves locked in a **stalemate**
You won't budge - can't work out a **compromise**
An **argument**, can't see eye to eye
A **viewpoint** I can't see
Let's work out a **solution**
But can we?

There's no need, no need for **violence**
Avoiding harm and **injury**
No need to bug and **irritate**
An **argument,** can't see eye to eye
A **viewpoint** I can't see
Let's work out a **solution**
But can we?

Interact, let's work it out face to face
React, speak out,
Lies only **mislead**
An **argument**, can't see eye to eye
But don't **Oppose** me
Let's **negotiate** a **solution**
But can we?

We will be **victorous** when we both win
insecurity plays on our fears

Negotiate a solution

But can we?

_____

Song Title: **But Can We?**
Artist / Performed by Fake Gimms
Vocals & Guitar: Joe Pfeiffer
Bass Guitar: Jared Duncan
Drums: Tom Morra
Lyrics by Joe Pfeiffer
Music composed by the Fake Gimms
Produced by Mike Pandolfo, Wonderful

Unit 2: Short Stories
Big Question Vocabulary—1
The Big Question: Can all conflicts be resolved?

Thematic Vocabulary

argument: *n.* a disagreement, often involving anger; other forms: *argue, arguing, argumentative*

compromise: *n.* a solution in which people agree to accept less than what they originally wanted; other forms: *compromised, compromising*

irritate: *v.* to make someone feel annoyed or impatient; other forms: *irritation, irritated, irritating*

oppose: *v.* to be against or to disagree; other forms: *opposition, opposing, opponent*

viewpoint: *n.* a person's way of thinking about a subject or issue

DIRECTIONS: *Answer the questions using the number of vocabulary words specified. You can use words more than once, but you must use all five Thematic Vocabulary words. You might use the "other forms" of the words, as shown above.*

Rosa and Ellen shared a bedroom at home. Their mother suggested that they repaint the walls, make new curtains, and rearrange the furniture. At first, the sisters were excited about the project. However, their differences of opinion soon brought a conflict.

"I hate the color pink!" Rosa stormed. "Why do we *always* have to do what *you* want?"

1. How might Ellen have responded? Use at least 2 vocabulary words in your answer.

   _____

   _____

Their older sister Paula heard them speaking angrily to each other. She tried to help.

2. What might Paula have said? Use at least 1 vocabulary word in your answer.

   _____

   _____

Paula got out a pencil and paper. She took notes as Rosa and Ellen each spoke about how she would like their room to look. Then, she made a suggestion.

3. What did she suggest? Use at least 2 vocabulary words in your answer.

   _____

   _____

Rosa wasn't totally satisfied, but at least Ellen had listened to some of her ideas.

4. How did the girls resolve their conflict? Use at least 1 vocabulary word in your answer.

   _____

   _____

Name _____ Date _____

Unit 2: Short Stories
Big Question Vocabulary—2

The Big Question: Can all conflicts be resolved?

Thematic Vocabulary

injury: *n.* damage caused by an accident or attack; other forms: *injured, injuring, injuries*

insecurity: *n.* the feeling of being unconfident or unsafe; other forms: *insecure, insecurities*

interact: *v.* to talk or work together; other forms: *interaction, interacting, interacted*

mislead: *v.* to lead in the wrong direction or give false information; other forms: *misled, misleading*

solution: *n.* a way of solving a problem or dealing with a difficult situation; other form: *solve*

A. DIRECTIONS: *On each line, write the Thematic Vocabulary word that best completes the sentence.*

1. Jane's _____ and nervousness before the play caused her to forget her lines.

2. Will the suspect tell the truth, or will he attempt to _____ the detective?

3. The football player had to leave the game due to an unfortunate _____.

4. At the press conference, the president will _____ with members of the news media.

5. A fair compromise is often the best _____ to a conflict.

B. DIRECTIONS: *Write the Thematic Vocabulary word that best completes each group of related words.*

1. communicate, cooperate, _____

2. pain, wound, _____

3. anxiousness, uncertainty, _____

4. answer, resolution, _____

5. deceive, trick, _____

Unit 2: Short Stories
Big Question Vocabulary—3

The Big Question: Can all conflicts be resolved?

Thematic Vocabulary

negotiate: *v.* to discuss, with the goal of settling a conflict; other form: *negotiation*

reaction: *n.* a response to a statement, event, or situation; other forms: *react, reacting*

stalemate: *n.* a standstill in a conflict, in which neither side can get an advantage

victorious: *adj.* triumphant; on the winning side; other forms: *victor, victory*

violence: *n.* behavior that is intended to cause someone physical harm; other form: *violent*

A. DIRECTIONS: *Respond to each item.*

1. Why is *violence* a poor way to try to solve a conflict? _____

_____

2. What would you do if you reached a *stalemate* while trying to solve a disagreement?

_____

3. Give an example of a situation in which someone might feel *victorious*. _____

_____

4. What skills are important for someone to have in order to *negotiate* successfully?

_____

5. Someone disagrees with you. Give an example of a constructive *reaction* you might express.

_____

B. DIRECTIONS: *Imagine that you are a police officer. On your way home, you see two young boys having a fist fight. You try to help them solve their conflict peacefully. Write a dialogue that takes place between you and the two boys. Use all five Thematic Vocabulary words.*

_____

_____

_____

_____

Name _____ Date _____

Unit 2: Short Stories
Applying the Big Question

Can all conflicts be resolved?

DIRECTIONS: *Complete the chart below to apply what you have learned about how and if conflicts are resolved. One row has been completed for you.*

Example	Type of Conflict	Opposing forces	Aids/ obstacles to resolution	Outcome	What I learned
From Literature	Charlie's struggle to be normal in "Flowers for Algernon"	Mental disability vs. science	Aid: surgery increases intelligence Obstacle: limits of science and technology	Charlie is still mentally disabled.	Some conflicts cannot be resolved.
From Literature					
From Science					
From Social Studies					
From Real Life					

Name _____

Unit 2: Short Stories Skills Concept Map—1

Can all conflicts be resolved?

Words you can use to discuss the Big Question

Literary Analysis:
Short Story

A Short Story → has → a setting → and → characters

(demonstrated in this selection)
Selection name:

(demonstrated in this selection)
Selection name:

Basic Elements of Short Stories
• Characters
• Setting
• Plot
• Theme
• Conflict

Literary Devices
• Foreshadowing
• Flashback
• Irony
• Point of View

Reading Skills and Strategies:
Compare and Contrast

You can compare and contrast characters → by → asking questions → and by → identifying each character's perspective

(demonstrated in this selection)
Selection name:

Informational Text:
Summary

Look for **similarities** and **differences** → to → compare a summary to an original text

Comparing Literary Works:
A Character

can be described as → static or dynamic

(demonstrated in these selections)
Selection names:
1.
2.

Student Log

Complete this chart to track your assignments.

Writing	Extend Your Learning	Writing Workshop	Other Assignments

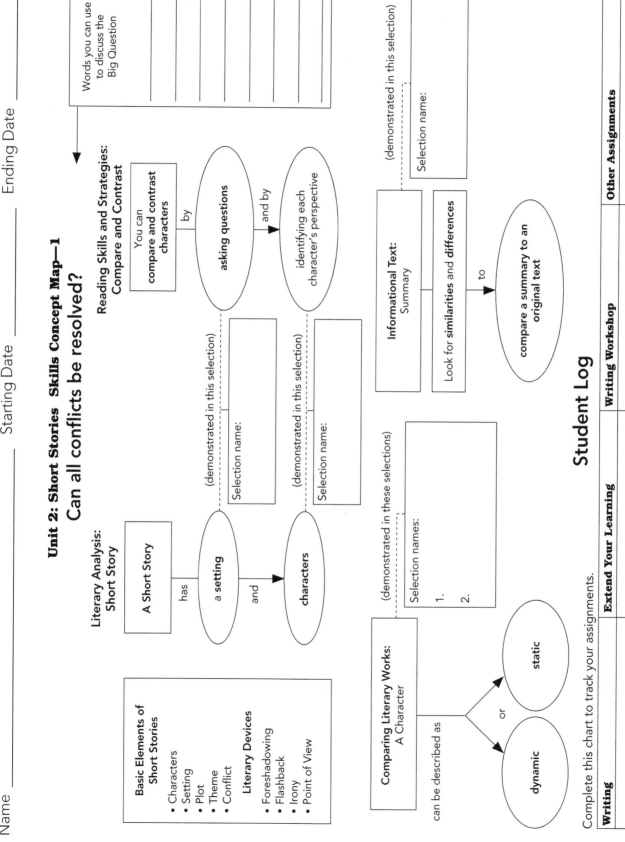

Vocabulary Warm-up Word Lists

Study these words from "An Hour With Abuelo." Then, apply your knowledge to the activities that follow.

Word List A

adults [uh DULTS] *n.* grown-ups
   Many <u>adults</u> still know the words of their favorite childhood songs.

dictionary [DIK shuh ner ee] *n.* book listing words alphabetically with their meanings
   I use the <u>dictionary</u> most often to see how to pronounce a word.

drafted [DRAF tid] *v.* selected for military service
   Once <u>drafted</u>, a person will join a branch of the armed services, such as the Marine Corps.

graduated [GRAJ oo ay tid] *v.* finished school and received a diploma
   My mother <u>graduated</u> from college with high honors.

ignorant [IG nur uhnt] *adj.* having a lack of knowledge and education
   Thanks to my economics class, I am no longer <u>ignorant</u> about the stock market.

obvious [AHB vee uhs] *adj.* easy to see and understand
   Her desire to get ahead was very <u>obvious</u> to me.

poetry [POH i tree] *n.* art of writing poems
   The book of <u>poetry</u> included two funny rhymes by Edward Lear.

wheelchairs [HWEEL chayrs] *n.* chairs mounted on wheels, used by people who can't walk
   At the Special Olympics, I saw amazing <u>wheelchairs</u> built for speed.

Word List B

ammonia [uh MOHN yuh] *n.* mixture of nitrogen and hydrogen with a very strong smell
   I was disgusted by the smell of <u>ammonia</u> in the dining area.

grandchildren [GRAND chil druhn] *n.* children of one's son or daughter
   I wonder what new inventions my <u>grandchildren</u> will see during their lives.

labor [LAY ber] *n.* hard work
   Building a bridge requires the <u>labor</u> of thousands.

material [muh TEER ee uhl] *n.* what something is made of or used for
   Our classroom <u>material</u> for social studies includes books, CD-ROMs, and posters.

maturity [muh CHOOR uh tee] *n.* state of being fully grown or developed
   True <u>maturity</u> comes only with both age and experience.

parchment [PARCH muhnt] *n.* animal skin used for writing on; paper resembling it
   Ancient stories were recorded on <u>parchment</u> and on clay tablets.

principal [PRIN suh puhl] *n.* head of a school
   Our new <u>principal</u> gave us a much stricter dress code.

suite [SWEET] *n.* group of rooms that are connected
   The wealthy woman rented a hotel <u>suite</u> bigger than my apartment.

"An Hour With Abuelo" by Judith Ortiz Cofer
Vocabulary Warm-up Exercises

Exercise A *Fill in the blanks using each word from Word List A only once.*

Don't you just love it when [1] _____ have to look up a word in the
[2] _____? After all, lots of grown-ups seem to think we kids are
[3] _____. They act so smart, explaining things like why people used
to get [4] _____ for the war. Don't they know we will have learned all
of this stuff by the time we have [5] _____ from high school? I'd rather
talk about today's issues, such as why all buildings should have ramps for
[6] _____. Or why can't we discuss [7] _____, movies, and
music? It's [8] _____ to me that parents could learn a lot from their children if they'd just listen more and talk less.

Exercise B *Answer the questions with complete explanations.*

1. Would you call pouting an act of <u>maturity</u>?

_____

2. Would a low-cost motel just off the freeway be likely to offer a <u>suite</u>?

_____

3. Would animal lovers who don't believe in eating meat be likely to write on real
<u>parchment</u>?

_____

4. Why should you open windows or use fans when cleaning with <u>ammonia</u>?

_____

5. Are your <u>grandchildren</u> likely to be amazed by space travel?

_____

6. What character traits do you think a <u>principal</u> should have?

_____

7. Why do people say, "<u>Labor</u> isn't hard if you love what you do"?

_____

8. What is your favorite kind of reading <u>material</u>?

_____

"An Hour With Abuelo" by Judith Ortiz Cofer
Reading Warm-up A

Read the following passage. Pay special attention to the underlined words. Then, read it again, and complete the activities. Use a separate sheet of paper for your written answers.

The Spanish-American War ended in 1898. That's when the island of Puerto Rico became a United States territory. In 1899, the United States Army formed the first battalion of Puerto Ricans. As the <u>dictionary</u> defines it, a *battalion* is "a large group of soldiers." These Puerto Rican soldiers worked to defend their island home.

In 1917, Puerto Ricans were given American citizenship. With this right, <u>adults</u> could vote in United States elections. Also, Puerto Rican men could be <u>drafted</u> for service in World War I. No longer protecting just their island, 18,000 Puerto Ricans served in this war. Many helped guard the Panama Canal against an enemy attack.

During World War II, 65,000 Puerto Ricans served in the military. More than one-third of them signed up as volunteers. However, it was during the Korean War that Puerto Rican military service became most <u>obvious</u>. In this conflict, 756 Puerto Ricans lost their lives—one out of every forty-two U.S. military persons killed came from the tiny island. One Puerto Rican soldier, Fernando Luis Garcia, received the Congressional Medal of Honor during the Korean War after he died in a heroic effort that allowed his fellow soldiers to live.

The proud military traditions of Puerto Ricans have continued. Island soldiers have served in every major conflict since the Korean War. Artworks, music, and <u>poetry</u> celebrate the soldiers' heroism. Throughout the island country, young people who have recently <u>graduated</u> from high school join elderly war veterans, some in <u>wheelchairs</u>, at coffee shops and other local places. They discuss courage, loyalty, and determination in the defense of democratic ideas. Puerto Rico does not want its children to grow up <u>ignorant</u>, or unaware, of the sacrifices that have been made. Truly, there have been many. As one army general has stated: "Puerto Rico has done for this nation more than its share."

1. Circle the verb that tells what a <u>dictionary</u> does. Explain why the writer used a *dictionary* while researching this piece.

2. Underline the words naming two things Puerto Rican <u>adults</u> could do after gaining citizenship. Then, explain if voting and being <u>drafted</u> were optional.

3. Circle the name of the war in which Puerto Rican military service became most <u>obvious</u>. Then, explain what *obvious* means.

4. Circle two other forms of expression in addition to <u>poetry</u>. Explain why *poetry* is often written to praise something.

5. How old is someone who has recently <u>graduated</u> from high school? How old might a veteran of the Korean War (1950–1953) be? Write a sentence explaining why these two groups of people might enjoy each other.

6. Circle the words that tell who might use <u>wheelchairs</u>. Explain why.

7. Circle the synonym for <u>ignorant</u>. Explain how Puerto Ricans can prevent their children from growing up *ignorant*.

"An Hour With Abuelo" by Judith Ortiz Cofer
Reading Warm-up B

Read the following passage. Pay special attention to the underlined words. Then, read it again, and complete the activities. Use a separate sheet of paper for your written answers.

When Lily decided to volunteer at Mountain View Retirement Home, she was actually making a selfish decision. Her high-school underline{principal} was always saying that colleges would look kindly on the applications of students who had been volunteers. Since Lily's application was lacking in certain key areas, she figured any volunteer efforts could help her out.

Lily's first three Saturdays at the home were spent doing hard physical underline{labor}. She cleaned windows, weeded gardens, and scrubbed floors. When she nearly fainted from the underline{ammonia} in the mop water, the director said she could begin assisting with the residents instead.

Lily showed up on the fourth Saturday ready to read to the residents. She soon found that the home had no decent reading underline{material}, however. The magazines were ancient, and the books were missing pages. So, Lily decided to entertain the residents by playing the piano. Sadly, most of them seemed to nod off or had trouble getting their hearing aids to stop squealing. After five or six songs, Lily sighed and got up from the piano bench.

On the fifth Saturday, Lily decided to organize an art class for the residents and visiting underline{grandchildren}. With her allowance, she bought beautiful underline{parchment}, wide brushes, and little pots of paint. She thought people could learn how to create Chinese symbols for words like *happiness* to display on their walls. But no one wanted to attempt it, not that day or the sixth Saturday, either.

On the seventh and eighth Saturdays, Lily slept in instead of going to the home. The next Monday, she was called to the underline{suite} of guidance offices at school. Imagine her surprise upon seeing the director of the home. He held a thick envelope, which he presented to her. Inside, Lily found letters written on the fancy paper she had bought. Each one requested that she please visit again. With a new underline{maturity}, Lily made an unselfish promise to show up next Saturday.

1. Explain why Lily's underline{principal} would know about college applications.

2. Underline the words that name the exact type of underline{labor} Lily did at the home. Describe the hardest *labor* you have ever done.

3. Explain why Lily nearly fainted while mopping with underline{ammonia}.

4. Circle two types of reading underline{material} Lily found at the home. Explain what you think is good reading *material*.

5. Circle the words that tell who the underline{grandchildren} were visiting. Why would Lily expect to see them at the home?

6. Circle words that suggest underline{parchment} is a kind of paper. Explain why Lily would choose *parchment* instead of regular paper.

7. Explain what the underline{suite} of guidance offices might look like.

8. Circle a word in the same sentence that might indicate a person's underline{maturity}. Then, describe how a high-school student might act with *maturity*.

Judith Ortiz Cofer
Listening and Viewing

Segment 1: Meet Judith Ortiz Cofer
- As a young child, what did Judith Ortiz Cofer learn about the power of storytelling? In what ways do you see stories as being powerful?

_____

_____

_____

_____

Segment 2: The Short Story
- What truth is revealed in a humorous manner in Judith Ortiz Cofer's short story? What do the themes she discusses in the story reveal about the importance of our elders?

_____

_____

_____

_____

Segment 3: The Writing Process
- What is Judith Ortiz Cofer's writing routine? Why do you think it is important for a writer to establish a routine?

_____

_____

_____

_____

Segment 4: The Rewards of Writing
- What is the goal of Judith Ortiz Cofer's writing? What have you learned about yourself from reading literature?

_____

_____

_____

_____

Learning About Short Stories

A **short story** is a brief work of fiction that contains many of these elements:

Conflict: a struggle between opposing forces In an **external conflict,** a character struggles against an outside force. An **internal conflict** takes place in the mind of a character.
Plot: the sequence of events in the story **Exposition** introduces the characters and setting. The **rising action** introduces the conflict and increases its intensity. The **climax** is the turning point of a story. The **falling action** is the part of the story when the conflict lessens in intensity. The **resolution** is the story's conclusion.
Setting: the time and place of the action in a story **Mood** is the emotional atmosphere that the setting sometimes conveys.
Characters: the people or other beings in a story **Character traits** are a character's qualities and attitudes. **Characterization** is the way the author reveals a character's traits. The author may state traits **directly** ("Ross is strong") or reveal traits **indirectly** by showing what the character says, thinks, and does.
Theme: the central message expressed in a story A theme may be **directly stated** by the author or **implied,** suggested indirectly through what happens to the characters.
Point of View: the perspective from which a story is told **First-person point of view:** a character in the story tells the story. **Third-person point of view:** a narrator outside the story tells the story.
Literary Devices: tools that writers use to enhance their writing **Foreshadowing** uses clues early in the story to hint at future events. A **flashback** interrupts the story to reveal past events. **Irony** is a contradiction between appearance and reality, between expectation and outcome, or between meaning and intention.

A. DIRECTIONS: *For each story detail, circle the letter of the term that best identifies it.*

1. Tom struggles to reach a decision.
   A. external conflict   B. internal conflict   C. mood
2. "Jo is a greedy girl."
   A. direct characterization   B. indirect characterization C. plot
3. A storm gets worse and worse.
   A. rising action   B. falling action   C. foreshadowing
4. "Kindness is often rewarded."
   A. irony   B. point of view   C. theme
5. "And they all lived happily after."
   A. exposition   B. climax   C. resolution

B. DIRECTIONS: *On a separate sheet of paper, briefly describe the setting, characters, conflict, and theme of a story or fairy tale that you know well.*

"An Hour with Abuelo" by Judith Ortiz Cofer
Model Selection: Short Story

Plot is the sequence of events in a story. The sequence usually unfolds in **chronological order,** the order of time. However, sometimes there is a **flashback** to an earlier time. Flashbacks can provide insight into a character's personality **traits,** or qualities, and **motivation,** the reasons behind the character's behavior.

The events of the plot usually center around one or more **conflicts,** or struggles, that the main character faces. Sometimes the conflict is **external,** pitting the character against an outside force. Sometimes the conflict is **internal,** taking place in the character's mind.

The story's conclusion is the **resolution,** in which the conflict is settled and the outcome is revealed. Sometimes the resolution is a **surprise ending** that the characters or readers do not expect. Surprise endings and other unexpected twists in the plot create **irony,** a contrast between what seems true and what turns out to be the real truth.

The perspective from which a story is told is called the **point of view.** In the **first-person point of view,** the story is told by a character in the story. In the **third-person point of view,** the story is told by a narrator outside the story. An **omniscient** narrator knows everything that each character thinks and feels. A third-person narrator also might be **limited** and only reveal the thoughts and feelings of a single character.

DIRECTIONS: *Answer these questions about "An Hour with Abuelo."*

1. What **internal conflict** does young Arturo have about visiting his grandfather?

   _____

   _____

2. Describe young Arturo's **traits** and **motivation** in life. What does he dislike about the attitude expressed in the Spanish saying *"Así es la vida,"* or "That's the way life is"?

   _____

   _____

   _____

3. In what way does Abuelo's autobiography *Así Es la Vida* serve as a **flashback**? From whose **point of view** is it told, and what does it help you understand about this character?

   _____

   _____

   _____

4. Explain the **irony** in Abuelo's behavior at the story's end. What did Arturo expect about his grandfather, and how did what he expected turn out not to be true?

   _____

   _____

   _____

"An Hour With Abuelo" by Judith Ortiz Cofer
Open-Book Test

Short Answer *Write your responses to the questions in this section on the lines provided.*

1. According to Judith Ortiz Cofer's remarks about jokes and short stories, both jokes and short stories contain an *a-ha* moment. In the short story, that moment is called an epiphany. When you are reading a short story, how can you recognize the epiphany? In other words, what is the main element of the *a-ha* moment, or the epiphany?

   _____

   _____

   _____

2. You are reading a short story in which the main character is thinking hard about a decision: Should he report a crime that involves a friend or tell the truth and probably lose the friendship? Is the character's main conflict external or internal? Explain your answer.

   _____

   _____

   _____

3. You are reading a short story, and the conflict is becoming more and more exciting, but it is not clear what will happen. Think about the five main parts in the plot of a short story. Which part are you reading, and how do you know?

   _____

   _____

   _____

4. You are reading a short story. The narrator is not one of the characters. You wish that the narrator would explain more about the characters, but the narrator does not seem to know what the characters are thinking. In what two ways should you describe the narrator's point of view? Explain your answer.

   _____

   _____

   _____

5. In "An Hour With Abuelo," Arturo does not want to go to the nursing home in Brooklyn, and he offers several excuses: He wants to prepare for an English class, he does not like the nursing home, and there are plenty of other relatives who visit his grandfather. Why might Arturo be offering so many excuses?

   _____

   _____

   _____

6. In reading from his notebook in "An Hour With Abuelo," Abuelo describes a major external conflict in his life. Describe that conflict, and explain how Abuelo responded to it.

_____

_____

_____

_____

7. In "An Hour With Abuelo," Arturo hears the expression *así es la vida* ("that's the way life is") from his mother and from his grandfather. How does Arturo feel about that expression? Cite two details from the story to support your answer.

_____

_____

_____

_____

8. Abuelo reads to Arturo from his notebook in "An Hour With Abuelo." In that way, readers learn that, as a young man, Abuelo dreamed of spending his life "around books." At the end of the story, readers learn how Abuelo keeps this dream alive in the nursing home. Use details from the story to describe how Abuelo does this.

_____

_____

9. At the end of "An Hour With Abuelo," a woman appears at the door to Abuelo's room. In describing her, what attitude does Arturo reveal? Cite details to support your answer.

_____

_____

10. When a story contains *irony*, there is a strong contrast between what the readers or the characters expect to happen and what actually happens. Explain why the end of "An Hour With Abuelo" is an example of irony. Cite at least two details from the story to support your answer.

_____

_____

_____

_____

_____

Essay

Write an extended response to the question of your choice or to the question or questions your teacher assigns you.

11. Write an essay about Arturo as he is described in "An Hour With Abuelo." Describe his thoughts and character traits at the beginning of the story. Then, describe how his thoughts and traits have changed by the end of the story.

12. In an essay, state what you think is the theme of "An Hour With Abuelo." Explain how events and details in the story point to that theme—the most important message or lesson that the story has to offer.

13. In the middle of "An Hour With Abuelo," Judith Ortiz Cofer presents Abuelo's life story. By doing so, she interrupts the flow of events and changes the point of view. In an essay, discuss why Cofer might have made this choice. Consider what the autobiography shows about Abuelo's background and values—and how that information helps convey important ideas about the story.

14. **Thinking About the Big Question: Can all conflicts be resolved?** Arturo wants to talk with his grandfather about "why he didn't keep fighting to make his dream come true," but he does not get the chance. Does Arturo think that his grandfather has an unresolved conflict? Use details from "An Hour With Abuelo" to support your answer.

Oral Response

15. Go back to question 5, 7, or 10 or to the question your teacher assigns you. Take a few minutes to expand your answer and prepare an oral response. Find additional details in "An Hour With Abuelo" that support your points. If necessary, make notes to guide your oral response.

"An Hour With Abuelo" by Judith Ortiz Cofer
Selection Test A

Learning About Short Stories *Identify the letter of the choice that best answers the question.*

____ 1. At the start of the story, what does Arturo's mother want him to do?
   A. visit his grandfather in a nursing home
   B. visit his grandfather in Puerto Rico
   C. watch his grandfather for one hour while she goes out
   D. cancel his visit to his grandfather and, instead, do his schoolwork

____ 2. How does Arturo feel about his mother's request?
   A. delighted
   B. frightened
   C. reluctant
   D. puzzled

____ 3. Which of these is a personality trait that Arturo displays when you first meet him?
   A. He is self-centered.
   B. He is generous with his time.
   C. He is very mischievous.
   D. He has no sense of humor.

____ 4. Which word best describes Arturo's attitude toward schoolwork?
   A. lazy
   B. ambitious
   C. bored
   D. confused

____ 5. From which point of view are the opening paragraphs presented?
   A. first person, narrated by Arturo
   B. first person, narrated by Arturo's mother
   C. first person, narrated by Abuelo
   D. third-person omniscient

____ 6. In what setting does most of the story take place?
   A. present-day Puerto Rico
   B. present-day Paterson, New Jersey
   C. Brooklyn about a hundred years ago
   D. present-day Brooklyn

___ 7. What special tie does Arturo have with his grandfather?
A. They were both born in the same town in Puerto Rico.
B. They both have trouble learning English.
C. Arturo is named after his grandfather.
D. Arturo is the grandfather's favorite grandchild.

___ 8. Where in the plot does the sequence of events flash back to an earlier time?
A. when Arturo's mother drops him off at the nursing home
B. when Arturo reaches Puerto Rico
C. when Abuelo reads Arturo part of his autobiography
D. when the woman in pink running shoes arrives

___ 9. Abuelo calls his story *"Así Es la Vida."* What does that mean?
A. Say "yes" to life.
B. That's the way life is.
C. Times have changed.
D. My life has been filled with hard times.

___ 10. What ambition did the grandfather have when he was a boy?
A. He wanted to leave Puerto Rico.
B. He wanted to be rich.
C. He wanted to be a famous poet.
D. He wanted to be around books all his life.

___ 11. After the war, why did Abuelo stop teaching school?
A. He wanted to please his father.
B. He preferred farming.
C. He did not have the required college degree.
D. He left Puerto Rico.

___ 12. How does Arturo's grandfather react to the woman in the pink jogging outfit?
A. He is annoyed by the interruption.
B. He perks up and speaks more strongly.
C. He does not remember who she is.
D. He teases her wickedly.

____ 13. What unexpected twist happens at the end?

   A. It turns out that the grandfather is writing poetry as well as an autobiography.

   B. The grandfather has been timing Arturo and is eager to go off and do something else.

   C. Though the grandfather seems in good physical shape, it turns out that he needs a wheelchair.

   D. Arturo decides that he would rather stay with his grandfather than go back home.

____ 14. Which of these is an external conflict in "An Hour With Abuelo"?

   A. Arturo's grandfather struggles to keep teaching and not go to war.

   B. Arturo's grandfather struggles to remember his past.

   C. Arturo struggles to make time for his grandfather.

   D. Arturo struggles to decide whether or not he will visit his grandfather.

____ 15. Which of these is a main theme of "An Hour With Abuelo"?

   A. Schoolwork is more important than family.

   B. If you work hard and "play by the rules," you can control what happens in your life.

   C. People can lead happy, fulfilling lives even if everything does not turn out as planned.

   D. If you do not exercise, you will regret it in old age.

Essay

16. Write a brief essay about the character of young Arturo in "An Hour With Abuelo." Describe his character traits and attitudes at the beginning of the story. Then, tell how he changes by the end.

17. Write a brief essay about some of the surprising twists in "An Hour With Abuelo." Explain how things often do not turn out as Arturo expects they will.

18. **Thinking About the Big Question: Can all conflicts be resolved?** Arturo wants to talk with his grandfather about "why he didn't keep fighting to make his dream come true," but he does not get the chance. Does Arturo think that his grandfather has an unresolved conflict? Explain your answer in an essay that uses details from the story.

"An Hour With Abuelo" by Judith Ortiz Cofer
Selection Test B

Learning About Short Stories *Identify the letter of the choice that best completes the statement or answers the question.*

____ 1. Which phrase best describes Arturo when you first meet him?
   A. shy and obedient
   B. kind and generous
   C. smart but lazy
   D. ambitious and self-absorbed

____ 2. Why is Arturo reluctant to visit his grandfather?
   A. He has little time and needs to use it to do the reading for a special class he hopes to take.
   B. He hates the nursing home where his grandfather is living.
   C. He feels that he really does not know his grandfather well.
   D. all of the above

____ 3. Why do you think Arturo's mother insists that he visit his grandfather?
   A. She wants him to know more of the man for whom he is named before it is too late.
   B. She wants him to help ease the burden on the rest of the family.
   C. She wants to encourage him to become a schoolteacher, like his grandfather once was.
   D. She wants him to learn writing skills from his grandfather.

____ 4. What mood or atmosphere does Arturo portray in his descriptions of the old-age home near the start of the story?
   A. a depressing mood
   B. a cheerful mood
   C. a nostalgic mood
   D. a mysterious mood

____ 5. Which of these remarks shows that Arturo has a sense of humor?
   A. "I'm going stupid in some of my classes, and Mr. Williams, the principal at Central, said that if I passed some reading tests, he'd let me move up."
   B. "I catch up on back issues of *Modern Maturity*."
   C. "It sometimes makes me mad that the adults I know just accept whatever is thrown at them because 'that's the way things are.'"
   D. "I slide into the hard vinyl chair by his bed."

____ 6. From the picture on the notebook the grandfather uses, what can you conclude about him?
   A. He is a fine artist.
   B. He is proud of his Puerto Rican heritage.
   C. He longs for the past.
   D. He does not realize he is in Brooklyn.

_____ 7. How is Abuelo's attitude toward learning different from Arturo's?
    A. Abuelo loves learning, while Arturo sees it as a means to a successful life.
    B. Abuelo has little use for book learning and prefers the "school" of experience.
    C. Abuelo believes all real learning must take place in Spanish, not English.
    D. Now that he is old and frail, Abuelo has lost the desire to learn and teach.

_____ 8. Which of these incidents is the best example of irony?
    A. A whole vanload of grandchildren visit their grandfather at Christmas.
    B. Arturo threatens to take the bus back to Paterson.
    C. When Arturo jokingly asks if Abuelo is writing his life story, it turns out that he is.
    D. Abuelo looks at his grandson as if he is trying to see into the boy's head.

_____ 9. What does Arturo dislike most about the saying, *"Así es la vida"*?
    A. He thinks it expresses a selfish attitude.
    B. He thinks it expresses an attitude that readily accepts defeat.
    C. He does not know what the saying means.
    D. He resents being forced to speak Spanish.

_____ 10. What surprises Arturo about Abuelo's condition?
    A. The grandfather is mentally very sharp.
    B. The grandfather is physically very strong.
    C. The grandfather sleeps most of the time.
    D. The grandfather needs a wheelchair.

_____ 11. What does Abuelo mean when he tells Arturo, "You have spoken the truth. *La verdad.* You have much time."
    A. You should make time to see your old grandfather.
    B. You have put in plenty of time studying; stop worrying about school.
    C. You are a young man with most of your life still ahead of you.
    D. You are boring me; I hope this visit ends soon.

_____ 12. In "An Hour With Abuelo," where is there a shift in point of view?
    A. when the mother drops Arturo off in Brooklyn
    B. when Arturo finds his grandfather's "suite"
    C. when the grandfather starts reading from his autobiography
    D. when the grandfather rolls down the hall with the woman in pink jogging clothes

_____ 13. In Cofer's "An Hour With Abuelo," which is an external conflict with society?
    A. Arturo struggles to find time for his grandfather.
    B. Arturo struggles to finish his summer reading.
    C. The grandfather struggles to farm the land.
    D. The grandfather struggles to remain a teacher.

_____ 14. From the details in the grandfather's autobiography, what can you infer about his values?
    A. He places great value on knowledge and learning.
    B. He places great value on obedience to his parents and conformity to society's wishes.
    C. He places great value on physical strength and endurance.
    D. He places great value on fame and fortune.

_____ 15. What does the sprinkling of Spanish words contribute to the story?
   A. They make the mother's and grandfather's speech seem more realistic.
   B. They add authentic local flavor to the setting.
   C. They stress the grandfather's pride in his heritage.
   D. all of the above

_____ 16. What does the incident with the woman in pink show about the grandfather's life in the nursing home?
   A. He is not respected.
   B. He hopes to be a famous poet.
   C. He is very bossy.
   D. He is still teaching.

_____ 17. What does Arturo reveal about himself with this remark?
   She is wearing a pink jogging outfit too. The world's oldest marathoner, I say to myself.
   A. He pays little attention to details.
   B. He is somewhat disrespectful toward elderly people.
   C. He has no sense of humor.
   D. He is always talking to himself.

_____ 18. What is the main irony in the resolution of "An Hour With Abuelo"?
   A. Arturo, who was in a hurry to leave his grandfather, finds that his grandfather is in a hurry to leave him.
   B. Arturo, who thinks that visiting a nursing home is depressing, finds that his grandfather is struggling with depression.
   C. Abuelo, who all his life wanted to teach and share ideas, finds that he is unable to do so in the nursing home.
   D. Abuelo, who did not want to move to the nursing home, is making the best of his life there.

Essay

19. In an essay, state what you feel is the main theme of "An Hour With Abuelo." Then, show how the details in the story point to that theme.

20. Write a brief essay in which you compare and contrast Arturo with his grandfather. Consider their character traits, their motivation, and their attitudes toward life and their own achievements.

21. In an essay, discuss Cofer's purpose in including Abuelo's autobiography in "An Hour With Abuelo." Consider how the autobiography interrupts the chronological flow of events and introduces a different point of view. Discuss what it shows about the grandfather's background, values, and motivation, and how it helps convey the story's themes.

22. **Thinking About the Big Question: Can all conflicts be resolved?** Arturo wants to talk with his grandfather about "why he didn't keep fighting to make his dream come true," but he does not get the chance. Does Arturo think that his grandfather has an unresolved conflict? Use details from "An Hour With Abuelo" to support your answer.

Vocabulary Warm-up Word Lists

Study these words from "Who Can Replace a Man?" Then, apply your knowledge to the activities.

Word List A

activity [ak TIV uh tee] *n.* situation in which a lot of things are happening
   There was no <u>activity</u> on the outdoor basketball courts because of the rain.

babble [BAB buhl] *n.* sounds that have no meaning
   The loud <u>babble</u> from my parents' party kept me awake all night.

communicate [kuh MYOO nuh kayt] *v.* to exchange ideas, feelings, or information
   Instant messaging is a quick way for friends to <u>communicate</u>.

complex [kuhm PLEKS] *adj.* having lots of parts or ideas
   Computer programming is <u>complex</u> work.

momentarily [moh muhn TER uh lee] *adv.* for a short time
   Before his last quick dash, the runner <u>momentarily</u> slowed down.

plainly [PLAYN lee] *adv.* clearly, with no mistake
   The quarterback could <u>plainly</u> see that there was nothing to do but run.

quantity [KWAHN ti tee] *n.* amount
   The school ordered a large <u>quantity</u> of popcorn for movie night.

superior [suh PEER ee ur] *adj.* greater in ability, rank, or quality
   The five-year-old's thinking was <u>superior</u> to that of most other youngsters her age.

Word List B

aimlessly [AYM luhs lee] *adv.* without a clear purpose or reason
   No one I knew was at the party, so I just moved around <u>aimlessly</u>.

berserk [ber SERK] *adj.* angry and violent; out of control
   After sentencing, the defendant went <u>berserk</u> and had to be restrained.

continuously [kuhn TIN yoo uhs lee] *adv.* without stopping
   The light bulb burned <u>continuously</u> for a month.

deduction [di DUHK shuhn] *n.* conclusion reached by using reasoning
   From the clues, Sherlock Holmes made a <u>deduction</u> that the butler committed the robbery.

distinction [dis TINGK shuhn] *n.* clear difference between things
   There is a <u>distinction</u> between a frozen, boxed meat patty and a freshly made burger.

mobile [MOH buhl] *adj.* able to move and be moved
   After breaking both legs, it was a while before he became <u>mobile</u> again.

mutual [MYOO choo uhl] *adj.* shared by two or more people
   It is to our <u>mutual</u> benefit if we work out an agreement.

routines [roo TEENZ] *n.* usual methods or ways of doing things
   Some people get upset when their daily <u>routines</u> are disturbed.

"Who Can Replace a Man?" by Brian W. Aldiss
Vocabulary Warm-up Exercises

Exercise A *Fill in the blanks using each word from Word List A only once.*

On the job, when you're puzzled by something [1] _____, it helps
to stop [2] _____ before asking a question. That way, you can
[3] _____ with a worker of [4] _____ rank in a clear, con-
cise way. If you have a large [5] _____ of questions, jot them down.
Then, you won't have to risk looking foolish and forgetful. What would people think
if they heard a strange [6] _____ coming out of you? These tips
[7] _____ apply not only to the workplace, but also to any situation
where there's a lot of [8] _____ going on and where you're expected to
learn quickly.

Exercise B *Revise each sentence so that the underlined vocabulary word from Word List B is
used in a logical way. Be sure to keep the vocabulary word in your revision.*

1. It is to our <u>mutual</u> benefit to walk away from the bargaining table.

   _____

2. The doctor made the <u>deduction</u> that her patient had gone <u>berserk</u> from happiness.

   _____

3. On weekday mornings, Martha's <u>routines</u> help her walk around <u>aimlessly</u>.

   _____

4. After George regained the use of his legs, he was happy not to be <u>mobile</u> any longer.

   _____

5. The machine runs <u>continuously</u> for twelve hours, so it stops often.

   _____

6. There is no <u>distinction</u> between apples and oranges.

   _____

"Who Can Replace a Man?" by Brian W. Aldiss
Reading Warm-up A

Read the following passage. Pay special attention to the underlined words. Then, read it again, and complete the activities. Use a separate sheet of paper for your written answers.

On the first day of school, my science-lab partner, Witherspoon, casually told me he was devising a robot that could underline communicate better than the average teenager. I asked him what a robot might have to say.

"You know, Montgomery, a robot is infinitely more complex than most people imagine. Those simple movie robots from the fifties and those one-task auto assembly robots are primitive. Fritz (his robot) is far superior."

"If you're suggesting that Fritz resembles one of those fantastic new movie robots," I shot back, "you are pulling my leg. They plainly do not exist in real life. That is something I am clear about—positive, actually."

"Where have you been?" Witherspoon asked, a quizzical expression momentarily flickering over his normally blank face. "They not only exist, but I have one, and I have loaded him with a huge quantity of words and phrases and an immense number of ways of using body language to express himself, too."

I was skeptical, so I asked Witherspoon if I could go over to his house and observe some of Fritz's activity. I was as interested in his body language as his verbal language. Witherspoon gleefully accepted.

Well, the big moment came. Witherspoon and I were alone in his basement, or so I thought. Then, from behind a large door, an enormous metallic machine lunged forward.

"Fritz," said Witherspoon, "this is Montgomery. Tell him what you have been doing all day." I waited anxiously. Instead of rattling off a list of chores or leisure pastimes, instead of even making an observation about the weather, Fritz said nothing meaningful, only babble.

Witherspoon turned red. "What's wrong?" I asked.

"I don't know," Witherspoon replied with fear in his eyes. "He has never done that before."

"Listen," I said reassuringly. "Maybe it is nothing. Maybe he is just 'on the fritz' today."

1. Circle two words that explain communicate. Write a sentence telling what it means to "*communicate* better than the average teenager."

2. Circle two words that mean the opposite of complex. Write a sentence about something that is *complex*.

3. Circle a word that suggests the opposite of superior. Explain in a sentence what it means that Fritz is *superior* to simple robots.

4. Underline the word in the next sentence that explains plainly. Write a sentence using *plainly*.

5. Explain in a sentence how the word *flickering* helps explain the meaning of *momentarily*.

6. Underline the synonym for quantity in the sentence. Then, use *quantity* in a sentence of your own.

7. Underline the phrases describing Fritz's activity. Describe the *activity* in your neighborhood.

8. Circle the phrase that suggests what babble is. Explain in a sentence why it's not good for Fritz to *babble*.

Name _____ Date _____

"**Who Can Replace a Man?**" by Brian W. Aldiss
Reading Warm-up B

Read the following passage. Pay special attention to the underlined words. Then, read it again, and complete the activities. Use a separate sheet of paper for your written answers.

A group at NASA, the United States space agency, researches, develops, and tests <u>mobile</u> robots. These are robots that roam about performing missions on Mars and the moon. Since early 2004, two rovers have been operating <u>continuously</u> on Mars, and they don't show signs of stopping.

Old-time movie robots might have wandered a planet <u>aimlessly</u> or even gone <u>berserk</u> when scientists lost control of them. However, NASA holds a tight rein on these rovers. By using their scientific capabilities, NASA experts can make many a <u>deduction</u> about the history of Mars. Scientists piece together evidence that the rovers gather.

The rovers have <u>routines</u> that allow them to get their work done. They climb hills of layered rock, test soil samples, and photograph the terrain. They do these things over and over in different places on the planet.

Rovers have been able to establish a <u>distinction</u> between the dry landscape of one location on Mars today and the landscape of that location many years ago. A long way back, the area was wet. It dried and eroded into a plain. Then, something hurtling from space struck the area with great force. After that, it seems to have become wet again. Then, the water disappeared once more, leaving a dry planet. As they receive more information, scientists can make more educated guesses about Martian history.

NASA scientists and students around the country work together to their <u>mutual</u> benefit. Each group gets something from the other. Students learn from world-class scientists. Some students actually get to analyze data, as well as create and test ideas. Some get to send commands to a rover here on Earth in preparation for the Mars mission. From the questions that students ask, scientists see their work in a new light. The researchers also get to "turn on" a new generation to the wonders of robots in space!

1. Underline two words or phrases that mean "mobile robots." Then, write a sentence about something you use that's *mobile*.

2. Circle the phrase that explains the word <u>continuously</u>. Write a sentence about something you know that stays on *continuously*.

3. Explain what a robot would be doing if it wandered <u>aimlessly</u>.

4. Circle the words that hint at the meaning of the word <u>berserk</u>. Write a sentence describing a robot gone *berserk*.

5. Underline the phrase that explains how a <u>deduction</u> is made. Write a sentence about a *deduction* you've made.

6. Explain how *routines* help robots work.

7. In a sentence, explain a <u>distinction</u> between one area on Mars today and that same area a long time ago.

8. Circle the sentence that explains what <u>mutual</u> means. Then, tell about something that was a *mutual* benefit to you and someone else.

"**Who Can Replace a Man?**" by Brian Aldiss
Writing About the Big Question

Can all conflicts be resolved?

Big Question Vocabulary

argument	compromise	injury	insecurity	interact
irritate	mislead	negotiate	oppose	reaction
solution	stalemate	victorious	viewpoint	violence

A. *Use a word from the list above to complete each sentence.*

1. Humans can avoid personal _____ in certain types of conflicts by using robots.

2. Robots can be programmed to _____ with one another to get jobs done.

3. To solve disagreements, people can _____, with each side giving a little to the other.

4. One _____ to the problem of boring jobs is to have robots do them.

B. *Follow the directions in responding to each of the items below. Answer in complete sentences.*

1. Describe two times that you had a conflict involving a machine. The conflict could be with another person or inside yourself.

   _____

   _____

2. Explain how you found a solution to one of those conflicts. Use at least two Big Question vocabulary words.

   _____

   _____

C. *In "Who Can Replace a Man?" machines in a futuristic world start to fight when their human masters disappear. Complete the sentence below. Then, explain how your answer connects to the big question.*

When people are not sure what to do, they often _____

   _____

   _____

   _____

"**Who Can Replace a Man?**" by Brian Aldiss
Reading: Ask Questions to Compare and Contrast

A **comparison** tells how two or more things are alike. A **contrast** tells how two or more things are different. **Asking questions to compare and contrast** helps you notice any similarities and differences in characters, settings, moods, and ideas. When you consider the similarities and differences in a work, you enrich your understanding of it.

Readers of "Who Can Replace a Man?" can tell right away that the character working in the field is not human. When the author refers to the character as "it," readers begin to look for clues as to what this character is, asking questions such as these:

- What does it look like?
- How does it move?
- How does it think?
- Are there any others like it?

As you read and discover more about the machines in the story, you can compare and contrast them with humans.

DIRECTIONS: *Answer the questions by using details given about the machines in the story and facts you know about humans.*

1. What do the machines look like? _____

   _____

   A. How are they similar to humans in appearance? _____

   _____

   B. How are they different? _____

   _____

2. How do the machines communicate with one another? _____

   _____

   A. How is their communication similar to that of humans? _____

   _____

   B. How is it different? _____

   _____

3. What kind of work do the machines do? _____

   _____

   A. How is their work similar to the work of humans? _____

   _____

   B. How is it different? _____

   _____

"Who Can Replace a Man?" by Brian Aldiss
Literary Analysis: Setting

The **setting** is the time and place of a story's action. A setting can create an emotional atmosphere, or *mood*. It also can give readers the sensation of living in a different time and place. As you read, notice details that make up the setting, including

- the customs and beliefs of the characters,
- the physical features of the land,
- the weather or season of the year, and
- the historical era in which the action takes place.

These details help readers not only picture the setting but also understand it better. For example, "Who Can Replace a Man?" takes place in a future time when machines operate at varying levels of independence. The setting changes as the machines act on information that man is extinct. In addition, readers learn about other places that exist in this Earth of the future.

A. DIRECTIONS: *Use the chart to list details you learn about the story's settings.*

Farm in the Country	City	Badlands

B. DIRECTIONS: *Write two or three sentences in which you compare and contrast the farm, where the story begins, and the Badlands, where it ends.*

_____

_____

_____

_____

Name _____ Date _____

"Who Can Replace a Man?" by Brian Aldiss
Vocabulary Builder

Word List

debris   deficiency   distinction   erosion   ravaged   respectively

A. DIRECTIONS: *On the line, write the letter of the word whose meaning is closest to that of the word from the Word List.*

___ 1. respectively
    A. orderly
    B. randomly
    C. gratefully
    D. urgently

___ 2. debris
    A. neatness
    B. dirt
    C. wreckage
    D. building

___ 3. ravaged
    A. ruined
    B. repaired
    C. hungry
    D. tired

___ 4. deficiency
    A. abundance
    B. lack
    C. defiance
    D. satisfaction

___ 5. distinction
    A. similarity
    B. distance
    C. closeness
    D. difference

___ 6. erosion
    A. devastation
    B. production
    C. formation
    D. usefulness

B. WORD STUDY   The Latin prefix *de-* means "away" or "from." Answer each of the following questions using one of these words containing *de-*: *debate, decrease, decode.*

1. How can having a *debate* help people avoid having a physical battle?

_____

2. How would a *decrease* in strength affect your ability to run fast?

_____

3. How does the ability to *decode* unfamiliar words help you understand what you read?

_____

Name _____ Date _____

Enrichment: Planning a Screenplay

When writers use a short story or a novel as the basis for a screenplay, they begin by asking: What will the setting look like? How will it change through the course of the film? What will the characters look like? How will they speak? The answers to these questions become specific directions to the director and the actors on how to portray the story visually and audibly.

The audience for a science-fiction film has not seen many of the people or places that the novel or short story writer has dreamed up. Therefore, a science-fiction screenplay must describe details realistically and entertainingly enough to grab and keep an audience's attention.

Imagine that you are planning to write a screenplay for "Who Can Replace a Man?" For each category below, list details that you would use in describing each place and machine to the actors and director. Look back in the story to be as specific as you can about how the original writer imagined the appearance of people and machines, personalities, voices, and so on. Add your own ideas as well.

Category	Details of Sights and Sounds for Actors and Director
Field Landscape	
Agricultural Station	
Badlands Landscape	
Field-minder	
Unlocker	

"Who Can Replace a Man?" by Brian Aldiss
Open-Book Test

Short Answer *Write your responses to the questions in this section on the lines provided.*

1. Where and when does "Who Can Replace a Man?" begin? Complete this chart with three details from the first four paragraphs of the story. Then, answer the question.

Time/Place	Evidence

How does the setting prove that this is a science-fiction story?

_____

_____

2. In "Who Can Replace a Man?" how have the penner and the field-minder been built to be alike? Explain how what they have in common sets them apart from the other machines.

_____

_____

_____

3. As "Who Can Replace a Man?" opens, the machines have not received their orders for the day. What does the machines' reaction suggest about their relationship to humans? How does that reaction provide a clue for readers about the ending of the story?

_____

_____

_____

4. In "Who Can Replace a Man?" what explanation does the radio operator give for the disappearance of humans? Why don't the other machines understand that explanation?

_____

_____

_____

5. Why do the machines in "Who Can Replace a Man?" want to rescue the radio operator from its room? How does that machine's difference make it valuable to the rest of the machines?

_____

_____

_____

_____

6. In "Who Can Replace a Man?" the countryside seems to be a safer place for the machines than the city. Despite that safety, why does it present a challenge for the machines as they travel?

_____

_____

_____

_____

7. Reread the first paragraph that describes the Badlands in "Who Can Replace a Man?" (It follows the penner's announcement of "South it is then!") What is another reason for the disappearance of humans? Cite evidence for your answer from the description of that setting. What do the two reasons, taken together, say about human beings?

_____

_____

_____

_____

8. The machines in "Who Can Replace a Man?" travel south with great plans. How and why do those plans change dramatically when they reach their destination?

_____

_____

_____

_____

9. Only one human appears in "Who Can Replace a Man?" How does he differ from the kind of people who probably built the machines? Why, then, do the machines react to him the way they do? Support your answer with details from the story.

_____

_____

_____

_____

10. Define *deficiency*. Then, describe two deficiencies that make the world of "Who Can Replace a Man?" a terrible place.

_____

_____

_____

Essay

Write an extended response to the question of your choice or to the question or questions your teacher assigns you.

11. Think about what has happened to the humans in "Who Can Replace a Man?" In an essay, discuss what you think the few remaining humans in that world wish they had done differently in the past. Consider what the story says about problems with the land and forests, and think about how those areas could have been treated differently. Refer to story details in your answer.

12. In "Who Can Replace a Man?" the machines' roles are determined by their brain class. How closely does this arrangement resemble the way our society is organized? Write an essay to compare and contrast the roles of the machines with the roles of people in our society. Use examples from the story and from real life to support your answer.

13. Almost all of the characters in "Who Can Replace a Man?" are machines, but the machines differ from one another. Write an essay in which you compare and contrast two of the machines. Discuss what the machines look like, what jobs they do, and how they think and act. Include details or examples from the story.

14. **Thinking About the Big Question: Can all conflicts be resolved?** As the machines in "Who Can Replace a Man?" discuss humans, the penner says, "It is better that men should never come back." Write an essay that responds to these questions: (1) Does the penner think that the tension between humans and machines has been resolved? (2) At the end of the story, is the penner proved right? Cite evidence from the story to explain your answers.

Oral Response

15. Go back to question 1, 3, or 9 or to the question your teacher assigns you. Take a few minutes to expand your answer and prepare an oral response. Find additional details in "Who Can Replace a Man?" that will support your points. If necessary, make notes to guide your response.

"Who Can Replace a Man?" by Brian W. Aldiss

Selection Test A

Critical Reading *Identify the letter of the choice that best answers the question.*

____ 1. Where is the field-minder working at the beginning of "Who Can Replace a Man?"
    A. on a green hill
    B. by a river
    C. in a gray field
    D. on a highway

____ 2. The seed-distributor in "Who Can Replace a Man?" cannot go into the storage area. Why not?
    A. The unlocker has not arrived.
    B. The seed-distributor has lost its keys.
    C. The seed-distributor cannot follow orders.
    D. Other machines damaged the area.

____ 3. In "Who Can Replace a Man?" how are the penner and the field-minder alike?
    A. Both are about the same size.
    B. Both are eager to start a war.
    C. Both have had some education.
    D. Both have the same level brain.

____ 4. In "Who Can Replace a Man?" what do the yard machines do when they do not receive orders?
    A. They play organized games.
    B. They shout and disrupt things.
    C. They ask the field-minder what to do.
    D. They try to escape.

____ 5. In "Who Can Replace a Man?" why have most of the humans died?
    A. They ran out of food.
    B. They killed one another in a world war.
    C. The water sources dried up.
    D. The sun lost its warming power.

____ 6. In "Who Can Replace a Man?" how do the machines release the radio operator from its room?
    A. The city machines direct them.
    B. They knock down the station wall.
    C. They get the unlocker to unlock the door.
    D. They bomb the building.

_____ 7. In "Who Can Replace a Man?" why is the radio operator able to think ahead?

    A. It went to school for many years.

    B. It spent most of its time with humans.

    C. It took a reasoning class in college.

    D. It has a higher-level brain.

_____ 8. How are the Badlands in "Who Can Replace a Man?" a problem for the machines?

    A. The hills are hard for them to climb.

    B. Grasses get caught in their low chassis.

    C. They get caught in the dried crevices.

    D. River water causes their parts to rust.

_____ 9. In "Who Can Replace a Man?" why do the machines leave the stranded or broken ones behind?

    A. They no longer like the broken ones.

    B. The servicer refuses to do its job.

    C. They are unable to lift or repair them.

    D. They do not notice that machines break.

_____ 10. In "Who Can Replace a Man?" what news about men does the flying machine tell the others before it crashes?

    A. The cities have been destroyed.

    B. A few men live in the mountains.

    C. There is food stored in mountain caves.

    D. Humans arrived from another planet.

_____ 11. At the end of "Who Can Replace a Man?" what does the man order the machines to do?

    A. to find food

    B. to carry him out

    C. to search for his friends

    D. to bring water from the stream

Vocabulary and Grammar

_____ 12. Which word is *never* a linking verb?

    A. is

    B. look

    C. were

    D. walk

____ 13. Which word is closest in meaning to *evidently*?
   A. sporadically
   B. loosely
   C. obviously
   D. doubtfully

____ 14. In which sentence is *dexterity* not used logically?
   A. The piano tuner used great dexterity to reglue the keys.
   B. With unusual dexterity, I was able to thread the needle.
   C. Luke juggled the oranges with dexterity.
   D. Sherry's dexterity was apparent when she fell down the stairs.

____ 15. Which of these sentences contains a linking verb?
   A. Where are the children?
   B. The baby slept peacefully.
   C. Colin painted with water colors.
   D. Kate hoped to visit Ireland.

Essay

16. The main characters in "Who Can Replace a Man?" are machines. Each machine has a particular appearance, function, and personality. Write a brief essay in which you compare and contrast two machines in the story. Describe such things as how each machine looks, what its job is, how it speaks or thinks, and so on. Include examples from the story.

17. Imagine that you are one of the last humans alive in "Who Can Replace a Man?" Write a journal entry explaining what you wish you had done differently on Earth. Consider the problems with the land and forests in the story, and think about how those areas could have been treated differently. Refer to details from the story in your answer.

18. **Thinking About the Big Question: Can all conflicts be resolved?** As the machines in "Who Can Replace a Man?" discuss humans, the penner says, "It is better that men should never come back." Does the penner think that the tension between humans and machines has been resolved? Support your opinion in an essay based on specific examples from the story.

"Who Can Replace a Man?" by Brian W. Aldiss
Selection Test B

Critical Reading *Identify the letter of the choice that best answers the question.*

_____ 1. At the start of "Who Can Replace a Man?" what is the setting?
   A. a green, lush hillside
   B. a gray, worn-out field
   C. a barren, cracked wasteland
   D. a remote mountain cave

_____ 2. What clue does the author of "Who Can Replace a Man?" give to suggest that the field-minder is not human?
   A. He makes the field-minder roll, not walk.
   B. He gives the field-minder clicking noises.
   C. He refers to the field-minder as "it."
   D. He calls the field-minder a robot.

_____ 3. In "Who Can Replace a Man?" what prevents the seed-distributor from giving seed potatoes to the field-minder?
   A. Its arms have become locked in place.
   B. The machine that unlocks the storage area has not arrived.
   C. The seed potatoes have been poisoned by chemicals.
   D. There are no seed potatoes left.

_____ 4. In "Who Can Replace a Man?" why does the field-minder turn over topsoil when the land should have time to rest between plantings?
   A. It thinks the land can produce a crop.
   B. It is forced to work by the penner.
   C. It loves its work.
   D. It follows the orders it was given.

_____ 5. In "Who Can Replace a Man?" why do some machines in the station yard shout and hoot?
   A. They are playing a game after work.
   B. They are starting a revolution.
   C. They have had no orders about work.
   D. They are laughing at the field-minder.

_____ 6. In "Who Can Replace a Man?" how is the penner different from the field-minder?
   A. It is smaller and does clerical work.
   B. It is smaller and works in the city.
   C. It has a Class One brain.
   D. It can read maps.

_____ 7. In "Who Can Replace a Man?" what has happened to the humans?
   A. They have started a world war.
   B. They are all living in the city.
   C. They have died of starvation.
   D. They have left for another planet.

_____ 8. In "Who Can Replace a Man?" what are machines with a higher-class brain able to do?

    A. They can move easily over the land.

    B. They have larger vocabularies and think ahead.

    C. They can read instructions and discuss strategy.

    D. They have a sense of humor.

_____ 9. In "Who Can Replace a Man?" why do the machines release the radio operator from its room?

    A. because it orders them to release it

    B. because they are friends with it

    C. because they want to smash its building

    D. because they want its company

_____ 10. How does the geography change as the machines in "Who Can Replace a Man?" travel cross-country?

    A. The fields become lusher.

    B. The climate gets warmer.

    C. The land becomes cracked and eroded.

    D. The machines cross shallow rivers.

_____ 11. Why does the quarrier in "Who Can Replace a Man?" keep repeating the same sentence?

    A. Its brain cannot go beyond a certain level.

    B. It thinks other machines did not hear it.

    C. It has been damaged in a fight.

    D. It is trying to become the leader.

_____ 12. In "Who Can Replace a Man?" how is the countryside safer for the machines than the city?

    A. The land is flatter and easier to negotiate.

    B. There are fewer machines to fight.

    C. Forested areas provide cover.

    D. Airplanes are dropping bombs in the city.

_____ 13. In "Who Can Replace a Man?" what information does the flying machine announce?

    A. Some men are still alive in the cities.

    B. Man has been replaced.

    C. More men have arrived from a far planet.

    D. Some men are still alive in the mountains.

_____ 14. In "Who Can Replace a Man?" how do the machines respond when the penner falls and breaks?

    A. They put it back on top of the quarrier.

    B. They leave it and continue on.

    C. The servicer repairs it.

    D. The flying machine lifts it out.

_____ 15. In "Who Can Replace a Man?" what do the machines do when the surviving man turns to them?
A. They destroy him.
B. They ask him for help.
C. They take him back to the city.
D. They follow his order to find food.

Vocabulary and Grammar

_____ 16. Someone who has *dexterity* is
A. afraid of change.
B. careless in ice and snow.
C. skillful with his or her hands.
D. receptive to new ideas.

_____ 17. Which sentence does *not* contain a linking verb?
A. She sang soprano in the choir.
B. Liz is my youngest sister.
C. Randy looked disappointed with his score.
D. I am the one who plays chess.

_____ 18. Which sentence contains an action verb?
A. The old dog appeared tired.
B. Adam is a talented pianist.
C. Sherry put the flowers in water.
D. The large crowd surprised Amy.

Essay

19. In "Who Can Replace a Man?" the machines' roles are determined by their brain class. Does this arrangement resemble the way our society is organized, or not? Write an essay in which you compare and contrast the roles of the machines with the roles of people in our society. Use examples from the story to support your answer.

20. Read the following quotation from "Who Can Replace a Man?":
> "It is better that men should never come back," said the penner. In its way, it was a revolutionary statement.

In a brief essay, discuss in what way the penner's comment can be seen as revolutionary. Consider what the machines have been doing up to the point where the story begins and what they are planning to do when the penner speaks. Use details from the story to support your answer.

21. **Thinking About the Big Question: Can all conflicts be resolved?** As the machines in "Who Can Replace a Man?" discuss humans, the penner says, "It is better that men should never come back." Write an essay that responds to these questions: (1) Does the penner think that the tension between humans and machines has been resolved? (2) At the end of the story, is the penner proved right? Cite evidence from the story to explain your answers.

Vocabulary Warm-up Word Lists

Study these words from "Tears of Autumn." Then, complete the activities.

Word List A

anxiety [ang ZY uh tee] *n.* feelings of fearful worry or nervousness
   I felt <u>anxiety</u> throughout my first day at the new school.

devoting [di VOH ting] *v.* giving time and effort to some person or purpose
   My dad was <u>devoting</u> his attention to removing the tick from our dog.

latitude [LAT uh tood] *n.* freedom to do or say as one pleases
   Our dance teacher gave us the <u>latitude</u> to choose our own music.

leaden [LED en] *adj.* feeling heavy and slow
   My <u>leaden</u> feet would hardly move as I walked to the principal's office.

officials [uh FI shuhlz] *n.* people holding important positions in organizations
   We talked to several <u>officials</u> at City Hall about building a new park.

spirited [SPEER uh tid] *adj.* full of energy or courage
   The <u>spirited</u> young horse was a joy to watch as it pranced through the pasture.

suitable [SOOT uh buhl] *adj.* appropriate; proper; right
   You should wear <u>suitable</u> clothes to a job interview.

ventured [VEN cherd] *v.* expressed at the risk of criticism
   The class groaned whenever Mr. Green <u>ventured</u> to tell a new joke.

Word List B

homeland [HOHM land] *n.* the country where a person was born
   I left my <u>homeland</u> of Ireland to start a new life in the United States.

investigation [in ves tuh GAY shuhn] *n.* official attempt to find out information
   My <u>investigation</u> of her statements about that night turned up a number of lies.

protective [pruh TEK tiv] *adj.* designed to keep something safe
   The children must wear <u>protective</u> gear whenever they skate.

recognition [rek uhg NI shuhn] *n.* knowing a person or thing on sight
   My <u>recognition</u> of my aunt in the crowd depended upon her wearing the hat.

relentless [ri LENT lis] *adj.* endless; without stopping or getting less severe
   The <u>relentless</u> barking of the neighbor's dog kept me up all night.

sallow [SAL oh] *adj.* looking yellow and unhealthy
   The boy's skin looked <u>sallow</u> when he got off the roller coaster.

tuberculosis [too ber kyuh LOH sis] *n.* serious, easily spread disease of the lungs
   People with <u>tuberculosis</u> are not supposed to be out in public.

varying [VAIR ee ing] *adj.* different
   The colors of the beautiful blanket included <u>varying</u> shades of blue and green.

"Tears of Autumn" by Yoshiko Uchida
Vocabulary Warm-up Exercises

Exercise A *Fill in the blanks using each word from Word List A only once.*

When [1] _____ at the zoo announced that panda bears would be on exhibit for a few months, I was thrilled. I had some [2] _____ about their stay at our zoo, though. Would a [3] _____ place for them to live be ready? Would enough workers be [4] _____ their time to the care of these amazing animals? I [5] _____ to express my fears in a letter to the zoo. As a strong supporter, I felt I should have the [6] _____ to give my opinions. Besides, I just needed a way to get rid of the [7] _____ feeling in my stomach whenever I thought about any harm befalling the panda bears. Happily, the zoo invited me to a [8] _____ session at which the community could discuss all of the preparations.

Exercise B *Circle T if the statement is true or F if the statement is false. Then, explain your answer.*

1. During summer you do not need to wear any <u>protective</u> clothing.
   T / F _____

2. A healthy child will have <u>sallow</u> skin after exercising outdoors.
   T / F _____

3. Your <u>homeland</u> can be different from that of your grandparents.
   T / F _____

4. A person with <u>tuberculosis</u> might have trouble breathing.
   T / F _____

5. An <u>investigation</u> can be done quickly with little attention to details.
   T / F _____

6. A good test can help a teacher see the students' <u>varying</u> levels of understanding.
   T / F _____

7. The rise and fall of ocean waves is <u>relentless</u>.
   T / F _____

8. Her resemblance to my mother helped with my <u>recognition</u> of a long-lost relative.
   T / F _____

"Tears of Autumn" by Yoshiko Uchida
Reading Warm-up A

Read the following passage. Pay special attention to the underlined words. Then, read it again, and complete the activities. Use a separate sheet of paper for your written answers.

In 1900, the United States reported that there were 24,326 Japanese Americans. Only 410 of them were women. Within 20 years, however, 20,000 more Japanese women had come to the United States. Many of them were "picture brides." Following the customs of Japan, the families of these women set up their marriages. A suitable man was chosen by his place in society and by his personality. The twist was that each picture bride was traveling to a new country to be with a husband she had never met. Imagine the anxiety a young woman would have on this trip across the sea.

Records show that one ship carried 75 Japanese picture brides to San Francisco. Just think of the spirited discussions they must have had! Holding a photograph, one bride might have ventured to say that her future husband was the most handsome. Little did she know that the picture could be quite old. It might even be a photograph of someone other than the man she was going to wed. Some brides might have been devoting their time to thoughts of the wealth to be found in America. As one of the immigration officials of the time said, the reality was much different. "One day they're picture brides, and the next day they're digging potatoes on a ranch."

Still, many Japanese Americans found the freedom and the latitude to start a new life in this country. Women worked alongside their husbands to earn money while raising families. Whether farming or starting businesses, the picture brides got right to work upon arrival. As the women became busy and their community grew, the leaden feelings they must have had as their ships steamed into port went away. The unpleasant emotions were replaced with a new sense of purpose and a drive to succeed. Hopefully, the picture brides also had feelings of warmth and love toward their new husbands.

1. Underline the words describing what would make a man a suitable husband. Then, explain what *suitable* means.

2. Circle the words that tell why a picture bride might feel anxiety. Then, write a sentence about an *anxiety* you've felt.

3. Rewrite the sentence with the word spirited, using a synonym for the word.

4. Underline the words telling what a bride might have ventured to say. Then, explain what *ventured* means.

5. Underline the thoughts to which many brides were devoting their time. Explain some activities to which you have been *devoting* your time.

6. Explain why immigration officials would know about the reality awaiting the picture brides.

7. Circle a word that means almost the same thing as latitude. Explain what having *latitude* meant for the picture brides.

8. Circle the words that mean almost the same thing as leaden feelings. Describe the *leaden* feelings of picture brides as they reached the United States.

"Tears of Autumn" by Yoshiko Uchida
Reading Warm-up B

Read the following passage. Pay special attention to the underlined words. Then, read it again, and complete the activities. Use a separate sheet of paper for your written answers.

Long before Angel Island was the first stop for people looking across San Francisco Bay to a new <u>homeland</u>, it was a place of great importance. Before Angel Island sheltered people with a contagious illness like <u>tuberculosis</u>, the place held secrets of healing. Before Angel Island had forts and ports, it was a peaceful place.

The Miwok Indians were the first to enjoy the beauty and resources of Angel Island. They crossed the bay by boat to reach it. An <u>investigation</u> of the island proved that it was a great place to hunt and fish. The Miwok never lived there permanently, but they built <u>protective</u> shelters. They would visit the island in good weather, staying as long as they wanted. Then, they would return to their small villages on the mainland.

Like all early peoples who lived by hunting and gathering, the Miwok had <u>varying</u> levels of success. The rich resources on the island helped them fight off hunger and remain in good physical condition. Unlike people with poor diets and <u>sallow</u> skin, the Miwok seemed to glow with health.

If the Miwoks visited Angel Island today, they would have an instant <u>recognition</u> of its natural beauty. As a modern visitor, you can hike the hilly trails and admire the many beautiful plants and trees. You can still feel the <u>relentless</u> wind as you stand high up on the island, looking out to sea. You might even get to watch sea lions playing on the waves. For fun, you could decide to gather some of the acorns on the ground. These are some of the same experiences the Miwok had when they lived on Angel Island. If you are lucky, you might even hear the sounds of their drums and flutes carried across time on the fresh ocean breezes.

1. Name the <u>homeland</u> described in the first sentence. Describe your *homeland*.

2. Underline the words that name what <u>tuberculosis</u> is. Write a sentence about *tuberculosis*.

3. Circle the words describing what an <u>investigation</u> of Angel Island proved. Explain what *investigation* means.

4. Explain why the Miwoks would have needed <u>protective</u> shelters. Use the meaning of *protective* in your explanation.

5. Rewrite the sentence with the word <u>varying</u>. Use a synonym for the word. Then, tell why they might have *varying* levels of success.

6. Underline one cause of <u>sallow</u> skin. What else might cause someone's skin to look *sallow*?

7. Explain why the Miwoks might have some <u>recognition</u> of Angel Island today.

8. What other natural element might be created by a <u>relentless</u> wind? Define *relentless*.

"Tears of Autumn" by Yoshiko Uchida
Writing About the Big Question

Can all conflicts be resolved?

Big Question Vocabulary

argument	compromise	injury	insecurity	interact
irritate	mislead	negotiate	oppose	reaction
solution	stalemate	victorious	viewpoint	violence

A. *Use a word from the list above to complete each sentence.*

1. In some cultures, families _____ terms for arranged marriages.

2. A matchmaker should not _____ a family about a young man's qualities.

3. If any family members _____ the arranged marriage, it might not take place.

4. A good _____ against an arranged marriage is that love might be lacking.

B. *Follow the directions in responding to each of the items below. Answer in complete sentences.*

1. Write two sentences about a time you had an inner conflict concerning a big change in your life.

_____

_____

2. In one or two sentences, explain how you resolved this inner conflict. Use at least two of the Big Question vocabulary words.

_____

_____

C. *In "Tears of Autumn," a young woman chooses a new life that is very different from what she has ever known. Complete the sentence below. Then, write a short paragraph in which you discuss the pros and cons of making big changes.*

Making a big change in one's life can cause conflicts because _____.

_____

_____

"Tears of Autumn" by Yoshiko Uchida
Reading: Ask Questions to Compare and Contrast

A **comparison** tells how two or more things are alike. A **contrast** tells how two or more things are different. **Asking questions to compare and contrast** helps you notice similarities and differences in characters, settings, moods, and ideas. When you consider similarities and differences in a work, you enrich your understanding of it.

To compare and contrast characters in "Tears of Autumn," ask these questions:

• What do readers know about Hana's three older sisters?
• How does Hana feel about following the paths of her sisters?
• What do readers know about Taro's life in America? About Taro as a person?

A. DIRECTIONS: *As you read the story, record details you learn about Hana, Hana's sisters, and Taro.*

Hana	Hana's Sisters	Taro

B. DIRECTIONS: *Write two or three sentences in which you compare and contrast Hana, Hana's sisters, and Taro. Use details from the chart.*

_____

_____

_____

"**Tears of Autumn**" by Yoshiko Uchida
Literary Analysis: Setting

The **setting** is the time and place of a story's action. A setting can create an emotional atmosphere, or *mood*. It also can give readers the sensation of living in a different time and place. As you read, notice details that make up the setting, such as

- the customs and beliefs of the characters,
- the physical features of the land,
- the weather or season of the year, and
- the historical era in which the action takes place.

These details help readers not only picture the setting but also understand it better. For example, "Tears of Autumn" takes place in the past, probably in the early twentieth century. There are three settings: Japan; the Japanese American community of San Francisco, California; and aboard a ship traveling between the two places.

A. DIRECTIONS: *Use the chart to list details you learn about the story's settings.*

Japan	Ship	Japanese American Community

B. DIRECTIONS: *Write two or three sentences in which you compare and contrast the three settings.*

_____

_____

_____

_____

_____

"Tears of Autumn" by Yoshiko Uchida
Vocabulary Builder

Word List

affluence   degrading   radical   recoiled   relentless   turbulent

A. DIRECTIONS: *For each sentence, think about the meaning of the underlined word. Then, answer the question.*

1. Why might someone want more <u>affluence</u> rather than less?

   _____

   _____

2. Why might some people find washing dishes in a restaurant <u>degrading</u>?

   _____

   _____

3. How might a change in the presidency from one political party to another be considered <u>radical</u>?

   _____

   _____

4. Why might a pilot be reluctant to fly in <u>turbulent</u> weather?

   _____

   _____

5. What would explain why a man <u>recoiled</u> at the sight of a rattlesnake?

   _____

   _____

6. Why might a child be <u>relentless</u> in his requests for a new toy?

   _____

   _____

B. WORD STUDY The Latin prefix *de-* means "down." Explain your answers to the following questions using one of these words containing *de-*: *despise, destruction, devalued.*

1. If you *despise* the actions of another person, how do you feel about them?

   _____

2. If you agree to the *destruction* of an old building, do you want it to stay as it is?

   _____

3. If the money of a country is suddenly *devalued*, can you buy more with it?

   _____

"Tears of Autumn" by Yoshiko Uchida
Enrichment: Documentary Film

"Tears of Autumn" is a fictional account of a young woman's journey from Japan to America. Through the experiences of fictional characters, readers learn about traditional ways of life and certain customs in Japan. They also learn something about what new immigrants experienced on arriving at Angel Island, off the California coast.

A documentary film, on the other hand, attempts to provide a nonfictional account. With firsthand reports from those who were there and visuals of the events as they actually happened, an audience can experience and learn about the subject in a different way.

DIRECTIONS: *Write your answers to the following questions on the lines provided.*

1. What do documentary films provide that fictional stories, poems, or other written accounts do not?

   _____

   _____

   _____

2. What advantages do encyclopedias and textbooks have over documentary films?

   _____

   _____

   _____

3. If documentary films existed in the days of early immigration to America, what would you have liked the following people to tell you on screen?

   A. teenager arriving in America

   _____

   _____

   B. Americans watching the new immigrants' arrival

   _____

   _____

4. Do you think documentaries would have influenced more or fewer people to emigrate to America? Give reasons for your answer.

   _____

   _____

   _____

   _____

   _____

"Who Can Replace a Man?" by Brian Aldiss
"Tears of Autumn" by Yoshiko Uchida
Integrated Language Skills: Grammar

Action and Linking Verbs

An **action verb** expresses physical or mental action.

Action: The man <u>shook</u> his head. The man <u>will say</u> "no."

A **linking verb** expresses a state of being. It links the subject of a sentence with a word or words that rename or describe the subject. Common linking verbs are forms of *be: be, am, is, are, was, were, has been, have been, is being, was being,* and so on.

Linking: His voice <u>was</u> loud and grating. He <u>is being</u> silly.

Other linking verbs are *seem, stay, become, turn, feel, taste, appear, remain, grow, look, sound, smell.* Some of these words also can function as action verbs. To determine whether a verb is an action verb or a linking verb, try replacing it with a form of *to be.* If the sentence still makes sense, the verb is a linking verb.

The car <u>turned</u> the corner. [*The car <u>was</u> the corner* makes no sense: Action Verb.]

The sky <u>turned</u> dark before the storm. [*The sky <u>was</u> dark* makes sense: Linking Verb.]

A. PRACTICE: *Read each sentence, and circle the verb or verb phrase. Then, on the line before the sentence, write AV if the verb or verb phrase is an action verb or LV if it is a linking verb.*

____ 1. The moon has been full for the past three nights.

____ 2. Our team played in the finals of the city softball tournament.

____ 3. Louisa is the captain of our softball team.

____ 4. The crowd's cheers sounded like a freight train approaching.

____ 5. Alan sounded the bell.

____ 6. Randy stared in wonder at the butterfly and the cocoon.

____ 7. Caterpillars are often beautiful themselves.

____ 8. Dana will become a famous ballerina.

____ 9. Lisle walked quickly home from school.

____ 10. We will eat lunch at twelve o'clock sharp.

B. Writing Application: *On the lines provided, write sentences in which you use and underline verbs as directed.*

1. a form of *look* as an action verb: _____

_____

2. a form of *look* as a linking verb: _____

_____

3. an action verb of your choice: _____

_____

"Who Can Replace a Man?" by Brian Aldiss
"Tears of Autumn" by Yoshiko Uchida

Integrated Language Skills: Support for Writing a Description

When you **write a description,** it is important to include specific details that help the reader imagine what you are describing. If you are describing a place, details should tell what the place looks like, who lives there, and what the inhabitants do there. If you are describing a person, details should tell about his or her personality, interests, appearance, and reactions.

To prepare for writing a description of your city or town as it might appear at the end of the twenty-first century, consider details about the town as it exists today. Then, imagine ways in which these details might change over the next hundred years. Use the chart to record your ideas.

Category	Detail Today	Detail in 100 Years
Land		
Buildings		
People		
Occupations		
Setting		
Technology		

Now, draft a description of the city or town 100 years in the future.

"**Who Can Replace a Man?**" by Brian Aldiss
"**Tears of Autumn**" by Yoshiko Uchida

Integrated Language Skills: Support for Extend Learning

Oral Report

Research and Technology: "Who Can Replace a Man?"

First, your group needs to decide on the work of a particular writer, artist, or filmmaker to study. You might ask your school librarian to help identify such people who also specialize in science fiction. When you have chosen a person whose work interests all group members, use the following questions to guide your research.

1. What medium (for example, print, paint, film) does the person use to portray his or her vision of the future?

_____

2. What methods make this person's portrayals unique or especially interesting?

_____

3. Describe the person's vision. Is it humorous, frightening, ugly, beautiful?

_____

_____

4. Which of the person's works is your favorite? Why?

_____

_____

Research and Technology: "Tears of Autumn"

To prepare for your group's oral report, gather factual information about Angel Island. Use the following questions to guide your research. Then, find supporting evidence by using the Internet or your library.

1. Who passed through Angel Island? Where were they from?

_____

2. Why did people leave their homeland?

_____

_____

3. Describe the conditions at Angel Island. What kinds of challenges did people face?

_____

4. How do people feel about the experience of passing through Angel Island?

_____

_____

"**Tears of Autumn**" by Yoshiko Uchida
Open-Book Test

Short Answer *Write your responses to the questions in this section on the lines provided.*

1. "Tears of Autumn" opens on a ship. Does most of the story take place in that setting? Explain your answer.

   _____

   _____

   _____

2. In the third paragraph of "Tears of Autumn," Hana recalls a setting in great detail. What do the details tell the reader about the time of the story and the place Hana comes from?

   _____

   _____

   _____

   _____

3. In the first four paragraphs of "Tears of Autumn," what emotions does Hana feel? Cite two details from the story that reveal Hana's feelings and her mood.

   _____

   _____

   _____

   _____

4. In "Tears of Autumn," Hana is not eager to marry any of the men her mother suggests to her. She is interested in Taro, however. What is the main difference between Taro and the other Japanese men Hana might marry?

   _____

   _____

5. In "Tears of Autumn," why does Hana's brother-in-law consider Hana's views "radical"? Base your answer on the meaning of *radical*.

   _____

   _____

   _____

6. In the middle of "Tears of Autumn," Taro writes to Hana for the first time. Why is his letter formal and impersonal? Cite a detail from Hana's response to the letter to support your answer.

   _____

   _____

   _____

7. In "Tears of Autumn," Hana agrees to marry Taro. When she first considers the marriage and just before she arrives in California, she considers how the marriage might improve her life. What improvements does she hope will result from the marriage? Support your response with two details from the story.

_____

_____

_____

8. In "Tears of Autumn," Hana spends two days at Angel Island. She is questioned by immigration officials and given medical examinations. Why does she find the experience degrading? Base your answer on the definition of *degrading*.

_____

_____

9. The conclusion of "Tears of Autumn" takes place on a ferry from San Francisco to Oakland. Explain how that setting helps give the story a positive, encouraging ending.

_____

_____

_____

10. Compare and contrast Hana and Taro. In the outer columns, write two details from "Tears of Autumn" that are unique to each character. In the middle column, write two things that the characters have in common. Then, on the line below, describe how something they have in common might help them adjust to their marriage.

Hana	Hana and Taro	Taro

_____

_____

Essay

Write an extended response to the question of your choice or to the question or questions your teacher assigns you.

11. There are three settings in "Tears of Autumn": Oka Village, the ship bound from Japan to California, and California itself. In an essay, compare and contrast those three settings. Support your ideas with details from the story.

12. In "Tears of Autumn," Hana approaches new surroundings and a new way of life. In a brief essay, tell whether you think Hana will be able to make the adjustment. Support your prediction with details from the story.

13. In "Tears of Autumn," Hana and Taro probably have different expectations of what their mate will be like. In a brief essay, compare and contrast those expectations. Use details from the story to support your ideas.

14. **Thinking About the Big Question: Can all conflicts be resolved?** In "Tears of Autumn," Hana has sometimes clashed with members of her family. Does her decision to marry Taro resolve those conflicts? Why or why not? Use evidence from the story to explain your response.

Oral Response

15. Go back to question 3, 4, or 9 or to the question your teacher assigns you. Take a few minutes to expand your answer and prepare an oral response. Find additional details in "Tears of Autumn" that will support your points. If necessary, make notes to guide your oral response.

"Tears of Autumn" by Yoshiko Uchida
Selection Test A

Critical Reading *Identify the letter of the choice that best answers the question.*

____ 1. Where does the opening scene of "Tears of Autumn" take place?
   A. in Japan
   B. in Oakland, California
   C. on a small ship
   D. in an airplane

____ 2. In "Tears of Autumn," why is Hana traveling?
   A. She is taking a vacation.
   B. She wants to see Europe.
   C. She is going to visit her sisters.
   D. She is traveling to America.

____ 3. Which word best describes Hana's mood as she travels toward her destination in "Tears of Autumn"?
   A. hopeless
   B. hopeful
   C. joyful
   D. relaxed

____ 4. Which characteristic of Hana's is conveyed in the following passage?
   She wanted to escape the smothering strictures of life in her village.
   A. conformity
   B. jealousy
   C. independence
   D. childishness

____ 5. In "Tears of Autumn," what career had Hana wanted to pursue?
   A. teaching
   B. farming
   C. business
   D. medicine

____ 6. Based on choices he has made in his own life, how will Taro react to Hana's decision to come to America?
   A. He will admire Hana's decision.
   B. He will criticize Hana's decision.
   C. He will be embarrassed by Hana's decision.
   D. He will try to change Hana's decision.

_____ 7. In "Tears of Autumn," from whom does Hana learn that Taro wants a wife?
   A. from her sisters
   B. from her mother
   C. from her uncle
   D. from her brother-in-law

_____ 8. Which of the following items do Hana and Taro of "Tears of Autumn" *not* have in common?
   A. a sense of humor
   B. a samurai father
   C. an independent spirit
   D. a childhood in Japan

_____ 9. In "Tears of Autumn," which custom plays an important part in Hana's future?
   A. Women do not take a husband's name.
   B. Most women seek higher education.
   C. Women can be trained as samurai.
   D. Many marriages are arranged.

_____ 10. What is Hana looking forward to when she agrees to marry Taro in "Tears of Autumn"?
   A. new and exciting surroundings
   B. more education
   C. working in a store
   D. a warmer climate

_____ 11. In "Tears of Autumn," which word best describes Hana's first reaction on meeting Taro in person?
   A. delight
   B. hatred
   C. amusement
   D. surprise

Vocabulary and Grammar

_____ 12. Which of the following sentences contains an action verb?
   A. My brother seems tired.
   B. My sister ran for a touchdown.
   C. My cousin will be here for lunch.
   D. My uncle is on a diet.

____ 13. Which word is closest in meaning to *degrading*?
   A. misgiving
   B. insulting
   C. honoring
   D. judging

____ 14. Which of the following verbs can *never* be a linking verb?
   A. am
   B. was
   C. appear
   D. walk

____ 15. In which sentence is *affluence* used incorrectly?
   A. The mansion reflected the affluence of the community.
   B. Her large wardrobe was a sign of her affluence.
   C. My father is an important affluence in our community.
   D. He pursued affluence in order to own luxury cars.

Essay

16. Imagine that you are Hana from "Tears of Autumn." Imagine that you have been in America for a few weeks. Write a letter that Hana might send to her mother. Include both positive and negative experiences.

17. Write an essay in which you compare and contrast the settings in "Tears of Autumn." Keep the three settings in the story in mind: a village in Japan, aboard a ship, and Oakland. Support your ideas with details from the story.

18. **Thinking About the Big Question: Can all conflicts be resolved?** In "Tears of Autumn," Hana has sometimes clashed with members of her family. Does her decision to marry Taro resolve those conflicts? Why or why not? Explain your answer in an essay that uses examples from the story.

Unit 2 Resources: Short Stories
58

"Tears of Autumn" by Yoshiko Uchida
Selection Test B

Critical Reading *Identify the letter of the choice that best completes the statement or answers the question.*

_____ 1. What are the settings in "Tears of Autumn"?
  A. Japan, an airplane, California
  B. Japan, California, China
  C. Japan, a ship, California
  D. a ship, California, Washington

_____ 2. In "Tears of Autumn," what does Hana recall about her homeland while she is traveling?
  A. fields of flowers, mountains, and her sleeping mat
  B. the salt in the air and the ocean
  C. her mother's cooking and the smell of the fireplace
  D. her father's house, the largest in the village

_____ 3. In "Tears of Autumn," what do Hana's relatives think is the most important thing to look for in a husband?
  A. looks
  B. personality
  C. sense of humor
  D. wealth

_____ 4. Why does the uncle in "Tears of Autumn" not immediately consider Hana as a possible wife for Taro?
  A. She is too young.
  B. She is unlikely to travel so far.
  C. She has not had enough education.
  D. She is already engaged.

_____ 5. Hana's brother-in-law in "Tears of Autumn" often claimed that Hana had
  A. just the right amount of education.
  B. no education.
  C. too little education.
  D. too much education.

_____ 6. Why does Hana in "Tears of Autumn" agree to marry Taro?
  A. She knew him as a child.
  B. She knows his family well.
  C. She wants a life unlike her sisters'.
  D. She wants to marry a wealthy man.

_____ 7. What does Hana in "Tears of Autumn" know about Taro before meeting him?
  A. nothing at all
  B. only his name
  C. very little
  D. a great deal

_____ 8. Which of the following words best captures Hana's feelings when she finally meets her husband-to-be in "Tears of Autumn"?
A. nervousness
B. horror
C. delight
D. emptiness

_____ 9. What change of setting lightens the mood at the end "Tears of Autumn"?
A. Hana and Taro step onto dry land.
B. Hana and Taro board a ferry for a short trip to Oakland.
C. Hana and Taro meet Taro's friends at their apartment.
D. Hana and Taro begin a long trip to Oakland.

_____ 10. According to "Tears of Autumn," what is the main difference between Taro and other Japanese men Hana has known?
A. Taro is older.
B. Taro is established in a business.
C. Taro is a family friend.
D. Taro has made a life outside Japan.

_____ 11. It is evident that at the time of "Tears of Autumn" Japanese women
A. enjoyed great individual freedom.
B. often entered into arranged marriages.
C. enjoyed equal rights with men.
D. received no education.

_____ 12. In "Tears of Autumn," what similarity in Hana and Taro bodes well for their marriage?
A. They have a sense of humor.
B. Their fathers had been samurai.
C. They are the same age.
D. They enjoy sailing.

_____ 13. In "Tears of Autumn," in what way will the setting of Hana's future be different from the setting of her past?
A. She is moving from a wealthy household to a poorer one.
B. She is leaving a teaching career to become a housewife.
C. She is moving from a country village to a large city.
D. She is starting a teaching career in another country.

_____ 14. Given what you know about Taro in "Tears of Autumn," how will his attitude toward Hana compare or contrast with that of her brother-in-law?
A. Taro probably will be critical of Hana's views about women's roles.
B. Taro probably will admire Hana's independent streak.
C. Taro probably will agree with Hana's brother-in-law about schooling for women.
D. Taro probably will agree that Hana's brain is "addled."

Unit 2 Resources: Short Stories
60

_____ 15. What historical time period do you think is the setting for "Tears in Autumn"?
   A. present
   B. early 1900s
   C. early 1800s
   D. early 1700s

Vocabulary and Grammar

_____ 16. Think about the definition of the word *degrading*. Which experience does Hana find degrading?
   A. having to work instead of going to school
   B. being forced into an arranged marriage
   C. having medical exams on Angel Island
   D. being poor after being born into wealth

_____ 17. In which sentence is *affluence* used correctly?
   A. Jacob tried to affluence the voters to support his candidate.
   B. Her large house was a sign of her affluence.
   C. My father was an important affluence in our community.
   D. Despite his affluence, Jack was able to afford a new car.

_____ 18. If someone's views are called *radical*, the person favors
   A. extreme change.
   B. minimal change.
   C. any change.
   D. no change.

_____ 19. Which sentence contains an action verb?
   A. My brother noticed the unusual bird.
   B. We were sure that we were right.
   C. I was afraid of the large dog.
   D. My friend is a comedian.

Essay

20. In "Tears of Autumn," Hana ventures toward new surroundings and a new way of life. In an essay, tell whether you think Hana will be able to make the adjustment. Use examples from the story to support your answer.

21. Taro and Hana in "Tears of Autumn" probably have different expectations about what their mate will be like. Write a brief essay in which you compare and contrast what each character's expectations might be. Use details from the story to explain your ideas.

22. **Thinking About the Big Question: Can all conflicts be resolved?** In "Tears of Autumn," Hana has sometimes clashed with members of her family. Does her decision to marry Taro resolve those conflicts? Why or why not? Use evidence from the story to explain your response

Vocabulary Warm-up Word Lists

Study these words from "Hamadi." Then, complete the activities that follow.

Word List A

available [uh VAY luh buhl] *adj.* can be gotten, had, or used
   We stopped at three motels before finding one with <u>available</u> rooms.

contagious [kuhn TAY juhs] *adj.* quickly spread from person to person
   I find that smiles and laughter are more <u>contagious</u> than frowns.

crates [KRAYTS] *n.* large boxes made of wooden slats
   Don't stack the <u>crates</u> too high, or they'll break under the weight.

international [in ter NASH uh nuhl] *adj.* relating to more than one country
   The <u>international</u> market had beautiful rugs from all over the world.

local [LOH kuhl] *adj.* having to do with the area in which you live
   Our <u>local</u> movie theater just put in comfortable new seats.

occasionally [uh KAY zhuh nuh lee] *adv.* sometimes, but not regularly
   My alarm clock <u>occasionally</u> fails to wake me.

particularly [puhr TIK yuh ler lee] *adv.* especially
   That pizza shop makes pies with a <u>particularly</u> thin crust.

purified [PYOOR uh fyd] *adj.* made pure or clean
   The air around Los Angeles seemed <u>purified</u> after the heavy rains.

Word List B

carolers [KA ruhl ers] *n.* people singing Christmas songs joyfully from house to house
   We always offer hot chocolate to <u>carolers</u> who visit our house.

dramatically [druh MAT ik uh lee] *adv.* in a way that shows imagination and emotion
   The band moved <u>dramatically</u> to show the meaning of their song.

focusing [FOH kuhs ing] *v.* giving or directing one's attention
   I was <u>focusing</u> on the teacher's words, but I still did not understand the concept.

giddy [GID ee] *adj.* silly, happy, and excited
   The ten-year-old was <u>giddy</u> when she got to meet her hero.

rickety [RIK uh tee] *adj.* in bad condition and likely to break with use
   We warned our guest not to sit in the <u>rickety</u> chair even though it looked comfortable.

significant [sig NIF i kuhnt] *adj.* important; having special meaning or value
   I made <u>significant</u> progress in my playing by practicing on the piano every day.

worldly [WUHRLD lee] *adj.* knowing a lot about people, based on life experiences
   My brother became much more <u>worldly</u> after just one month of college.

wry [RYE] *adj.* twisted to one side; cleverly or dryly humorous
   It was his <u>wry</u> smile that told us that he was not pleased with our performance.

"Hamadi" by Naomi Shihab Nye
Vocabulary Warm-up Exercises

Exercise A *Fill in the blanks using each word from Word List A only once.*

Dad had planned a great feast for our guests. The [1] _____ market did not have all of the ingredients we knew were [2] _____, so we drove to a bigger store. This one had a large [3] _____ section with bags, bottles, and [4] _____ of food from all around the world. Dad's excitement as we shopped was [5] _____, causing me to smile along with him. He [6] _____ liked the spices. I [7] _____ suggested that he think twice before buying some of the stranger items. For example, why did we need pickled grapes packed in [8] _____ water?

Exercise B *Answer the questions with complete explanations.*

1. Why might a person feel <u>giddy</u> about riding a roller coaster for the first time?

   _____

2. When have you recently shared a <u>significant</u> moment with someone you love?

   _____

3. Why do great movies often begin and end <u>dramatically</u>?

   _____

4. If you were riding in a <u>rickety</u>, old car, what sounds might you hear?

   _____

5. If you disliked your new haircut, would you show your feelings in a <u>wry</u> or a serious way?

   _____

6. Why wouldn't you describe a young child as <u>worldly</u>?

   _____

7. If you were <u>focusing</u> your attention on <u>carolers</u>, what emotions might you feel?

   _____

"Hamadi" by Naomi Shihab Nye
Reading Warm-up A

Read the following passage. Pay special attention to the underlined words. Then, read it again, and complete the activities. Use a separate sheet of paper for your written answers.

Throughout the world, spring is a season when people welcome warmer weather. They like to be outside, enjoying the delightful air that seems somehow <u>purified</u> in the bright sunshine. Spring is also a time to enjoy special <u>local</u> foods, grown and produced by individuals in the area nearby.

In Palestine, a spring feast includes many traditional foods. People really look forward to eating certain dishes. In case you never get to a city with <u>international</u> restaurants that offer delicious treats from around the world, here's a taste of what a spring feast in Palestine is like.

Diners might begin with a thick, colorful soup made from beans, peas, tomatoes, onions, and lots of spices. Palestine is known for the leafy green vegetables of spring that sprout up everywhere. Surely a salad would be next on the menu. Flavored with lemon, olive oil, and spices, the greens also <u>occasionally</u> are served with nuts on top. What a special treat that is!

Next comes the main course. If diners are lucky, they will be served lamb with some sort of rice. Roasted lamb is considered a <u>particularly</u> special meal. The Palestinian sauces for lamb are truly delicious! Diners also might be treated to a dish made from artichoke hearts. The season for growing this special vegetable is short in Palestine, so artichokes are not always <u>available</u>. In fact, <u>crates</u> of these delicacies are emptied almost as soon as they reach the markets.

Of course, a meal would not be complete without bread. The bread in Palestine is thin and usually baked over hot stones. Nothing beats this hot, fresh treat, except perhaps dessert. Many different sweets are popular in Palestine. However, most feature pastry, honey, nuts, cream, and powdered sugar. The love for these ingredients is certainly <u>contagious</u> among all who try the desserts.

1. Underline the word that tells what seems <u>purified</u>. Then, explain what **purified** means.

2. Circle the words that tell the meaning of <u>local</u>. Write a sentence about a **local** food that is popular in your area.

3. Circle the phrase that means the same thing as <u>international</u>. Explain why you might need to go to an **international** restaurant to enjoy Palestinian food.

4. Circle the word that tells what is <u>occasionally</u> served on top of spring salads in Palestine. Then, describe something you have **occasionally** seen served on salads.

5. Underline the words naming a <u>particularly</u> special main course in Palestine. Then, describe a meal that is **particularly** special to you.

6. Circle the vegetable that is <u>available</u> only for a short time. Write about what types of food are often **available** in **crates** in grocery stores.

7. Circle the words describing what is <u>contagious</u>. Then, explain what **contagious** means.

Name _____   Date _____

"Hamadi" by Naomi Shihab Nye
Reading Warm-up B

Read the following passage. Pay special attention to the underlined words. Then, read it again, and complete the activities. Use a separate sheet of paper for your written answers.

My name is Helen Silvestri. I'm eighty-five years old, and I live in one of those fancy new retirement homes. As my children and grandchildren like to say to me, often and very <u>dramatically</u>, I am lucky that I can afford to live in such a place during my "twilight years."

Don't get me wrong. Even though at times I may be accused of being <u>wry</u> about my circumstances, I know I am fortunate. I have no <u>significant</u> problems with my thinking or ability to function, but it's this <u>rickety</u> old body of mine that led the young people to believe I should no longer live alone. I did fall down a couple of times, mostly because I'm not used to <u>focusing</u> only on my body parts while moving about. I used to do a dozen things at once, but now I need to concentrate on walking and only walking if that's what I'm doing. Or, if I'm buttoning up my coat, my fingers are slow and stiff. People can't rush me. I don't need help; I just need for people to have patience so that I can do things at the right pace for me.

Anyway, I've been at the home for a few weeks now, and the first community event of interest to me is tonight. Apparently, some young <u>carolers</u> are coming to sing holiday tunes for us old folks. I hope these young people will perk us up. I'd love to see some truly <u>giddy</u> teenagers, laughing and carefree. I know everyone says young people are too <u>worldly</u> these days and bored with life. Still, I don't see many differences between today's sixteen-year-olds and myself at that age. The whole idea that your life is ahead of you and the world is at your feet . . . how could that feeling really ever change? I know I'll sense it tonight, as the young people sing their songs of joy.

1. Underline the words Helen's children say <u>dramatically</u>. Describe how one might say something **dramatically**.

2. Explain why the writer might be <u>wry</u>.

3. Circle two things with which the writer has no <u>significant</u> problems. Explain why **significant** is important in this sentence.

4. Describe what problems you might have if your body were <u>rickety</u>.

5. Explain what the writer is <u>focusing</u> on when she puts on her coat.

6. Underline the words describing what the <u>carolers</u> will be doing. Then, write a sentence about whether you'd like to be one of the **carolers**.

7. Circle words in the sentence with <u>giddy</u> that help to define it. In your own words, define **giddy**.

8. Explain why someone described as <u>worldly</u> might be bored with life.

Name _____ Date _____

"**Hamadi**" by Naomi Shihab Nye
Writing About the Big Question

Can all conflicts be resolved?

Big Question Vocabulary

argument	compromise	injury	insecurity	interact
irritate	mislead	negotiate	oppose	reaction
solution	stalemate	victorious	viewpoint	violence

A. *Use one or more words from the list above to complete each sentence.*

1. Unable to come to a verdict, the jurors told the judge they were at a

   _____.

2. The trial involved a man who had caused a serious _____ to another man.

3. It was unclear which man had let the verbal _____ turn into physical _____.

4. The judge's _____ to the jury's statement was to declare a mistrial.

B. *Follow the directions in responding to each of the items below. Answer in complete sentences.*

1. Write two sentences about a conflict you had concerning a holiday celebration. Use at least two of the Big Question vocabulary words.

   _____

   _____

2. How did you solve the conflict? Explain your solution in two sentences.

   _____

   _____

C. *Complete the sentence below. Then, write a short paragraph in which you state and explain some wise advice to apply to emotional conflict.*

   Resolving emotional conflicts can be difficult because _____

   _____

   _____

   _____

   _____

"**Hamadi**" by Naomi Shihab Nye
Reading: Compare and Contrast

When you **compare and contrast characters,** you look for similarities and differences among the people in a story. One strategy for comparing is to **identify each character's perspective**—that is, to consider the way each person understands the world.

- As you read, note details about the main character.
- To compare, consider whether the main character's actions, emotions, and ideas are similar to or different from those of other characters.
- Finally, decide whether you can trust what the character says and does.

One of the main ways readers understand the characters' perspectives in "Hamadi" is by looking closely at the characters' reactions to the same person, topic, or event. Notice the very different reactions to Hamadi in these passages:

Susan's father: "Riddles. He talks in riddles. I don't know why I have patience with him."

Susan: "He says interesting things. He makes me think."

DIRECTIONS: *Answer the following questions. Think about each character's perspective on the topic.*

Topic: staying in touch with friends and relatives

1. How does Susan's father stay in touch with his relatives in the Middle East?

   _____

2. How does Hamadi keep in touch with his relatives in the Middle East?

   _____

3. How does Susan keep in touch with her friend Hamadi?

   _____

Topic: the caroling outing

4. How does Susan's father react when she invites Hamadi to go caroling?

   _____

   _____

5. How does Hamadi react to the invitation?

   _____

   _____

6. Why does Susan want to invite Hamadi to carol?

   _____

   _____

Name _____ Date _____

"**Hamadi**" by Naomi Shihab Nye
Literary Analysis: Character Traits

Character traits are the personal qualities, attitudes, and values that make a character unique. For example, one character may be joyless, while another finds pleasure in everything.

- *Round characters* are complex, showing many different character traits.
- In contrast, *flat characters* are one-dimensional, showing just a single trait.

Writers sometimes state character traits directly, but more often they reveal them through details such as a character's actions, appearance, speech, and the reactions of others to the character. In "Hamadi," readers learn about Saleh Hamadi in all these ways. For example, this passage from the story reveals that Hamadi observes closely and enjoys language.

> Hamadi liked to use Spanish words. They made him feel expansive, worldly. He'd learned them when he worked at the fruits and vegetables warehouse on Zarzamora Street, marking off crates of apples and avocados on a long white pad.

A. DIRECTIONS: *On the chart below, list at least three details the author gives about Saleh Hamadi and what trait each detail reveals.*

Detail	Trait Revealed

B. DIRECTIONS: *Choose two of the details you recorded about Hamadi. Write a few sentences describing him.*

_____

_____

_____

_____

_____

"Hamadi" by Naomi Shihab Nye
Vocabulary Builder

Word List

expansive   melancholy   obscure   refugee   surrogate   tedious

A. DIRECTIONS: *Mark each statement below with T for true or F for false. Then, explain your answers.*

____ 1. One would expect a *refugee* to have made a personal choice to live away from his or her homeland.

_____

_____

____ 2. If a good friend moved to another state, you would probably be *melancholy*.

_____

____ 3. Most people look forward to *tedious* tasks.

_____

_____

____ 4. A person who is feeling *expansive* would probably donate generously to charity.

_____

____ 5. Zoos sometimes provide *surrogate* mothers to orphaned baby animals.

_____

_____

____ 6. An *obscure* fact is one that most people know.

_____

B. WORD STUDY: The suffix *-ee* refers to someone who receives an action or has been put in a certain position. Revise each sentence so that the underlined word containing the prefix *-ee* is used logically. Be sure not to change the underlined word.

1. The *absentee* list included the names of all those who were present at the meeting.

_____

_____

2. The *payee* wrote a check to pay the bill.

_____

_____

3. The *employee* benefits apply only to those who do not work here.

_____

_____

Name _____ Date _____

Enrichment: Using an Encyclopedia as a Resource

Hamadi lived in Lebanon until he immigrated to the United States at age eighteen. Usually, the place one grows up in has a significant influence on the ways in which one views the world.

To increase your understanding of Hamadi's background and perspectives, do some research about the country of Lebanon. Use an encyclopedia, either printed or online, to find and record information about Lebanon's geography (including land and climate), people, and history.

DIRECTIONS: *Use the chart to record the information you find in each category.*

Geography	People	History

"**Hamadi**" by Naomi Shihab Nye
Open-Book Test

Short Answer *Write your responses to the questions in this section on the lines provided.*

1. Susan's father urges Hamadi to move to a better apartment, but Hamadi refuses. Why is he content to live at the Traveler's Hotel? Refer to story details to explain your answer.

   _____

   _____

   _____

2. Once, when Susan and her father visit Hamadi, Susan asks about the "Love" stamps on his desk. Why does he like the stamps? At the end of the story, how does he show that he believes in their message?

   _____

   _____

3. In "Hamadi," Eddie's feelings and actions are important to Tracy. How are Susan's interests different from Tracy's? What does the narrator say about Susan that leads you to your answer?

   _____

   _____

   _____

4. After Susan talks to Tracy about Eddie, Tracy says, "Sometimes you remind me of a minister." Is that a compliment? Explain your answer.

   _____

   _____

   _____

5. Susan invites Hamadi to go caroling with her English Club. How does Hamadi react to Susan's invitation? Why might he feel the way he does?

   _____

   _____

   _____

6. Susan says of her uncles, "Anyone who watches TV more than twelve minutes a week is uninteresting." What does this comment tell you about Susan's personality? Name another detail from "Hamadi" in which Susan shows the same trait.

   _____

   _____

   _____

   _____

7. What does Susan mean when she calls Hamadi her "surrogate grandmother"? What similarity does she see between Hamadi and her grandmother?

_____

_____

_____

_____

8. In a story, a flat character is one-sided, demonstrating only one trait. In "Hamadi," is Tracy a flat character? Use details from the story to explain your answer.

_____

_____

9. Think about ways in which Susan and Hamadi are similar and ways in which they are different. Complete this chart. Then, on the line below, state whether the similarities or the differences seem more important to the relationship. Briefly explain your answer.

Similarities	Differences
Both talk about Kahlil Gibran.	He is an older man from Palestine; she is a teenage girl from the United States.
Both offer Tracy support.	

_____

10. Is Hamadi a melancholy character? Explain your answer based on the definition of *melancholy*.

_____

_____

Essay

Write an extended response to the question of your choice or to the question or questions your teacher assigns you.

11. Hamadi often gives advice. He talks about drinking a glass of water each morning. He also talks about going on with life when one has been hurt. In a brief essay, explain how his advice helps show that he is a round character rather than a flat one. Begin by defining the term *round character*.

12. Hamadi enjoys being with other people, but he spends much of his time alone. In an essay, describe the way Hamadi lives and his beliefs about what is important in life. Mention his home, his interests, and his personality.

13. Reread the very first sentence of "Hamadi." Then, in a brief essay, explain why Susan might have become interested in Hamadi at this point in her life. Support your response with information from the story.

14. **Thinking About the Big Question: Can all conflicts be resolved?** Reread the advice that Hamadi gives at end of the story, when he says, "We go on." In an essay, explain how Hamadi might respond to the question, Can all conflicts be resolved? Use Hamadi's advice and details about his life to support your response.

Oral Response

15. Go back to question 3, 6, or 7 or to the question your teacher assigns you. Take a few minutes to expand your answer and prepare an oral response. Find additional details in "Hamadi" that support your points. If necessary, make notes to guide your response.

"**Hamadi**" by Naomi Shihab Nye
Selection Test A

Critical Reading *Identify the letter of the choice that best answers the question.*

____ 1. In the story "Hamadi," where was Susan's father born?
  A. Palestine
  B. Lebanon
  C. India
  D. England

____ 2. In "Hamadi," how does Susan's father stay in touch with his relatives in the Middle East?
  A. He calls them on the phone every week.
  B. He visits his relatives on holidays.
  C. He travels back to his homeland once a year.
  D. He writes frequent letters.

____ 3. In "Hamadi," why does Susan find her uncles dull?
  A. They always talk about business.
  B. They mostly shop and watch television.
  C. They talk only about the past.
  D. They take no interest in her life.

____ 4. Hamadi chooses to live in an old hotel rather than in a more modern apartment. What does this choice tell you about him?
  A. He values simplicity more than outward appearances.
  B. He regrets not being able to afford a newer place to live in.
  C. He is embarrassed about not having much furniture.
  D. He does not want to make the effort to move.

____ 5. What character trait does the author reveal about Susan when she writes, "Susan didn't want a boyfriend"?
  A. shyness
  B. unpleasantness
  C. snobbism
  D. independence

_____ 6. How would you describe Hamadi based on this excerpt from the story?

"A white handkerchief spread across a tabletop, my two extra shoes lined by the wall, this spells 'home' to me, this says 'mi casa.' What more do I need?"

A. content

B. lazy

C. jealous

D. bitter

_____ 7. Which of the following terms best describes Hamadi's relationship to Susan?

A. uncle

B. grandfather

C. role model

D. tutor

_____ 8. What advice does Hamadi give to people he meets?

A. People should eat six small meals a day.

B. Everyone should read Kahlil Gibran's works.

C. It is important to sing carols loudly to attract listeners.

D. You must visit people in order to know them.

_____ 9. Susan visits Hamadi, invites him caroling, and comforts her friend Tracy. What do these things tell you about her?

A. She is a popular companion.

B. She is generous and compassionate.

C. She makes friends easily.

D. She enjoys people of all ages.

_____ 10. Why does Susan invite Hamadi to go caroling with her and her friends?

A. She feels sorry that he is all alone during the holidays.

B. She wants to teach him about American traditions.

C. She is tired of being with the same people all the time.

D. She misses her grandmother.

_____ 11. How does Hamadi react to Susan's invitation to go caroling?

A. He is thrilled.

B. He worries about traveling to her house.

C. He asks her to pick him up.

D. He says he read about the custom.

Vocabulary and Grammar

___ 12. Which sentence contains the past tense of a verb?
   A. She finished the book yesterday.
   B. She reads quickly.
   C. He likes to read mysteries.
   D. He rides his bike to school.

___ 13. Which word best describes the meaning of *distinctions*?
   A. wealth
   B. happiness
   C. details
   D. differences

___ 14. Which sentence contains the present participle form of a verb?
   A. Melanie ate dinner with her friends.
   B. Nate walks a mile each day.
   C. James is raking leaves today.
   D. Mary mowed the lawn last weekend.

___ 15. In which sentence is *melancholy* used correctly?
   A. Jack felt melancholy when his team won the game.
   B. The pleasant, sunny day at the beach made Judy feel melancholy.
   C. I feel melancholy when I think of a friend who moved away.
   D. Sue felt melancholy as she laughed at the comedy.

Essay

16. In a brief essay, explain with which character in "Hamadi" you identified more, Susan or Tracy. Use examples from the story to explain your answer.

17. Hamadi is a person who enjoys people, but he chooses to spend much of his time alone. Write an essay in which you describe the way Hamadi lives and his beliefs about what is important in life. Include details about his home, his interests, and his personality.

18. **Thinking About the Big Question: Can all conflicts be resolved?** Reread the advice that Hamadi gives at the end of the story, when he says, "We go on." In an essay, explain how Hamadi might respond to the question, Can all conflicts be resolved? Use Hamadi's advice and details about his life to support your response.

"Hamadi" by Naomi Shihab Nye
Selection Test B

Critical Reading *Identify the letter of the choice that best answers the question.*

____ 1. In "Hamadi," when the author calls the women in the school counselor's office "brittle," she is describing
    A. the theme.
    B. a character trait.
    C. the mood.
    D. a prediction.

____ 2. How does Hamadi first become acquainted with Susan's father?
    A. They met through Kahlil Gibran.
    B. They met at Susan's school.
    C. They were childhood friends.
    D. They just drifted together.

____ 3. Where did Hamadi grow up?
    A. England
    B. India
    C. Lebanon
    D. the United States

____ 4. What does Susan in "Hamadi" mean when she says: "I want fat beans. If I imagine something, it's true, too. Just a different kind of true."
    A. She is hungry for dinner.
    B. Her grandmother has made her interested in gardening.
    C. She values imagination.
    D. She is imagining returning to the countryside of Palestine.

____ 5. What does the following passage from "Hamadi" tell you about Susan?
    Susan carried *The Prophet* around on top of her English textbook and her Texas history.

    A. She likes to impress others with her reading material.
    B. She is behind in her school reading.
    C. She enjoys reading books beyond those assigned by her teachers.
    D. She needs the book for her work on the literary magazine.

____ 6. In "Hamadi," Susan's friend Tracy is upset because
    A. another girl is competing with her for the attention of a boy.
    B. her parents want her to quit the literary magazine.
    C. she secretly finds Gibran boring, but cannot bring herself to tell Susan.
    D. her grades have dipped because of her involvement with extracurricular activities.

____ 7. In "Hamadi," Eddie's feelings and actions are important to Tracy. How are Susan's interests different?
    A. Susan would rather become a cheerleader.
    B. Susan is not interested in how others feel.
    C. Susan would rather read books than talk with Tracy.
    D. Susan is not interested in having a boyfriend.

___ 8. From the choices, pick the word that best describes the character trait of Hamadi conveyed in the following passage.

> Two thin streams of tears rolled down Tracy's face. . . . Hamadi peered into Tracy's face, inquiring, "Why? Is it pain? Is it gratitude? . . ."

A. cluelessness
B. compassion
C. nosiness
D. weariness

___ 9. Why is Hamadi content to live in the Traveler's Hotel?
A. It is convenient to his place of work.
B. He does not care much about appearances and possessions.
C. It reminds him of his home in the Middle East.
D. It is in a very interesting neighborhood.

___ 10. What does Susan in "Hamadi" mean by the following statement?

> "Anyone who watches TV more than twelve minutes a week is uninteresting."

A. She is critical of all television.
B. She finds most people uninteresting.
C. She wants Hamadi to watch less television.
D. She disapproves of passive behavior.

___ 11. What does Hamadi mean when he says, "I married the wide horizon"?
A. He loves to travel the world.
B. He loves books that inspire his imagination.
C. He loves to read about air travel.
D. He loves to study different landscapes.

___ 12. When Susan asks Hamadi if he met Kahlil Gibran in a book or in person, Hamadi says,

> "Make no such distinctions, my friend."

What does this remark tell you about Hamadi?
A. He would rather read about people than talk with them.
B. He cannot tell the difference between imagination and reality.
C. He values a person's ideas more than a person's physical presence.
D. He did not get along with Kahlil Gibran.

___ 13. Susan finds in Hamadi some of the traits she enjoyed in her grandmother, who lives near Jerusalem. What similarity does Susan find most compelling?
A. Both live simply and thoughtfully.
B. Both are elderly.
C. Both come from the Middle East.
D. Both enjoy visiting with friends.

_____ **14.** How do Susan's friends react on meeting Hamadi?
   A. They ask questions about his homeland.
   B. They find his formal manners amusing.
   C. They teach him the words to the carols.
   D. They welcome him graciously.

Vocabulary and Grammar

_____ **15.** Which of the following words is closest in meaning to *melancholy*?
   A. queasy
   B. harmonious
   C. sad
   D. determined

_____ **16.** Which sentence contains the past tense of a verb?
   A. Tom rides his bike to school each day.
   B. Today, Tom locked the bike to a fence.
   C. Tom's brother has been riding it home.
   D. His brother had asked to ride the bike.

_____ **17.** Which verb form is a present participle?
   A. gather
   B. gathered
   C. gathering
   D. had gathered

Essay

18. In "Hamadi," the author describes Susan's and Hamadi's character traits through their personal qualities and attitudes. She also shows reactions of others to Susan and Hamadi. Write an essay in which you describe Susan and Hamadi. Support your answer with examples from the story.

19. Nye writes, "Susan didn't really feel interested in Saleh Hamadi until she was a freshman in high school carrying a thousand questions around." In a brief essay, discuss why Susan might have become interested in Hamadi at this point in her life. Use details from the story.

20. Hamadi tells Tracy:

   "We go on. On and on. We don't stop where it hurts. We turn a corner. It is the reason why we are living. To turn a corner."

Write an essay in which you explain how Hamadi's advice might be helpful to Tracy in the story. Then, explain how it would prove useful to Susan in later years.

21. **Thinking About the Big Question: Can all conflicts be resolved?** Reread the advice that Hamadi gives at end of the story, when he says, "We go on." In an essay, explain how Hamadi might respond to the question, Can all conflicts be resolved? Use Hamadi's advice and details about his life to support your response.

Vocabulary Warm-up Word Lists

Study these words from "The Tell-Tale Heart." Then, complete the activities.

Word List A

boldly [BOHLD lee] *adv.* with confidence or daring
Despite his sister's anger, Brandon knocked <u>boldly</u> on her door.

chatted [CHAT id] *v.* talked in a friendly, informal way
Dr. Anderson always <u>chatted</u> with new patients, to put them at ease.

distinct [dis TINGKT] *adj.* clear
The mountains in the distance became more <u>distinct</u> as the fog lifted.

enthusiasm [en THOO zee az uhm] *n.* strong feeling of enjoyment and interest
Our soccer coach values <u>enthusiasm</u> about the game more than skill.

grief [GREEF] *n.* deep sadness or emotional pain
I searched an hour for the right card to express my <u>grief</u> over the death of her aunt.

hideous [HID ee uhs] *adj.* horrible or extremely ugly
I had <u>hideous</u> nightmares after watching the true crime show.

instinct [IN stingkt] *n.* way of behaving or reacting that one is born with
When a car slides on ice, avoid the <u>instinct</u> to hit the brakes.

undid [uhn DID] *v.* opened; untied
The room became bright and cheerful once I <u>undid</u> the shutters.

Word List B

agony [AG uh nee] *n.* great suffering or severe pain
The <u>agony</u> caused by his sore knee showed on the runner's face.

arises [uh RYZ ez] *v.* comes up; moves upward; appears
When smoke <u>arises</u> from most chimneys, you know that winter has come.

continually [kuhn TIN yoo uhl lee] *adv.* again and again on a regular basis
I <u>continually</u> dialed the number, but it was always busy.

detected [di TEKT id] *v.* noticed or discovered something
When I <u>detected</u> a bad smell, I remembered my uneaten sandwich.

raved [RAYVD] *v.* spoke in a wild or angry way
The poor woman <u>raved</u> about the sudden loss of her baby.

suspicion [suh SPI shuhn] *n.* an idea, not based on facts, that something is wrong
I had a <u>suspicion</u> that he planned to cheat on the test.

vexed [VEKST] *v.* annoyed
The child who kept pulling my hair greatly <u>vexed</u> me.

wary [WAIR ee] *adj.* cautious; watchful
Small animals grow <u>wary</u> as night falls and owls fly.

"The Tell-Tale Heart" by Edgar Allan Poe
Vocabulary Warm-up Exercises

Exercise A *Fill in the blanks using each word from Word List A only once.*

When I was six, my mom's [1] _____ was to keep me away from the

scary Fun House. As we drove to the fair, she [2] _____ about everything

else we would do there. However, my [3] _____ about visiting the Fun

House was strong. My older brother had described its supposedly

[4] _____ horrors in [5] _____ detail, and I decided

that I could handle it. Soon, we were standing before the Fun House, and I

[6] _____ handed my ticket to the clown at the door. As he

[7] _____ the curtains hiding the thrills inside, I looked at my mom and

saw only [8] _____ on her face. I now know it was because her youngest

child was growing up.

Exercise B *Revise each sentence so that the underlined vocabulary word is used in a logical way. Be sure to keep the vocabulary word in your revision.*

1. With ease, I <u>detected</u> the lizard in the grass because it had changed its color to green.

   _____

2. The police officer's <u>suspicion</u> deepened as the clues all proved false.

   _____

3. As the woman slept peacefully, you could see the <u>agony</u> of her constant back pain.

   _____

4. I didn't mind that my friend <u>continually</u> walked home after school without me.

   _____

5. The calm man <u>raved</u> about waiting so long for his meal.

   _____

6. My grandmother loved watching us since we often <u>vexed</u> her.

   _____

7. As the whale <u>arises</u> toward the depths of the ocean, it gets ready to blow.

   _____

8. A <u>wary</u> driver never checks the rearview mirror.

   _____

"The Tell-Tale Heart" by Edgar Allan Poe
Reading Warm-up A

Read the following passage. Pay special attention to the underlined words. Then, read it again, and complete the activities. Use a separate sheet of paper for your written answers.

I was sure that my sister was lying about my missing jacket. I had noticed several <u>distinct</u> signs that she loved that jacket and wanted it for her own. The first time I wore it, her eyes were like magnets, drawn to the sparkling rhinestones and metal studs. She even <u>boldly</u> reached out her hand to touch the jacket. That went against our strict "hands off my stuff" rule.

My <u>grief</u> upon losing my jacket was matched only by my sister's <u>enthusiasm</u> in helping me try to find it. Since my sister probably wouldn't lift a finger to help me on my deathbed, I found her offers to look for my jacket quite strange. Then, as my mom and she <u>chatted</u> about other things, she casually asked if we had a small suitcase that locked. I figured that the suitcase had to be the hiding place for my stolen jacket.

Perhaps you think I'm a <u>hideous</u> person for doubting my sister's innocence. Let's just say I had my reasons. These involved other experiences with certain items of clothing that went missing. Indeed, it would be odd if I didn't doubt my sister in this case.

So, one night when my sister was out, I snuck into her room. I found the suitcase under her bed. I know my sister well, so by <u>instinct</u>, I found the hidden key. As I slid the key into the lock, I prepared myself to once again see my favorite jacket. Then, just as I <u>undid</u> the lid, my eyes fell on something entirely different. It was a small stash of money, coins and dollar bills zipped up in plastic bags. I guess it was my sister's babysitting money and allowance. To my great surprise, one bag was clearly labeled "To help Lizzie buy a new jacket."

1. Underline two groups of words that describe <u>distinct</u> signs that the sister liked the jacket.

2. Underline the sentence that explains why the gesture of touching the jacket is described by the word <u>boldly</u>. Then, write a sentence using both **distinct** and **boldly**.

3. Circle the reason for the narrator's <u>grief</u>. Explain how **grief** and **enthusiasm** could be viewed as opposite feelings.

4. Why is **casually** a good word to use when describing how people <u>chatted</u>?

5. Underline the words that give a possible reason why the reader might think the writer is <u>hideous</u>. Then, describe something you would find **hideous** in a person.

6. Underline the word that identifies what the writer <u>undid</u>. Write a sentence of your own using **undid**.

7. Circle the words describing what the writer did by <u>instinct</u>. Then, write a sentence telling about something you can do by **instinct**.

"The Tell-Tale Heart" by Edgar Allan Poe
Reading Warm-up B

Read the following passage. Pay special attention to the underlined words. Then, read it again, and complete the activities. Use a separate sheet of paper for your written answers.

Mental health is something many people take for granted. In fact, until mental illness strikes a family, few people really understand it at all. They don't know that sickness can affect thinking and emotions as well as physical health. Not knowing the facts about mental illness can cause added <u>agony</u> for those who have it and for their loved ones.

One of the most serious types of mental illness is known as *psychosis*. People who <u>continually</u> have trouble understanding what is going on around them have this condition. For example, some people with psychosis are <u>vexed</u> because they imagine others are talking about them or wanting to harm them. They might believe that they have <u>detected</u> unusual things going on that are not really happening. When people have a constant unfounded <u>suspicion</u> that someone could harm them, these people are said to suffer from *paranoia*.

Possibly, you have seen a person with this problem as he or she <u>raved</u> about strange topics while standing on a street corner. Seeing this type of behavior can make you feel especially <u>wary</u>. Having such a feeling is not unusual. However, the best overall action to take is to become more educated about mental illness.

Mentally ill people, like all who suffer from sickness, need kindness. They require help from a doctor in order to get better. The help might come in the form of medicine. It might involve regular sessions with trained professionals to talk about whatever <u>arises</u> that may be upsetting the person. Other treatments are also helpful. Perhaps most important, however, is for everyone to have an awareness of mental illness and to understand the importance of healthy relationships and having a sense of self-worth.

1. Underline the words that describe what can cause <u>agony</u>. Then, explain what *agony* means.

2. Circle the word naming the condition of <u>continually</u> not knowing what is going on. Describe something in the world that happens *continually*.

3. Write about some actions of a person with psychosis that might help a doctor recognize the illness. Use the words *vexed*, *detected*, and *raved*.

4. Underline the words describing a <u>suspicion</u> a person with paranoia might have. Then, explain what *suspicion* means.

5. Explain why someone might feel <u>wary</u> when observing such behavior.

6. Circle the words that refer to what <u>arises</u> that mentally ill people might want to talk about. Then, explain what *arises* means.

"The Tell-Tale Heart" by Edgar Allan Poe
Writing About the Big Question

Can all conflicts be resolved?

Big Question Vocabulary

argument	compromise	injury	insecurity	interact
irritate	mislead	negotiate	oppose	reaction
solution	stalemate	victorious	viewpoint	violence

A. *Use a word from the list above to complete each sentence.*

1. Sometimes, another person's bad habits can really _____ someone else.

2. Someone's bad habit might cause a serious _____ with a roommate.

3. From my _____, you should try to control bad habits that annoy others.

4. Some bad habits, like nail-biting, suggest that a person suffers from _____.

B. *Follow the directions in responding to each of the items below. Answer in complete sentences.*

1. Describe two things other people do that you find really irritating.

_____

_____

2. In two sentences, explain how you handle one of those situations when it occurs. Use at least two of the Big Question vocabulary words.

_____

_____

C. *In "The Tell-Tale Heart," a murderer describes his mental conflicts before and after he has committed the crime. Complete the sentence below. Then, write a short paragraph in which you give advice to a person torn between doing right and wrong.*

When torn between doing right and wrong, a person may _____

_____

_____

_____

"The Tell-Tale Heart" by Edgar Allan Poe
Reading: Compare and Contrast

When you **compare and contrast characters,** you look for similarities and differences among the people in a story. One strategy for comparing is to **identify each character's perspective**—that is, to consider the way a person understands the world.

- As you read, note details about the main character.
- To compare, consider whether the main character's actions, emotions, and ideas are similar to or different from those of other characters.
- Finally, decide whether you can trust what the character says and does.

One of the main ways readers understand the characters' perspectives in "The Tell-Tale Heart" is by looking closely at the characters' reactions to the same person, topic, or event. In this story, readers get most of their information about the old man's reactions from the narrator's point of view. Notice the different reactions to the story's events in the following passages.

> The old man (from the narrator's point of view): "Presently I heard a slight groan, and I knew it was the groan of mortal terror. It was not a groan of pain or of grief—oh, no!—it was the low stifled sound that arises from the bottom of the soul when overcharged with awe."

> The narrator: "I knew what the old man felt, and pitied him, although I chuckled at heart."

DIRECTIONS: *Answer the following questions. Think about each character's perspective on the events of the night.*

1. How does the narrator describe his feelings and actions as he looks in on the old man sleeping each night?

   _____

2. How does the old man react on the eighth night when he hears a noise at the door?

   _____

3. How does the narrator feel when he sees the old man's eye in the ray of light? What does the narrator hear?

   _____

   _____

4. What has the old man been doing and feeling during the hour after hearing the noise?

   _____

   _____

5. How does the old man react when the narrator leaps into his room?

   _____

6. How does the narrator describe his feelings after killing the old man?

   _____

Name _____ Date _____

"The Tell-Tale Heart" by Edgar Allan Poe
Literary Analysis: Character Traits

Character traits are the personal qualities, attitudes, and values that make a character unique. For example, one character may be joyless, while another finds pleasure in everything.

- *Round characters* are complex, showing many different character traits.
- In contrast, *flat characters* are one-dimensional, showing just a single trait.

Writers sometimes state character traits directly, but more often they reveal them through details such as a character's actions, thoughts, appearance, speech, and the reactions of others to the character. In "The Tell-Tale Heart," readers learn about the narrator through his own description of his thoughts and feelings. For example, this passage from the story reveals that the narrator sees himself as both nervous and calm. He defends his health and sanity, yet refers to things that suggest insanity.

> True!—nervous—very, very dreadfully nervous I had been and am; but why *will* you say that I am mad? The disease had sharpened my senses—not destroyed—not dulled them. Above all was the sense of hearing acute. I heard all things in the heaven and in the earth. I heard many things in hell. How, then, am I mad? Hearken! and observe how healthily—how calmly I can tell you the whole story.

A. DIRECTIONS: *On the chart below, list at least three details the author gives about the narrator and what trait each detail reveals.*

Detail	Trait Revealed

B. DIRECTIONS: *Choose two of the details you recorded about the narrator. Write a few sentences describing him.*

_____

_____

_____

_____

86

Name _____ Date _____

"The Tell-Tale Heart" by Edgar Allan Poe
Vocabulary Builder

Word List

audacity cunningly derision resolved stealthily vex

A. DIRECTIONS: *Revise each sentence so that the underlined vocabulary word is used logically. Be sure to keep the vocabulary word in your revision.*

1. When the basketball player made the difficult shot look easy, the crowd shouted with <u>derision</u>.

_____

_____

2. Sheila's <u>audacity</u> showed in the way she shyly held back.

_____

_____

3. Simon's good behavior continued to <u>vex</u> his mother.

_____

4. Becca never tried to complete anything she had <u>resolved</u> to do.

_____

_____

5. Because Armando had acted so <u>cunningly</u>, everyone knew what he was up to.

_____

_____

6. Cindy moved very <u>stealthily</u>, banging on a drum as she went along.

_____

_____

B. WORD STUDY: The suffix *-ity* indicates a noun meaning "a quality or state of being." Explain your answers to the following questions using one of these words containing the suffix *-ity*: *possibility, necessity, tranquillity.*

1. Is there a *possibility* that you could travel back in time to before you were born?

_____

2. What kind of experience would give you a feeling of *tranquillity?*

_____

3. Why is drinking water a *necessity* when you are taking a long hike?

_____

_____

"The Tell-Tale Heart" by Edgar Allan Poe
Enrichment: Designing a Set

A suspense story such as "The Tell-Tale Heart" is scary, in part, because of its setting, or the time and place of the action. Edgar Allan Poe's description of a darkened room, shadows, and creaky flooring creates an atmosphere of tension. In movies, a set designer creates the proper mood, or atmosphere, through the selection and arrangement of scenery, lighting, and props (props can include things to dress the scene or things someone in the scene can use—anything from rugs to coffee mugs).

Imagine yourself as the set designer of a horror film. Your set design will provide moviegoers with their first frightening glimpse of where the action will take place.

A. DIRECTIONS: *Design your set by providing details in each of the following areas. Make your descriptions as specific as possible.*

Setting: Describe the location where the action will take place (for example, outside or inside; a forest, a basement, a kitchen, an attic, and so forth).

_____

_____

_____

Props: Describe some specific items in the scene (for example, a rusty wheelbarrow, a torn couch, an area rug, a vase of flowers, and so forth).

_____

_____

_____

Lighting: Describe how the scene will be illuminated (for example, by moonlight, lamplight, direct sunlight, shadows, and so forth).

_____

_____

_____

B. DIRECTIONS: *Think of your favorite movie. Describe the most memorable scene in detail, noting the setting, props, and lighting as you remember them.*

_____

_____

_____

_____

_____

"Hamadi" by Naomi Shihab Nye
"The Tell-Tale Heart" by Edgar Allan Poe
Integrated Language Skills: Grammar

Principal Parts of Regular Verbs

Each verb has four **principal parts,** or main forms.

Present (Base Form)	Past	Present Participle	Past Participle
gather(s)	gathered	gathering	gathered
move(s)	moved	moving	moved

- The present participle usually appears after forms of the helping verb *be.* To form the present participle, add *-ing* to the base form. If the verb ends in a consonant plus *e,* drop the *e* before adding *-ing.*

    Ruby is <u>fastening</u> the straps of her backpack.

    Jack is <u>exercising</u> great care with the delicate ship model.

- The past participle is used most often after forms of the helping verb *have.* To form the past participle of regular verbs, add *-ed* to the base form. If the verb ends in a consonant plus *e,* drop the *e* before adding *-ed.*

    No one has <u>warned</u> Eric of the approaching hurricane.

    By Saturday, she had <u>moved</u> into her new apartment.

A. PRACTICE: *Complete each sentence by providing the form of the verb indicated in parentheses.*

1. (present participle of *sell*) Firewood was _____ at forty dollars a cord.

2. (past participle of *notice*) Bart had _____ a used computer at the yard sale.

3. (present participle of *figure*) Cass was _____ out the sum without a calculator.

4. (present form of *tower*) The basketball player _____ over me.

5. (past tense of *halt*) Stanley _____ his dog team before it reached the river.

6. (present form of *search*) Fran always _____ for lost earrings.

B. Writing Application: *Write four sentences to illustrate the principal parts of shiver. Your sentences should be about a person who is highly sensitive to cold.*

1. _____

2. _____

3. _____

4. _____

"Hamadi" by Naomi Shihab Nye
"The Tell-Tale Heart" by Edgar Allan Poe

Integrated Language Skills: Support for Writing a Character Profile

To prepare for **writing a character profile** of either Saleh Hamadi or the narrator in "The Tell-Tale Heart," use the chart and gather specific details about his personality. Think about Hamadi's choice of lifestyle, the things he says to Susan, and his reaction to Tracy's unhappiness while they are caroling. Alternatively, recall how the narrator describes his relationship with the old man and his reasons for deciding to kill him. Then, think about the various emotions the narrator experiences and describes— nervousness, anxiety, happiness, anger—as he carries out his plan and, finally, confronts the police officers.

Character Trait	How the Trait Affects Plot and Resolution

Name _____ Date _____

"**Hamadi**" by Naomi Shihab Nye
"**The Tell-Tale Heart**" by Edgar Allan Poe

Integrated Language Skills: Support for Extend Your Learning

Listening and Speaking: "Hamadi"

To prepare for your oral response, write down your feelings about the characters and topics below. Then, write a question you had while reading "Hamadi." You might need to refer back to the story to refresh your memory. Read your question aloud to the class, and discuss with your classmates.

Feelings about characters: _____

_____

_____

Mood/atmosphere: _____

_____

_____

Narrative techniques: _____

_____

_____

Question: _____

_____

_____

Listening and Speaking: "The Tell-Tale Heart"

To prepare for your oral response, write down your feelings about the characters and topics below. Then, write a question you had while reading "The Tell-Tale Heart." You might need to refer back to the story to refresh your memory. Read your question aloud to the class, and discuss with your classmates.

Feelings about characters: _____

_____

Mood/atmosphere: _____

_____

Narrative techniques: _____

_____

Question: _____

_____

_____

Name _____ Date _____

"**The Tell-Tale Heart**" by Edgar Allan Poe

Open-Book Test

Short Answer *Write your responses to the questions in this section on the lines provided.*

1. Before the murder, the narrator of "The Tell-Tale Heart" greets the old man cheerfully each morning. What does the old man fail to understand about this greeting?

   _____

   _____

   _____

2. What does the narrator of "The Tell-Tale Heart" assume that the reader thinks about him? Explain. How does his reason for killing the old man suggest that his assumption is correct?

   _____

   _____

   _____

   _____

   _____

   _____

3. In the third paragraph of "The Tell-Tale Heart," the narrator says, "You fancy me mad." According to that passage, what character traits does the murderer pride himself on?

   _____

   _____

   _____

   _____

4. On the night of the murder, as he waits for the old man to lie down, the narrator of "The Tell-Tale Heart" chuckles. Why does he chuckle? What does his laughter show about his personality?

   _____

   _____

   _____

5. On the eighth night, the narrator of "The Tell-Tale Heart" accidentally wakes the old man. How do the narrator's feelings that night contrast with the old man's feelings? Cite details to support your answer.

   _____

   _____

   _____

6. Just before he is murdered, the old man groans. What are the two ways in which the narrator of "The Tell-Tale Heart" describes the groans? How does he identify himself with both of those explanations?

_____

_____

_____

_____

7. Think about the events in "The Tell-Tale Heart" that occur between the murder and the confession. Then, use details from the story to complete this cause-and-effect flowchart.

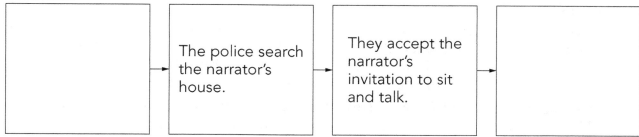

	The police search the narrator's house.	They accept the narrator's invitation to sit and talk.	

8. As "The Tell-Tale Heart" progresses, the narrator's mood changes. At the end, how is the narrator's personality different from what it was at the beginning? Support your answer with details from the story.

_____

_____

_____

_____

9. As "The Tell-Tale Heart" reaches its climax, why does the narrator think that the police officers are treating him with derision? Base your answer on the definition of *derision.*

_____

_____

_____

10. At the end of "The Tell-Tale Heart," the sound of a heartbeat drives the murderer to confess. Is he correct in thinking that the sound he hears is the sound of the old man's heart? Explain your response.

_____

_____

Essay

Write an extended response to the question of your choice or to the question or questions your teacher assigns you.

11. Did you figure out the ending of "The Tell-Tale Heart" in advance? In an essay, explain whether you think most readers can tell how the story will end. Consider the narrator's character traits in your answer. Did his personality influence your prediction? Explain.

12. "The Tell-Tale Heart" is narrated by the murderer. Can the reader trust his account? Would the story be more effective if it were narrated by a character outside the story? Answer these questions in an essay. Cite details from the story to support your points.

13. As "The Tell-Tale Heart" begins, the narrator mentions that he has been suffering from a disease. In an essay, describe the difference between what the narrator thinks the disease has done to him and what you think the disease may have done to him. Cite details from the story to support your points.

14. **Thinking About the Big Question: Can all conflicts be resolved?** As "The Tell-Tale Heart" reaches its climax, the narrator becomes more and more nervous. In an essay, respond to these questions: What internal conflict is making the narrator nervous? At the end of the story, is the conflict resolved? Support your response with evidence from the story.

Oral Response

15. Go back to question 2, 3, or 8 or to the question your teacher assigns you. Take a few minutes to expand your answer and prepare an oral response. Find additional details in "The Tell-Tale Heart" that support your points. If necessary, make notes to guide your response.

Vocabulary Warm-up Word Lists

Study these words from "Up the Slide" and "A Glow in the Dark." Then, complete the activities.

Word List A

ascent [uh SENT] *n.* act of climbing or rising
   Our <u>ascent</u> up the mountain wasn't scary—if we didn't look down.

barren [BA ruhn] *adj.* bare; having no plant life
   The desert was <u>barren</u> as far as we could see.

ebbed [EBD] *v.* faded little by little
   The light, once so strong, had <u>ebbed</u> to just a faint glow.

firewood [FYR wood] *n.* wood to be burned on a fire
   Because the cabin did not have central heating, we gathered <u>firewood</u>.

gully [GUHL ee] *n.* small, narrow valley
   Between the two hills was a <u>gully</u> through which a stream flowed.

pose [POHZ] *v.* present; put forth
   The roughness of the road did not <u>pose</u> a problem for our all-terrain vehicle.

pulse [PUHLS] *v.* move in a rhythmic way
   The light was not steady; it seemed to <u>pulse</u> with a regular rhythm.

rig [RIG] *n.* a cart pulled by animals
   The dogs did not seem to mind pulling the <u>rig</u> through the snow.

Word List B

consumed [kuhn SOOMD] *v.* used up completely
   Getting ready for the ski slope <u>consumed</u> nearly half an hour.

convulsively [kuhn VUL siv lee] *adv.* with jerking and uncontrollable movements
   As Tim started to fall, he <u>convulsively</u> grabbed for the railing.

eerie [EER ee] *adj.* strange or weird and frightening
   The soundtrack set an <u>eerie</u> tone for the horror film.

favorable [FAY ver uh buhl] *adj.* helpful; likely to bring success
   Because the winds were <u>favorable</u>, our boat reached land quickly.

nausea [NAW zee uh] *n.* sick feeling in the stomach
   After eating ten hot dogs, Martin was overcome with <u>nausea</u>.

outcropping [OWT krahp ing] *n.* portion of a substance that sticks out from the surface
   The <u>outcropping</u> of rock gave us something solid to hold on to as we climbed.

treacherous [TRECH er uhs] *adj.* extremely dangerous
   The river's white water can become <u>treacherous</u>.

upright [UHP ryt] *adj.* standing or sitting straight up; vertical
   Even in the darkness, we could make out the snowman's <u>upright</u> form.

"**Up the Slide**" by Jack London
"**A Glow in the Dark**" *from* **Woodsong** by Gary Paulsen
Vocabulary Warm-up Exercises

Exercise A *Fill in each blank in the paragraph below with an appropriate word from Word List A. Use each word only once.*

The dogs pulling the [1] _____ were eager to race across the frozen,

[2] _____ land. Here, there were no forests to get lost in or even

any small trees to use as [3] _____ for a warm fire. This did not

[4] _____ a problem to Martin because he planned to reach the village

before dark. There were small rises in the land, but the [5] _____ caused

the team no difficulty. There were low areas, too, but nothing you could call even a

ditch, let alone a [6] _____. Martin must have figured the distance

wrong because now the sunlight [7] _____ and darkness closed in. As he

watched the stars appear and begin to [8] _____ in the sky, he felt confi-

dent that the dogs would get him to the village before long.

Exercise B *Decide whether each statement below is true or false. Circle T or F. Then, explain your answer.*

1. If your homework <u>consumed</u> ten minutes, then you did not spend enough time on it.
   T / F _____

2. An <u>outcropping</u> can be a <u>favorable</u> place for a mountain climber to get a grip.
   T / F _____

3. A nightlight with an <u>eerie</u> glow would comfort a young child.
   T / F _____

4. Extreme <u>nausea</u> can cause a person to throw up <u>convulsively</u>.
   T / F _____

5. A winter snowstorm can be <u>treacherous</u> to drive in.
   T / F _____

6. An <u>upright</u> sign is one that fell over because of high winds.
   T / F _____

Name _____ Date _____

"Up the Slide" by Jack London
"A Glow in the Dark" *from* Woodsong by Gary Paulsen
Reading Warm-up A

Read the following passage. Pay special attention to the underlined words. Then, read it again, and complete the activities. Use a separate sheet of paper for your written answers.

In 1896, three men found gold in a stream that emptied into the Klondike River in Canada's Yukon Territory. Newspapers ran stories about the fortune to be made.

In the summer of 1897, thousands of people seeking gold boarded ships in ports along the Pacific Coast and headed north. Little did they know that something had occurred that would <u>pose</u> a problem to their dreams of becoming rich. People before them had already staked their claim to most of the gold fields.

Do you have a picture in your mind of these gold seekers? Are they driving a team of dogs, hooked up to a <u>rig</u>? Are they on a frozen, <u>barren</u> landscape? That was not the reality. Many started out in summer. Their trip included the difficult <u>ascent</u> and descent of mountains. Treasure hunters had to carry a year's worth of gear on their backs, up and down the steep trails. Often, they had to prevent it, their pack animals, and themselves from falling down into a <u>gully</u>.

Those who made it to Dawson, the town near the gold fields, were not pleased to find they had come for nothing. People who sold supplies to would-be gold seekers, however, did well. They provided food, clothing, and medical care. Sawmills could barely keep up with the demand for lumber to build houses and for logs that would be used as <u>firewood</u>. Prices for everything rose steeply.

Within a year, nearly twenty thousand people had crowded into Dawson. Lights seemed to <u>pulse</u> like bright stars in the night from buildings where those who had struck gold spent it so fast it was like water trickling through their fingers. Those who had nothing to show for their efforts watched with envy. Soon, most of the disappointed adventurers packed up and went home. In time, the brilliance of the lights <u>ebbed</u>, and Dawson lost most of its residents. A chapter in gold rush history came to a close.

1. Circle the sentence that tells what would <u>pose</u> a problem to the gold seekers. Write about something that might *pose* a problem in your life.

2. Underline the words that help you picture a <u>rig</u>. Tell whether you would like to drive a dog *rig*.

3. Circle the word that gives you a clue to the meaning of <u>barren</u>. Write about an area of the world that is *barren*.

4. Underline the antonym for <u>ascent</u>. Tell what would be a difficult *ascent* for you.

5. Underline the words that help you figure out what a <u>gully</u> is. Describe a *gully* you know or that you can imagine.

6. Circle the two smaller, words in <u>firewood</u>. Describe a time when you might use *firewood*.

7. Circle the words that tell to what the lights that <u>pulse</u> are compared. Write about something else that would *pulse*.

8. Underline what <u>ebbed</u>. Explain what *ebbed* means.

"Up the Slide" by Jack London
"A Glow in the Dark" *from* **Woodsong** by Gary Paulsen
Reading Warm-up B

Read the following passage. Pay special attention to the underlined words. Then, read it again, and complete the activities. Use a separate sheet of paper for your written answers.

If you are ever hiking with a group in the dark woods, you might see an underline eerie light coming from a tree or a log. Neither of them is haunted; it is only foxfire—wild mushrooms that are glowing with their own natural light.

As you draw closer, you will be able to see an underline outcropping of mushrooms on an underline upright tree. On a fallen log, you may see the mushrooms growing on both the outside and the inside of the dying wood.

Unlike plants, mushrooms—which belong to a group of living things called *fungi*—do not make their own food. They get it from other living things. Sometimes mushrooms can grow on a tree without destroying it; sometimes they eat away at it until it dies. Other times, the tree is already dying, and the mushroom helps it break down, or decay.

Why do mushrooms glow? They probably shine at night to attract insects. Then, the insects brush up against the mushrooms or eat them, picking up spores, which are the part of the mushroom that makes new mushrooms. It is underline favorable to the mushroom to spread its spores, and flying insects can help out.

Some mushrooms that glow in the dark are edible, including the honey mushroom. Just because you can eat it, however, does not mean it tastes good. Another mushroom, the jack-o'-lantern, is poisonous. Its bright color and attractive appearance mask the fact that it is underline treacherous to pick and eat. You should never pick any wild mushroom without an expert's OK.

People who eat a jack-o'-lantern mushroom do not die but become very sick. They will feel great underline nausea in their stomachs and throw up underline convulsively.

So, if you ever "see the light" of a mushroom, walk up to it and snap a picture, but do not take it home for dinner. Still, don't feel that the hike has underline consumed your time for nothing. You can always buy mushrooms at the store and know that they are safe to eat.

1. Circle the word in the next sentence that suggests the meaning of underline eerie. Describe something *eerie* that you have seen.

2. Rewrite the sentence beginning, "As you draw closer," using different words for underline outcropping and underline upright. Do not change the meaning of the sentence.

3. Circle the words that hint at what underline favorable means. Write about something that is *favorable* to you.

4. Underline the word in the paragraph that suggests the meaning of underline treacherous. Tell about something *treacherous* that you know of.

5. Underline the words in the paragraph that help explain underline nausea and underline convulsively. Tell what else might make someone feel *nausea* and throw up *convulsively*.

6. Circle the word that tells what was underline consumed. Tell about a situation in your life that *consumed* this thing.

Unit 2 Resources: Short Stories

Name _____ Date _____

Writing About the Big Question

Can all conflicts be resolved?

Big Question Vocabulary

argument	compromise	injury	insecurity	interact
irritate	mislead	negotiate	oppose	reaction
solution	stalemate	victorious	viewpoint	violence

A. *Use a word from the list above to complete each sentence.*

1. For a _____ end to a dangerous situation, you need to be very careful.

2. If a man wants $40 for something and you offer $20, he might _____ at $30.

3. Sled dogs must _____ well as they follow their lead dog.

4. A sudden _____ by a group of sled dogs might indicate danger.

B. *Follow the directions in responding to each of the items below. Answer in complete sentences.*

1. In two sentences, describe your reaction if you realized you were lost in an unfamiliar and icy environment.

_____

_____

2. Write two sentences explaining why you would or would not like to work with a sled-dog team in a race. Use at least two of the Big Question vocabulary words.

_____

_____

C. *In both of these narrations, an individual struggles against natural dangers. Complete the sentence below. Then, write a short paragraph in which you connect this sentence to the Big Question.*

Nature's beauty can mislead. It often hides dangers for those who _____

_____

_____

_____

_____

"Up the Slide" by Jack London
"A Glow in the Dark" *from* **Woodsong** by Gary Paulsen

Literary Analysis: Fictional and Nonfictional Narratives

A **narrative** is any type of writing that tells a story. In a **fictional narrative,** the author tells a story about imaginary characters and events. "Up the Slide" is a fictional narrative. Because it does not describe real events, the author had complete control over the basic story elements of *character, setting,* and *plot.*

In a **nonfictional narrative,** such as "A Glow in the Dark," the author tells a story about real characters and events. The author of this work describes an event that actually happened to him. Although he cannot alter any of the details, he does emphasize some of them to give the story a kind of excitement.

DIRECTIONS: *Read each passage, and answer the questions that follow.*

from **"Up the Slide"** by Jack London

For, coming up from the Siwash village the previous day, he [Clay] had noticed a small dead pine in an out-of-the-way place, which had defied discovery by eyes less sharp than his. And his eyes were both young and sharp, for his seventeenth birthday was just cleared.

A swift ten minutes over the ice brought him to the place, and figuring ten minutes to get the tree and ten minutes to return made him certain that Swanson's dinner would not wait.

Just below Dawson, and rising out of the Yukon itself, towered the great Moosehide Mountain, so named by Lieutenant Schwatka long ere the Yukon became famous.

1. Which elements of this fictional narrative did the author make up? Identify two.

_____

2. Which details did the author borrow from real life? Identify two. _____

_____

from **"A Glow in the Dark"** by Gary Paulsen

They were caught in the green light, curved around my legs staring at the standing form, ears cocked and heads turned sideways while they studied it. I took another short step forward and they all followed me, then another, and they stayed with me until we were right next to the form.

It was a stump.

A six-foot-tall, old rotten stump with the bark knocked off, glowing in the dark with a bright green glow. Impossible. . . . I found out later that it glowed because it had sucked phosphorus from the ground up into the wood and held the light from day all night.

3. What detail provides a clue that this is a nonfictional narrative? _____

_____

What kind of detail is this? _____

4. What details give the narrative a fictional feel? Why? _____

_____

"Up the Slide" by Jack London
"A Glow in the Dark" *from* Woodsong by Gary Paulsen
Vocabulary Builder

Word List

ascent   descent   diffused   exertion   maneuver   sustain

A. DIRECTIONS: *Complete each sentence in a way that proves you know the meaning of the italicized word.*

1. When we completed our *ascent,* _____
_____

2. _____ requires great *exertion.*

3. It is difficult to *sustain* _____
_____

4. The upward-facing lampshade *diffused* _____
_____

5. Before our *descent,* _____
_____

6. Using a careful *maneuver,* _____
_____

B. DIRECTIONS: *Circle the letter of the word or phrase that is most nearly* opposite *in meaning to the word in CAPITAL LETTERS.*

1. ASCENT
   A. flight
   B. leap
   C. descent
   D. tumble

2. SUSTAIN
   A. let go
   B. strengthen
   C. reject
   D. maintain

3. DIFFUSED
   A. confused
   B. weakened
   C. diluted
   D. condensed

4. MANEUVER
   A. manipulate
   B. bumble
   C. trick
   D. stunt

"**Up the Slide**" by Jack London
"**A Glow in the Dark**" *from* **Woodsong** by Gary Paulsen

Integrated Language Skills: Support for Writing to Compare Use of Details in Narratives

Before you draft your essay comparing and contrasting the use of details in these narratives, complete the graphic organizers below. First, list details that reveal aspects of each character. Then, tell specifically what each detail reveals about the character. Finally, discuss how the details affect your view of the character and his challenges.

Clay Dilham in "Up the Slide"	
Invented Details	What They Reveal About the Character
How do these details affect your view of the character's challenge?	

Gary Paulsen in "A Glow in the Dark"	
True Details	What They Reveal About the Character
How do these details affect your view of the character's challenges?	

Now, use your notes to write an essay comparing and contrasting the use of details in the two narratives.

Unit 2 Resources: Short Stories
108

"Up the Slide" by Jack London
"A Glow in the Dark" by Gary Paulsen
Open-Book Test

Short Answer *Write your responses to the questions in this section on the lines provided.*

1. In the opening of "Up the Slide," Clay Dilham reveals his plan to fetch firewood. The opening also reveals the setting of the story. What details in this section of the story seem realistic? Cite two details to support your answer.

   _____

   _____

   _____

2. In "Up the Slide," Clay Dilham realizes that he must climb up a mountainside in order to get down. What information in the narrative explains why this is so.

   _____

   _____

   _____

3. Near the end of "Up the Slide," Swanson has a "hearty laugh" at Dilham's expense. Does Swanson find Dilham's adventure funny? What might Swanson actually be feeling? Cite a detail from the narrative to support your opinion.

   _____

   _____

   _____

4. Near the beginning of "A Glow in the Dark," we learn that because some of the dogs were young, they "could not sustain a long run." Why are young dogs unable to sustain a long run? Base your answer on the meaning of *sustain.*

   _____

   _____

   _____

5. In "A Glow in the Dark," the dogs react to the green glow. What is their reaction? Cite a detail from the narrative that indicates how the dogs feel about the glow.

   _____

   _____

6. In "A Glow in the Dark," Gary Paulsen sees "an eerie green-yellow glow." Since Paulsen is describing an event that actually occurred, what can you predict about the source of the glow?

   _____

   _____

   _____

7. One important difference between "Up the Slide" and "A Glow in the Dark" is in the narrator, the person or character who tells the story. Who is the narrator of "Up the Slide," and who is the narrator of "A Glow in the Dark"? Explain how you can tell.

_____

_____

_____

8. Sled dogs are characters in both "Up the Slide" and "A Glow in the Dark." In which narrative do they play a more important part? Support your answer by telling what each story is about.

_____

_____

_____

9. "Up the Slide" is a work of fiction, and "A Glow in the Dark" is a work of nonfiction. What are two ways in which the fictional story differs from the nonfictional story?

_____

_____

_____

10. In what significant ways are Clay Dilham in "Up the Slide" and Gary Paulsen in "A Glow in the Dark" similar? Answer this question by filling in the following chart with details from the narratives.

Similarities   **Evidence**

	→	
	→	

Essay

Write an extended response to the question of your choice or to the question or questions your teacher assigns you.

11. In a short essay, explain the differences between a fictional narrative and a nonfictional one. In your essay, answer these questions: How free is the author of a work of fiction to invent the characters, plot, and setting ? How free is the author of a work of nonfiction to invent the characters, plot, and setting? Give examples from "Up the Slide" and "A Glow in the Dark" to illustrate your ideas.

12. The way a person acts in the face of danger can reveal a great deal about him or her. What do you learn about Clay Dilham in "Up the Slide" and about Gary Paulsen in "A Glow in the Dark"? Answer this question in a brief essay. Support your opinion with examples from the two narratives.

13. Both "Up the Slide" and "A Glow in the Dark" are exciting stories, yet one is a fictional narrative and one is a nonfictional narrative. Do you think that fictional narratives are always more exciting than nonfictional narratives? Do you think that nonfictional narratives are always more exciting? Do you think that other factors, besides the type of narrative, might affect the excitement you feel as you read these types of literature? Address these questions in a short essay. Refer to "Up the Slide" and "A Glow in the Dark" to support your points.

14. **Thinking About the Big Question: Can all conflicts be resolved?** Clay in "Up the Slide" and the narrator of "A Glow in the Dark" both face an internal conflict—a struggle that takes place within them. In an essay, describe the characters' internal conflicts and what happens as a result. Then explain whether you think the conflict each character faces can be resolved.

Oral Response

15. Return to question 2, 5, or 7 or to the question or questions your teacher assigns you. Take a few minutes to expand your answer and prepare an oral response. Find additional details in "Up the Slide" and/or "A Glow in the Dark" that support your points. If necessary, make notes to guide your oral response.

"Up the Slide" by Jack London
"A Glow in the Dark" *from* Woodsong by Gary Paulsen
Selection Test A

Critical Reading *Identify the letter of the choice that best answers the question.*

____ 1. Which word best describes Clay at the beginning of "Up the Slide"?
A. playful
B. confident
C. fearful
D. wise

____ 2. Based on the events of "Up the Slide," how long did Clay's trip take?
A. about thirty minutes
B. two days
C. more than two hours
D. ten minutes

____ 3. Which detail in "Up the Slide" comes from real life?
A. the Yukon River
B. Clay's climb
C. Clay's slide down the slope
D. Swanson

____ 4. In "Up the Slide," what does Swanson believe?
A. Firewood is plentiful and easily found.
B. Clay is a stronger, braver man than he.
C. Traveling to the Yukon was a huge mistake.
D. Clay will not return as quickly as he predicts.

____ 5. In "Up the Slide," what does Clay do with the tree after he cuts it down?
A. He uses it to build a fire.
B. He sells it for firewood.
C. He leaves it on the mountain.
D. He uses it to build a shelter.

____ 6. In "A Glow in the Dark," why does Paulsen run his dogs at night without a light?
A. to improve the dogs' eyesight
B. because he has an emergency
C. because his head lamp goes out
D. to get away from the glow

_____ 7. In "A Glow in the Dark," what do Paulsen's actions *after* he sees the glow tell the reader?
   A. He is curious.
   B. He is foolish.
   C. He is confident.
   D. He is cowardly.

_____ 8. In "A Glow in the Dark," what does the strange shape turn out to be?
   A. a dog
   B. moonlight
   C. a lantern
   D. a tree stump

_____ 9. What phrase best describes "A Glow in the Dark"?
   A. a fictional story about phosphorus
   B. a fictional story about a frightening event
   C. a nonfiction piece about the danger of traveling at night
   D. a nonfiction piece about an event in the author's life

_____ 10. Which word best describes both Clay of "Up the Slide" and the narrator of "A Glow in the Dark" at the end of the stories?
   A. afraid
   B. relieved
   C. puzzled
   D. regretful

_____ 11. What is true of Clay Dilham in "Up the Slide" and Gary Paulsen in "A Glow in the Dark"?
   A. They both exist in real life.
   B. They are both writers.
   C. They both travel by sled.
   D. They are both loggers.

_____ 12. What is true of a fictional narrative such as "Up the Slide"?
   A. It can borrow details from real life.
   B. It must contain only facts.
   C. It cannot tell a story.
   D. It must contain only made-up details.

____ 13. Despite differences between "Up the Slide" and "A Glow in the Dark," what is true of both works?
A. They are both speeches.
B. The both deal with mysteries.
C. They are both adventure tales.
D. They are both written in the third person.

Vocabulary

____ 14. In "Up the Slide," where does Clay Dilham go on his *descent*?
A. up the slide
B. around rocks
C. into a river
D. down a mountain

____ 15. To approach the strange glow, what does Gary Paulsen have to *sustain*?
A. his dogs
B. his courage
C. his fear
D. his sled

Essay

16. A character's actions and decisions tell a great deal about his or her personality. In an essay, identify two actions or decisions made by the main character of "Up the Slide" and two actions or decisions by the narrator of "A Glow in the Dark." What does each action or decision tell you about the character? Which character do you find more likable? Why?

17. In a short essay, explain the difference between a fictional narrative and a nonfictional one. How can one type of narrative resemble the other? Give examples from both "Up the Slide" and "A Glow in the Dark" to illustrate your ideas.

18. **Thinking About the Big Question: Can all conflicts be resolved?** An internal conflict is a struggle that takes place within a character. Clay in "Up the Slide" and the narrator of "A Glow in the Dark" both face an internal conflict. In an essay, describe the internal struggle the characters have. Tell what happens as a result. Then, explain what each character does to resolve the conflict.

Unit 2 Resources: Short Stories
114

"**Up the Slide**" by Jack London
"**A Glow in the Dark**" *from* **Woodsong** by Gary Paulsen
Selection Test B

Critical Reading *Identify the letter of the choice that best completes the statement or answers the question.*

____ 1. Which word best describes Clay's attitude toward his mission in "Up the Slide"?
   A. confident
   B. vengeful
   C. negative
   D. insecure

____ 2. In "Up the Slide," why has the tree Clay discovers escaped the eyes of others?
   A. It is covered by a thick blanket of snow.
   B. It is hidden by thick cloud cover.
   C. It is in an area patrolled around the clock by soldiers.
   D. Its gray color blends with the surrounding rock.

____ 3. Based on the information in "Up the Slide," a reader can conclude that Clay's venture took
   A. less than thirty minutes.
   B. less than an hour.
   C. more than two hours.
   D. just under two hours.

____ 4. Which aspect of Clay's character is revealed in this passage from "Up the Slide"?
   Fully ten minutes passed ere he could master these sensations and summon sufficient strength for the weary climb. His legs hurt him and he was limping, and he was conscious of a sore place in his back, where he had fallen on the ax.

   A. pride
   B. cowardice
   C. eagerness
   D. determination

____ 5. In "Up the Slide," the act of felling the tree turns out to be
   A. very time consuming.
   B. easy.
   C. impossible.
   D. difficult.

____ 6. The author of "Up the Slide" borrowed which story element from real life?
   A. the setting
   B. the main character
   C. the plot
   D. the conclusion

____ **7.** In "A Glow in the Dark," why is Paulsen running his dogs?
   A. to keep them warm
   B. to get to the nearest town
   C. to train them
   D. to get away from the glow

____ **8.** In "A Glow in the Dark," Paulsen's actions *after* he sees the glowing form show that he is
   A. less brave than readers are first led to believe.
   B. more curious than afraid.
   C. less adventuresome than readers are first led to believe.
   D. more afraid than curious.

____ **9.** The mysterious green form in "A Glow in the Dark" turns out to be
   A. a rock.
   B. the Northern Lights.
   C. a lantern.
   D. a tree stump.

____ **10.** Read this passage from "A Glow in the Dark."
   Two more steps, then one more, leaning to see around the corner and at last I saw it and when I did it was worse.
   It was a form. Not human. A large, standing form glowing in the dark. . . .
   I felt my heart slam up into my throat.

   Which of the following descriptions of the passage is most accurate?
   A. a nonfictional passage with details that make it seem fictional
   B. a fictional passage about something strange that occurs in nature
   C. a fictional passage with details that makes it seem nonfictional
   D. a nonfictional passage about a fictional event

____ **11.** Which is *not* true of a fictional narrative?
   A. The author may invent characters, settings, and plots.
   B. Some of its details can be borrowed from real life.
   C. The author may only tell about real people and events.
   D. It is usually told in chronological order.

____ **12.** Which word best describes both Clay Dilham of "Up the Slide" and Gary Paulsen of "A Glow in the Dark" at the end of the narratives?
   A. desperate
   B. self-critical
   C. remorseful
   D. relieved

____ **13.** How are both "Up the Slide" and "A Glow in the Dark" organized?
   A. They present the most important idea first.
   B. They move back and forth in time.
   C. They do not follow a set pattern.
   D. They are told in time order.

____ 14. Which phrase best describes "Up the Slide" and "A Glow in the Dark"?
   A. narrative essays
   B. first-person narratives
   C. adventure stories
   D. science fiction

____ 15. In what way are fictional and nonfictional narratives alike?
   A. They can both have conflict.
   B. They both use made-up characters.
   C. They are both factual.
   D. They always have flashbacks.

Vocabulary

____ 16. In "Up the Slide," during his *ascent*, Clay Dilham must go
   A. up the slide.   C. into the gully.
   B. down the mountain.   D. around the rock outcropping.

____ 17. To accomplish his goal, Clay Dilham in "Up the Slide" has to use a complicated
   A. exertion.   C. descent.
   B. maneuver.   D. sustain.

____ 18. Smoke might be *diffused* by
   A. batteries.   C. the wind.
   B. the sun's rays.   D. water.

____ 19. To win the Iditarod or any other sled race, the dogs must put forth great
   A. exertion.   C. descent.
   B. sustain.   D. maneuver.

Essay

20. Facing danger can reveal a great deal about someone's personality. What is revealed about Clay Dilham in "Up the Slide" and Gary Paulsen in "A Glow in the Dark" by the danger each faces? Do you think the two men are admirable or foolish? Write your answer in a brief essay, and support your opinions with examples from the text.

21. In an essay, define *narrative*. Then, tell whether "Up the Slide" is a fictional or a nonfictional narrative and whether "A Glow in the Dark" is fictional or nonfictional. What elements make each story fictional or nonfictional? What elements does each story borrow from the other type of narrative?

22. **Thinking About the Big Question: Can all conflicts be resolved?** Clay in "Up the Slide" and the narrator of "A Glow in the Dark" both face an internal conflict—a struggle that takes place within them. In an essay, describe the characters' internal conflicts and what happens as a result. Then, explain whether you think the conflict each character faces can be resolved.

Name _____ Date _____

Writing Workshop—Unit 2, Part 1
Response to Literature: Critical Review

Prewriting: Choosing Your Topic

Use the chart below to take notes on two literary works that you have found while browsing. These two works should have enough similarities to make connections between them and to draw comparisons.

Story	Author	Idea and Purpose	Characters	Response

Drafting: Using an Outline

Use the graphic organizer below to help you organize the details of your review.

Introduction State your central idea and identify both works.	
Body Paragraphs Develop your ideas about each work separately.	
Conclusion Evaluate each work, noting similarities and differences, and restate your reaction.	

Unit 2 Resources: Short Stories
© Pearson Education, Inc. All rights reserved.
118

Writing Workshop—Unit 2, Part 1
Critical Review: Integrating Grammar Skills

Revising Irregular Verbs

For regular verbs, the past tense is formed by adding *-ed* or *-d* to the present form, as in *smile, smiled*. **Irregular verbs** have past and past participle forms that do not follow a predictable pattern. You have to memorize them.

Some Irregular Verbs

Present	Present participle	Past	Past participle
bring	(am) bringing	brought	(have) brought
buy	(am) buying	bought	(have) bought
cost	(am) costing	cost	(have) cost
bid	(am) bidding	bid	(have) bid

Identifying Irregular Verbs

A. DIRECTIONS: *Circle the letter of the correct irregular verb form for each sentence.*

1. The director has _____ the cast.
   A. choose   B. chose   C. chosen

2. She _____ to us about being on time for rehearsals.
   A. speak   B. spoke   C. spoken

3. People have _____ all the tickets.
   A. buy   B. bought   C. buying

4. We are _____ time to practice every day.
   A. taking   B. took   C. taken

Fixing Faulty Use of Irregular Verbs

B. DIRECTIONS: *On the lines provided, rewrite these sentences to correct the verbs. There may be more than one way to correct a sentence.*

1. The lights have began to dim.

   _____

2. The curtain has rise on the first scene.

   _____

3. The scene is lay in New York City.

   _____

4. The actors immediately drawn the audience into the performance.

   _____

Unit 2 Resources: Short Stories
119

Unit 2: Short Stories
Benchmark Test 3

MULTIPLE CHOICE

Reading Skill: Compare and Contrast

1. Which of the following sentences expresses a comparison?
    A. Many tourists visit Brazil during the festival known as Carnival.
    B. Rio de Janeiro is a large city in Brazil, although it is not the capital.
    C. Like Rio de Janeiro, São Paolo is a large city on the coast of Brazil.
    D. People in Brazil speak Portuguese, for Brazil was once a colony of Portugal.

2. Which of the following statements expresses a contrast?
    A. The Nile, like the Amazon, is a very long river.
    B. The Nile is in Africa, while the Amazon is in South America.
    C. Both rivers have always been important to the people along their banks.
    D. Only some portions of the Nile and the Amazon are easily navigated.

Read this selection, and then answer the four questions that follow it.

Most people have heard of Sherlock Holmes, the fictional London detective created by Sir Arthur Conan Doyle. Fewer people know, however, that Doyle borrowed the idea for Holmes from American author Edgar Allan Poe. Several decades before Doyle wrote, Poe created Inspector Dupin of Paris, France, a detective who used his amazing intellect to solve puzzling crimes. The similarities can be seen in one of the very first Sherlock Holmes stories, "A Scandal in Bohemia," which involves a stolen document in a plot quite similar to the plot of Poe's earlier tale, "The Purloined Letter."

3. What basic comparison does the selection make between Sir Arthur Conan Doyle and Edgar Allan Poe?
    A. Neither author's works are well known today, though detective stories remain popular.
    B. Both authors wrote detective stories with similar characters and plot elements.
    C. Each author borrowed ideas from the other.
    D. Both were important American authors.

4. According to the selection, how is the character of Inspector Dupin like the character of Sherlock Holmes?
    A. He is French.
    B. He lives in London.
    C. He is based on a real person.
    D. He is very clever.

5. Which words show that the second sentence of the selection contrasts with the first?
    A. *fewer* and *however*
    B. *however* and *idea*
    C. *borrow* and *idea*
    D. *fewer* and *people*

6. What similarity or difference between Doyle's and Poe's works does the selection point out?
   A. "A Scandal in Bohemia" has events similar to those of "The Purloined Letter."
   B. Both works are set in Paris.
   C. "A Scandal in Bohemia" has no similarities with "The Purloined Letter."
   D. Both works are set in London.

Reading Skill: Compare an Original to a Summary

7. If you were writing a summary of a mystery story, which of the following details could be left out?
   A. names of the main characters
   B. names and motives of suspects
   C. details that describe the story's settings
   D. details that describe how the crime was committed

8. Which answer choice describes a good story summary?
   A. It includes all the words in the original story that convey mood.
   B. It includes an analysis that helps readers interpret the original.
   C. It repeats all the dialogue that the original contains.
   D. It includes the important details contained in the original.

9. How is a good summary similar to or different from the work it summarizes?
   A. It is more interesting to read than the work it summarizes.
   B. It is the same length as the work it summarizes.
   C. It includes the main ideas of the work it summarizes.
   D. It discusses the underlying meaning of the work it summarizes.

Literary Analysis: Setting

Read the selection. Then, answer the questions that follow.

The road was a dead end into the heart of the country. Where the woodland broke into a field, the sun poured down like honey from the vivid blue sky. Usually this was a quiet spot, but today—the first really warm day of spring—was a little different. A flock of goldfinches sailed overhead, singing as they swooped and flew. Their lemon-yellow and deep black feathers flashed in the sun. They sounded as melodious as a dozen wind chimes in a light breeze, and seemed to carry the spirit of spring itself on their wings.

10. Which aspect of the setting is most important to the description in this selection?
    A. the customs and beliefs of the characters and the writer's attitude toward the location
    B. the physical features of the land and the weather or season of the year
    C. the weather or season of the year and the historical era in which the action takes place
    D. the physical features of the land and the customs of the characters

11. What do details about the setting help to establish in a work?
   A. plot
   B. mood
   C. character traits
   D. resolution

12. What atmosphere does the setting in the reading passage help create?
   A. a blissful and peaceful atmosphere
   B. an eerie, somewhat frightening atmosphere
   C. a strange but cheerful atmosphere
   D. a tense and hectic atmosphere

Literary Analysis: Character Traits

13. Which answer choice describes a complex character?
   A. a flat, static character
   B. a flat, dynamic character
   C. a round, static character
   D. a round, dynamic character

14. For which of these purposes do writers often use static characters?
   A. to serve as the main character
   B. to create conflict for the main character
   C. to show how people change and grow
   D. to help establish the mood of a story

15. Which of the following character traits does Leona display in the sample text below?

   Leona was a goodhearted, outgoing person, but she did like to gossip. Her gossip was never unkind; she liked to spread the news, not make snide comments about it.

   A. sociability
   B. shyness
   C. nastiness
   D. sensitivity

Literary Analysis: Comparing Narratives

16. Which of these elements must a narrative contain?
    A. plot
    B. dialogue
    C. figurative language
    D. fictional characters

17. Which of the following is a type of nonfiction narrative?
    A. a novel
    B. a poem that tells a story
    C. a stage drama
    D. a biography

18. In what way might a nonfiction narrative be similar to a fictional narrative?
    A. It might include invented characters and events.
    B. It might take place in an imaginary setting.
    C. It might emphasize certain details to add excitement.
    D. It might be highly imaginative.

Vocabulary: Prefixes and Suffixes

19. What is the meaning of the prefix *de-* in the word *deficiency*?
    A. from   C. equal
    B. toward   D. within

20. Which definition best fits the word *returnees* in the following sentence?

    After the war, many returnees found it hard to find jobs.

    A. people exchanging items
    B. people coming back from somewhere
    C. people being forced to go somewhere
    D. people turning in a particular direction

21. What is the meaning of the suffix *-ity* in the word *curiosity*?
    A. lacking or missing
    B. able to
    C. quality or state
    D. native of

22. What is the definition of *descending* in the following sentence?

    Felicia did not laugh with the others because she did not feel like descending to their level.

    A. rising
    B. ignoring
    C. respecting or honoring
    D. sinking

23. What does the suffix -ee mean in the word *employee*?
    A. one who receives
    B. one who does
    C. one who goes
    D. one who studies

24. *Clarity* is related to the word *clear.* Which of the following sentences uses the word *clarity* correctly?
    A. The clarity of the directions made them very confusing.
    B. Henry's main weakness as a speaker was that he spoke with clarity.
    C. I do not understand what you are saying because your answer lacks clarity.
    D. Fewer people would respond to you if you expressed yourself with greater clarity.

Grammar

25. Identify the action verb in this sentence:

    The twins usually arrive on time for the gym class, but today they are late.

    A. arrive
    B. time
    C. gym
    D. are

26. Identify the sentence in which the verb in italics is a linking verb.
    A. As he walked through the garden, he *smelled* the roses.
    B. The garden *seemed* well-tended.
    C. He *saw* several new bushes in the corner by the trellis.
    D. Some of the bushes *had grown* very tall.

27. Identify the linking verb in the following sentence.

    Charles was in the back of the room, watching his cousin address the audience.

    A. was
    B. back
    C. watching
    D. address

28. Which of the following is the past participle tense of the verb *talk*?
    A. talk   C. had talked
    B. talking   D. was talking

29. In the following sentence, which verb tense is used?

    The professor is *describing* the process of osmosis to the class today.

    A. past participle   C. present
    B. past   D. present participle

30. Which of the following is the past tense of the verb *hurry*?
   A. to hurry
   B. hurried
   C. was hurrying
   D. has hurried

31. Which of the following is the past tense of the verb *break*?
   A. breaked
   B. breaking
   C. broke
   D. broken

32. Which sentence uses the past participle of the verb *bring*?
   A. I have brought my diary with me every day except today.
   B. I brought my dairy with me yesterday.
   C. I am bringing my diary today.
   D. I will bring my diary tomorrow.

33. Which of the following is the past tense of the verb *bid*?
   A. bidded
   B. bidding
   C. bid
   D. will bid

WRITING

34. Think of a place that you really like or really dislike. Then, on a separate piece of paper, write a one-paragraph description of this setting.

35. Think of a fictional character who made a strong impression on you. It could be a character you encountered in a TV show or film, or it could be someone in a book or story. On a separate piece of paper, write a one-paragraph profile of this character.

36. Consider what you liked or did not like about two movies or TV shows you have seen recently. You might choose to address elements such as the realism of the characters, the excitement of the plot, or the beauty of the setting. On a separate piece of paper, jot down your ideas for a critical review of the two movies. Then, write a two-paragraph or three-paragraph review.

Name _____

Unit 2: Short Stories Skills Concept Map—2
Can all conflicts be resolved?

Words you can use
to discuss the
Big Question

Literary Analysis:
Short Story

Reading Skills and Strategies:
Make Inferences

You can
make inferences

by

using details

and by

identifying connections
to make inferences about
the author's meaning

(demonstrated in this selection)

Selection name:

(demonstrated in this selection)

Selection name:

Informational Text:
Advertisements

You can think critically about
advertisements

by

evaluating persuasive appeals

(demonstrated in this selection)

Selection name:

A Short Story

has

a point of view

and

a theme

(demonstrated in this selection)

Selection name:

(demonstrated in this selection)

Selection name:

**Basic Elements of
Short Stories**

• Characters
• Setting
• Plot
• Theme
• Conflict

Literary Devices

• Foreshadowing
• Flashback
• Irony
• Point of View

Comparing Literary Works:
Symbols

add

insight

depth

(demonstrated in these selections)

Selection names:

1.
2.

Student Log

Complete this chart to track your assignments.

Writing	Extend Your Learning	Writing Workshop	Other Assignments

Vocabulary Warm-up Word Lists

Study these words from "Flowers for Algernon." Then, complete the activities.

Word List A

artificial [ahr ti FISH uhl] *adj.* not real or natural
  The two angry sisters put on an <u>artificial</u> display of politeness.

association [uh soh see AY shuhn] *n.* group united for a common purpose
  Dylan belonged to an <u>association</u> that worked to improve the environment.

consciousness [KAHN shuhs nes] *n.* a person's mind, thoughts, and ideas
  The death was so painful that Mario could not allow it to enter his <u>consciousness</u>.

emotional [i MOH shuh nuhl] *adj.* having to do with or showing feelings
  Dee became <u>emotional</u> in response to the piece of music.

function [FUNGK shuhn] *n.* use or purpose
  One <u>function</u> of the liver is to make bile.

motivation [moh tuh VAY shuhn] *n.* desire and determination to achieve a goal
  Lee had a strong <u>motivation</u> to learn, and the rewards helped keep him going.

processes [PRAH se siz] *n.* series of actions or mental activities
  Cassie's thought <u>processes</u> were not sharp early in the morning.

technique [tek NEEK] *n.* special way of doing something
  Ray played the piano with unmatched <u>technique</u> but no feeling.

Word List B

application [ap luh KAY shuhn] *n.* use of something for a specific purpose
  One <u>application</u> of *pi* is finding the distance around a circle.

contribution [kahn tri BYOO shuhn] *n.* something that one gives or does
  Mei's <u>contribution</u> to the picnic was a cold noodle salad.

equations [i KWAY zhuhnz] *n.* mathematical statements that two quantities are equal
  Ms. Coe wrote two <u>equations</u> on the board and said, "Solve them!"

experimental [ek sper uh MEN tuhl] *adj.* used for or related to scientific tests
  The medicine, still in the <u>experimental</u> stage of research, is not yet approved for use.

hypothesis [hye PAHTH uh sis] *n.* suggested but unproven explanation
  Early people's <u>hypothesis</u> about Earth's being round proved true.

indications [in di KAY shuhnz] *n.* signs or signals that something exists or is true
  There are <u>indications</u> in the sky that the rain may stop soon.

intellectual [in tuh LEK choo uhl] *adj.* showing great intelligence; scholarly
  Jamal's <u>intellectual</u> gifts were noticeable from an early age.

symptoms [SIMP tuhmz] *n.* physical signs of illness
  A runny nose, a cough, and a fever are <u>symptoms</u> of a cold.

"Flowers for Algernon" by Daniel Keyes
Vocabulary Warm-up Exercises

Exercise A *Fill in the blanks using each word from Word List A only once.*

Dr. Muddleton bragged to his professional [1] _____ that he had pio-
neered a new [2] _____ by which people could control their negative
thought [3] _____. He said it was the perfect remedy for people who
felt they were too high-strung, or [4] _____. He insisted that patients
of his with enough [5] _____ could learn to monitor their own
[6] _____ so that no unpleasant thoughts could creep in. The moment
they felt down, they were to replace an unpleasant thought with a happy one. Critics
claimed that Muddleton's method was [7] _____ and that all he was
teaching his patients was to deny their true feelings. They suggested that he take
another hard look at brain [8] _____.

Exercise B *Write a complete sentence to answer each question. For each item, use a word
from Word List B to replace each underlined word without changing its meaning.*

1. <u>Signs of illness</u> such as a fever and pain may be <u>signals</u> of severe illness.

   _____

2. Pavlov's <u>gift</u> to science was his <u>use</u> of responses as a way of understanding
   the brain.

   _____

3. The page was filled with <u>mathematical statements showing pairs of equal numbers</u>.

   _____

4. <u>Scholarly</u> matters interested Rolf, but he also participated in sports.

   _____

5. Her data, which was still <u>being used in the scientific tests</u>, seemed to support her
   <u>suggested explanation</u>.

   _____

Name _____ Date _____

Read the following passage. Pay special attention to the underlined words. Then, read it again, and complete the activities. Use a separate sheet of paper for your written answers.

Are you smart? Does that question puzzle you? Does it make you feel uncomfortable? You're not alone. Scientists in one professional <u>association</u> or another, as well as nonscientists, have been debating the nature of intelligence for years. That debate doesn't show signs of stopping.

Intelligence testing is almost one hundred years old. Over the years, many people have complained that testing is highly <u>artificial</u> because it looks at only a narrow range of ability. Tests have overlooked <u>emotional</u> intelligence. Feelings are important, these people have said. So is testing the ability to build, draw, dance, play soccer, and lead the student council.

Even though recent tests are based on current theories of brain <u>function</u>, many people think that they remain too limited. They still assess too few kinds of thought <u>processes</u>, which are quite complicated. Also, even though the <u>technique</u> of giving tests has greatly improved, the newer method hasn't helped learners much. The tests still don't show how to supply <u>motivation</u> for learners so that they can try harder and do better. They don't provide a road map to understanding human <u>consciousness</u>. So much of the waking mind lies beyond the reach of the tests.

There probably will always be the need to make judgments about people's ability. However, testing shows only the capacity for a certain kind of intelligence, overlooks achievement, and fails to assess the whole range of human brainpower. The solution may not be to get rid of intelligence testing. Rather, we need to find ways to develop tests so that they cover a broader range of interests and abilities. After all, we do want people to be all they can be.

1. Underline the word that tells who belongs to an <u>association</u>. Then, write a sentence about an *association* you know of.

2. Underline why some think testing is <u>artificial</u>. Then, write a sentence in which you tell about something *artificial*.

3. Circle the word in the next sentence that gives a hint to the meaning of <u>emotional</u>. Then, write a sentence using *emotional*.

4. Write a sentence explaining the <u>function</u> of your heart. Define *function*.

5. Circle the word that describes thought <u>processes</u>. Describe your own thought *processes* when you get nervous.

6. Circle the word that is a synonym for <u>technique</u>. Tell about something you know that requires special *technique*.

7. Circle phrases that show what students with <u>motivation</u> are likely to do. Write about something for which you have great *motivation*.

8. Circle the words in the next sentence that explain <u>consciousness</u>. Then, use *consciousness* in a sentence.

"Flowers for Algernon" by Daniel Keyes
Reading Warm-up B

Read the following passage. Pay special attention to the underlined words. Then, read it again, and complete the activities. Use a separate sheet of paper for your written answers.

To tell you the truth, I had never thought about my cat's <u>intellectual</u> life. Mittens seemed happy chasing a ball of aluminum foil and occasionally his tail, scratching the furniture, and sleeping eighteen hours a day. I hadn't realized I was keeping him from a life of the mind.

That was until I read about Dr. Nutkin, animal educator. His <u>hypothesis</u>, along with claims of <u>experimental</u> results, gave all <u>indications</u> that he could make Mittens my mental equal. I didn't want to deprive my cat of such a chance or the world of Dr. Nutkin's <u>contribution</u> to science. So I sent the doctor an e-mail.

Dr. Nutkin replied almost at once and assured me his work had great <u>application</u> to human intelligence as well as animal intelligence. Within a week, Mittens and I were sitting in his office, the walls of which were covered with mathematical <u>equations</u> that looked a little like algebra.

We had a thorough interview, during which Mittens was either silent or answered "meow" to questions. Then, Dr. Nutkin sent us home with a bunch of DVDs, which we were supposed to watch together every night before bed. He said the purpose was to achieve a "mind meld," in which we would start thinking together. He warned me, however, that if I showed any <u>symptoms</u> of illness, I should call him immediately.

What kind of illness might I get from DVDs? Dr. Nutkin's plan sounded ridiculous, and Dr. Nutkin himself sounded like a nut. Still, I figured there was no harm in trying the DVDs. After a week of staring at nature films like you find on the science channels, I woke up hungry in the middle of the night and went into the kitchen. Mittens was sitting at the table, reading the paper. I poured myself a bowl of milk, lapped it up, and curled up on the rug.

"What a quack that Nutkin is," I thought.

"Why do you say that?" Mittens asked, and then returned to his paper without waiting for an answer.

1. Underline the words in the paragraph that hint at the meaning of <u>intellectual</u>. Then, write a sentence that tells about something that is a part of *intellectual* life.

2. Write a sentence that explains the opposite of a <u>hypothesis</u> and gives an example of it.

3. Circle the word that tells what is <u>experimental</u>. Then, write a sentence for *experimental*.

4. Give a synonym for <u>indications</u>. Then, write a sentence, using the word *indications*. Check to see if you can replace it with its synonym.

5. Tell what Dr. Nutkin claims as his <u>contribution</u> to science. Then, write about a *contribution* you make to your school.

6. Write a sentence in which you tell the two things to which Dr. Nutkin's work has an <u>application</u>.

7. Give two examples of <u>equations</u>.

8. Write a sentence describing the <u>symptoms</u> of an illness.

"Flowers for Algernon" by Daniel Keyes
Writing About the Big Question

Can all conflicts be resolved?

Big Question Vocabulary

argument	compromise	injury	insecurity	interact
irritate	mislead	negotiate	oppose	reaction
solution	stalemate	victorious	viewpoint	violence

A. *Use a word from the list above to complete each sentence.*

1. Some people interested in animal rights _____ experiments that harm animals.

2. Results of animal experiments can _____ us into thinking the same results would occur in humans.

3. Some experiments can cause a seriou_____ to an animal.

4. The conflict between animal-rights _____ some scientists seems to have no good _____.

B. *Follow the directions in respond_____ of the items below. Answer in complete sentences.*

1. What are two uses of animals _____ conflict in our society?

   _____

   _____

2. What is your reaction to one of the_____ conflicts? Use at least two of the Big Question vocabulary words.

   _____

   _____

C. *Complete the sentence below. Then, write a short paragraph in which you comment on the conflicts you might feel about a friend who changes.*

When someone I know changes, it is _____

   _____

   _____

   _____

   _____

"Flowers for Algernon" by Daniel Keyes
Reading: Notice Details to Make Inferences

Making inferences means **noticing details** that an author provides and using them to make logical assumptions about the events, settings, themes, and other story elements that the author leaves unstated. Consider these details that author Daniel Keyes has Charlie tell us:

> I had a test today. I think I faled it. and I think that maybe now they wont use me. What happind is a nice young man was in the room and he had some white cards with ink spilled all over them. He sed Charlie what do you see on this card. I was very skared even tho I had my rabits foot in my pockit because when I was a kid I always faled tests in school and I spilled ink to.

From these details, you might make the following inferences:

- Charlie is no longer of school age.
- Charlie has a learning disability, so he had a hard time when he was in school.
- Charlie is superstitious.
- Charlie very much wants to pass a test and be used in an experiment.

DIRECTIONS: *In the chart below, the left column gives quotations from the story. Each quotation provides several details. From each group of details, make at least one inference, and list it on the right.*

Details	Inferences
1. They said how come you went to the adult nite scool all by yourself Charlie. How did you find it. I said I askd pepul and sumbody told me where I shud go to lern to read and spell good.	
2. Their really my friends and they like me. Sometimes somebody will say hey look at Joe or Frank or George he really pulled a Charlie Gordon. I dont know why they say that but they always laff.	
3. Dr. Nemur wanted to publish the results of the experiment at the end of this month. Dr. Strauss wanted to wait a while longer to be sure. Dr. Strauss said that Dr. Nemur was more interested in the Chair of Psychology at Princeton than he was in the experiment.	

"Flowers for Algernon" by Daniel Keyes
Enrichment: Intelligence Tests

Modern intelligence testing is based largely on the work of Alfred Binet and Théodore Simon, who in 1905 introduced the Binet-Simon Intelligence Scale as a way of detecting mental retardation. Later (in 1916), Binet's work was developed by Lewis Terman into the Stanford-Binet Intelligence Test, which assigned children of all abilities to appropriate class groups and was supposed to predict their abilities in the classroom. The child's performance on the test resulted in a numerical value called an Intelligence Quotient, or IQ. The average IQ score is 100. People like Charlie (at the beginning of the story) usually score below 70.

Some people doubt that the tests are meaningful because studies have shown that cultural differences, rather than intelligence alone, help determine scores. Other critics point out that some people are intelligent in some areas but not others—a person with weak language skills may still have strong musical skills, for example—so the tests, they claim, cannot possibly measure overall intelligence fairly.

DIRECTIONS: *Write your answers to the following questions on the lines provided.*

1. Do you think we should pursue means for increasing intelligence as shown in the experiment involving Charlie and Algernon? Why or why not?

   _____

   _____

   _____

   _____

2. Was Charlie happier when he became smarter? Explain your answer.

   _____

   _____

   _____

3. Why might intelligence tests be helpful?

   _____

   _____

   _____

4. Why might intelligence tests be harmful?

   _____

   _____

   _____

   _____

"**Flowers for Algernon**" by Daniel Keyes
Open-Book Test

Short Answer *Write your responses to the questions in this section on the lines provided.*

1. Reread Ch_____ _____ progris riport 1" in "Flowers for Algernon." What can readers _____ _____ Charlie _____ ersonality? How can they tell?

_____

_____

_____

_____

2. In _____ _____ in "_____ _____ Algernon," Charlie writes about the many tests he _____ and his comp_____ with _____ lgernon. Choose two important points from that entry _____ _____ _____ _____ server's point of view.

_____

_____

_____

_____

3. In "progris ript 5" in "Flowers for Algernon," Charlie describes his fear. Why is Charlie afraid at this moment? Explain how he fights his fear.

_____

_____

_____

4. What can readers infer about the relationship between Dr. Strauss and Dr. Nemur in "Flowers for Algernon"? Cite two details from Charlie's reports for March 8 and April 27 to support that inference.

_____

_____

_____

5. In the report of March 25 in "Flowers for Algernon," how does the first-person point of view help readers understand things about Charlie's life that Charlie himself does not understand?

_____

_____

_____

6. Complete this chart with details from the April 6 report in "Flowers for Algernon." Then, on the line below, explain why readers are likely to infer that Charlie feels closer to the mouse than to many people.

Inference	Detail Supporting Inference
Charlie is enthusiastic.	
Charlie values friendships.	
Charlie knows right from wrong.	

_____

7. In the beginning of "Flowers for Algernon," how well does Charlie understand that mental deterioration is possible? Base your answer on the definition of *deterioration*.

_____

_____

8. How would you describe the relationship between Charlie and Miss Kinnian? Support your response with three details from "Flowers for Algernon."

_____

_____

_____

_____

9. Before the operation, Charlie relies on good luck charms to help him face the new experience. Why does he refer to those items again in his final report in "Flowers for Algernon"?

_____

_____

10. Suppose that Miss Kinnian were narrating "Flowers for Algernon." Given what you know of her personality, how would her first-person point of view differ from Charlie's first-person point of view? Use details from the story to explain your answer.

_____

_____

_____

_____

Unit 2 Resources: Short Stories
137

Essay

Write an extended response to the question of your choice or to the question or questions your teacher assigns you.

11. At different points in "Flowers for Algernon," Charlie is asked to analyze inkblots. Using details from the entries of March 7 and April 22, write an essay that contrasts Charlie's emotional reactions to the tests.

12. In "Flowers for Algernon," is there a major difference in Charlie's personality after the operation? If so, is it for the better? In what way, if any, does Charlie remain the same after the operation? Respond to these questions in a brief essay, giving clear reasons for your opinions. Be sure to support your ideas with details from the story.

13. In an essay, explain how the title "Flowers for Algernon" relates to the events, characters, and themes of the story. In your opinion, why did the author use Algernon's name, and not Charlie's, in the title? Address this question in your essay, and be sure to cite details from the story to support your opinions and conclusions.

14. **Thinking About the Big Question: Can all conflicts be resolved?** In the April 30 progress report of "Flowers for Algernon," Charlie writes that there is "a wedge between me and all the people I once knew and loved." In an essay, explain what the wedge is and what, if anything, Charlie could have done to avoid its coming between him and the other people. Then, explain why the resolution of the problem leaves readers feeling sad rather than happy.

Oral Response

15. Go back to question 5, 6, or 9 or to the question your teacher assigns you. Take a few minutes to expand your answer and prepare an oral response. Find additional details in "Flowers for Algernon" that support your points. If necessary, make notes to guide your oral response.

Vocabulary Warm-up Word Lists

Study these words from "Charles." Then, apply your knowledge to the activities that follow.

Word List A

enormously [i NAWR muhs lee] *adv.* in an extremely large way
　It is <u>enormously</u> important for citizens to vote in elections.

identified [eye DEN tuh fyd] *v.* recognized
　At the station, Wilson <u>identified</u> the police officer who had helped him the day before.

influence [IN floo uhns] *n.* effect; the power to have an effect on someone
　The new shop teacher had a positive <u>influence</u> on the students.

kindergarten [KIN dur gart uhn] *n.* school class for children aged four to six years old
　For children in <u>kindergarten</u>, playing is often learning.

privileges [PRIV uh li jiz] *n.* special rights or advantages
　Students in the school earn <u>privileges</u> if they behave themselves.

respectfully [ri SPEKT fuh lee] *adv.* politely; courteously
　"Ms. Dahl, I believe you forgot to carry the one when you added," Janine said <u>respectfully</u>.

toughness [TUHF nuhs] *n.* the quality of being strong and determined
　Dwayne's <u>toughness</u> served him well as he struggled to become a world-champion swimmer.

warily [WAIR uh lee] *adv.* cautiously
　Carlos glanced <u>warily</u> around the corner to be sure the dog had left.

Word List B

corduroy [KAWR duh roy] *adj.* thick cotton cloth with raised lines on one side
　<u>Corduroy</u> pants are more suitable for cold weather than shorts.

elaborately [i LAB uhr it lee] *adv.* with great care or detail
　We were impressed with how <u>elaborately</u> the young author wrote.

era [EER uh] *n.* long period of time
　High-school graduation marked the end of Tamara's student <u>era</u>.

haggard [HAG urd] *adj.* careworn; exhausted
　The family in the hospital waiting room looked <u>haggard</u>.

institution [in sti TOO shuhn] *n.* well-established tradition
　Potluck picnics are a summer <u>institution</u> in our neighborhood.

passionately [PASH uh nit lee] *adv.* in a way that shows strong feelings
　Some families argue <u>passionately</u>, but it doesn't mean they're angry.

prayerfully [PRAYR fuh lee] *adv.* in a hopeful way
　"Please don't think badly of me until you hear the whole story," Darlene said <u>prayerfully</u>.

scornfully [SKAWRN fuh lee] *adv.* without respect
　"You can't ride those waves," Chad told his little brother <u>scornfully</u>.

"Charles" by Shirley Jackson
Vocabulary Warm-up Exercises

Exercise A *Fill in the blanks using each word from Word List A only once.*

The [1] _____ was unlike any other group of students I'd ever known. I
[2] _____ several children in the class who were from the neighborhood,
but the rest were strangers. They eyed me [3] _____, as if I were going
to do something unpleasant. I had never seen such [4] _____ in
children so young, but then you might say I had lived a sheltered life full of love
and [5] _____. I hoped [6] _____ that my childhood
experiences could have an [7] _____ on them. But I wasn't sure whether
even that would do the trick. Oh, they treated me [8] _____ enough, but
trust was absent. I told myself hopefully that all it would take was time.

Exercise B *Circle* T *if the statement is true or* F *if the statement is false. Then, explain your answer.*

1. A person who asks for something <u>passionately</u> and <u>prayerfully</u> is indifferent.
   T / F _____

2. A <u>haggard</u> individual looks fresh and full of energy.
   T / F _____

3. Someone who acts <u>scornfully</u> is being nice.
   T / F _____

4. You were born in the <u>era</u> in which cars first became an <u>institution</u>.
   T / F _____

5. An <u>elaborately</u> designed hat is fancy.
   T / F _____

6. People don't wear <u>corduroy</u> suits to formal events.
   T / F _____

7. A family <u>institution</u> rarely occurs.
   T / F _____

Name _____   Date _____

"Charles" by Shirley Jackson
Reading Warm-up A

Read the following passage. Pay special attention to the underlined words. Then, read it again, and complete the activities. Use a separate sheet of paper for your written answers.

Friedrich Froebel was a German educator of the 1800s. In 1837, he invented <u>kindergarten</u>, which means "child's garden." In his kindergarten, teachers trained little children to think by playing. Many Germans took to Froebel's ideas <u>warily</u> because they didn't see how playing could lead to learning. Still, he remained confident in his ideas.

Froebel's method was to present children with "gifts," which were neither presents nor special <u>privileges</u> but a series of wooden shapes and other objects. A child played freely with one gift until he or she ran out of ideas. Then, the teacher suggested other ways of playing with it. Finally, the child moved on to the next gift.

Froebel <u>identified</u> three important categories in which the gifts could be used. The first was "forms of knowledge." A child used them to work out such ideas as number and order. The second was "forms of life." A child used the gifts to stand for objects in the world, such as houses and trees. The third category was "forms of beauty." A child arranged blocks on a grid to make a pattern for decorative purposes.

Froebel began training teachers in 1849. His ideas caught on <u>enormously</u> in Europe and the United States, and soon kindergartens were opening in many countries. While many earlier schools had relied on the <u>toughness</u> of teachers to rein in an unruly group of students, kindergarten classes gently encouraged a child's natural curiosity. Of course, children in kindergarten were expected to act <u>respectfully</u> toward the teacher and toward one another; play did not mean a free-for-all.

Froebel would probably not recognize most kindergartens today. With the big push to teach children to read, write, and do arithmetic, they have strayed far from his ideas. His methods do live on in some preschools, however. There's no denying that he has had a strong <u>influence</u> on the idea that young children should be educated.

1. Underline the words that explain what <u>kindergarten</u> means. Then, tell about something you did in *kindergarten*.

2. Circle the words that explain why many Germans acted <u>warily</u>. Then, write your own definition of *warily*.

3. Underline the word that tells that <u>privileges</u> are not ordinary things. Then, write about *privileges* you have.

4. Write your own sentence that tells what Froebel <u>identified</u>.

5. Circle the phrase that hints at the meaning of <u>enormously</u>. Then, write your own sentence for *enormously*.

6. Underline the words that give hints to the meaning of <u>toughness</u>. Write a sentence telling when *toughness* is useful.

7. Circle the words that tell toward whom children were supposed to act <u>respectfully</u>. Describe how you behave when you act *respectfully*.

8. Underline the idea upon which Froebel had a strong <u>influence</u>. Write about someone who has had a strong *influence* on you.

Name _____ Date _____

"Charles" by Shirley Jackson
Reading Warm-up B

Read the following passage. Pay special attention to the underlined words. Then, read it again, and complete the activities. Use a separate sheet of paper for your written answers.

When my little brother, Dan, was in kindergarten, his teacher, Ms. Dunne, announced that each student was to adopt a tree for the school year. She handed out a detailed list of things the students could do. Since my mother was busy with the baby, I was enlisted to tackle the <u>elaborately</u> drawn up list and help figure out what was doable.

The first thing Dan had to do was choose a tree. Now, we had several perfectly good trees in front of our building—a maple, two oaks, and a few sycamores. Yet, Dan dismissed them <u>scornfully</u> and argued <u>passionately</u> for something more unusual. So we walked around the neighborhood for what seemed like hours. Finally, Dan found something that suited him. It was an ancient weeping beech, as I found out later by looking in the field guide. It stood at one corner of an empty lot about a mile from home. <u>Haggard</u> but relieved, we headed home to dinner.

From season to season, I helped Dan trace the changes, gathering leaves and seeds and making bark rubbings. Tending to the tree—which Dan had named Phyllis, for no good reason—became an <u>institution</u> in our household. At the end of the school year, Dan handed in a hefty "tree book," accompanied by a tape he'd made himself. At that moment, I felt that we were truly at the end of an <u>era</u>.

The summer came and went, and it was deep fall—<u>corduroy</u> overalls time—for Dan, that is. I casually asked Dan if he wanted to visit his tree. He looked puzzled for a moment, then his eyes lit up. So we walked the mile or so once again. As we neared the corner, we heard the racket that only tree trimmers make. "Oh, let it be some other tree," I mumbled <u>prayerfully</u>. I guess when you adopt a tree, it's yours forever.

1. Underline a word in the paragraph that explains <u>elaborately</u>. Then, write a sentence about something you know that was *elaborately* done.

2. Circle the words that tell what Dan did <u>scornfully</u>. Then, write a sentence using *scornfully*.

3. Write a sentence that shows the meaning of <u>passionately</u>.

4. Write a synonym for <u>haggard</u>. Then, write a sentence about a time you were *haggard*.

5. Circle the words that tell what became an <u>institution</u> in the house. Write about something that is an *institution* at your house.

6. What was the <u>era</u> of the "adopt a tree" program? Write a sentence about an *era* in history.

7. Circle the word that tells what is made of <u>corduroy</u>. Describe something that is *corduroy*.

8. Why did the narrator mumble <u>prayerfully</u>? Write a sentence using *prayerfully*.

Name _____ Date _____

Writing About the Big Question

Can all conflicts be resolved?

Big Question Vocabulary

argument	compromise	injury	insecurity	interact
irritate	mislead	negotiate	oppose	reaction
solution	stalemate	victorious	viewpoint	violence

A. *Use a word from the list above to complete each sentence.*

1. Children often experience a sense of _____ about starting kindergarten.

2. They may find it frightening to _____ with so many new people at once.

3. A normal _____ to this stress is to put on a show of bravado.

4. If this show of bravado becomes too extreme, it can _____ other people.

B. *Follow the directions in responding to each of the items below. Answer in complete sentences.*

1. Describe a conflict you once felt that was related to school. Use at least two of the Big Question vocabulary words.

   _____

   _____

2. Write two sentences explaining how you dealt with the conflict.

   _____

   _____

C. *Complete the sentence below. Then, write a short paragraph in which you suggest how a person can handle the inner conflicts that new situations sometimes create.*

Adjusting to new situations is _____

_____

_____

_____

_____

"Charles" by Shirley Jackson
Reading: Notice Details to Make Inferences

Making inferences means **noticing details** that an author provides and using them to make logical assumptions about the events, settings, themes, and other story elements that the author leaves unstated. Consider these details that Shirley Jackson provides about Laurie:

> The day my son Laurie started kindergarten he renounced corduroy overalls with bibs and began wearing blue jeans with a belt; I watched him go off the first morning with the older girl next door, seeing clearly that an era of my life was ended, my sweet-voiced nursery-school tot replaced by a long-trousered, swaggering character who forgot to stop at the corner and wave good-bye to me.

From these details, you might make the following inferences:

- Before starting kindergarten, Laurie was a fairly sheltered and well-behaved child.
- Laurie grows less polite and more self-important, perhaps to mask his nervousness about starting kindergarten.
- Laurie is a strong-willed child able to insist on his own way.
- Laurie's mother feels some regret as she recognizes that her son is growing up.

DIRECTIONS: *In the chart below, the left column gives quotations from the story. Each quotation provides several details. From each group of details, make at least one inference, and list it on the right.*

Details	Inferences
1. He came home the same way, the front door slamming open, his cap on the floor, and the voice suddenly become raucous shouting, "Isn't anybody *here*?"	
2. The third day—it was Wednesday of the first week—Charles bounced a see-saw on the head of a little girl and made her bleed, and the teacher made him stay inside during recess. Thursday Charles had to stand in a corner during story-time because he kept pounding his feet on the floor.	
3. "You know what Charles did today?" Laurie demanded at the lunch table, in a voice slightly awed. "He told a little girl to say a word and she said it and the teacher washed her mouth out with soap and Charles laughed."	

"Charles" by Shirley Jackson
Literary Analysis: Point of View

Point of view is the perspective from which a story is told. In a story told from the **first-person point of view,** the narrator is a character in the story who refers to himself or herself with first-person pronouns like *I* and *me.* In a story told from the **third-person point of view,** the narrator stands outside the story and refers to all the characters with third-person pronouns like *he, she,* and *they.* A first-person narrator can tell only what he or she sees, hears, knows, thinks, or feels. "Charles" is told from the first-person point of view of Laurie's mother.

A. DIRECTIONS: *On the lines provided, answer these questions about the story.*

1. Briefly explain the narrator's situation at the start of "Charles" by telling how she feels about Laurie's going off to school.

   _____

   _____

   _____

2. Would you say the narrator has a sense of humor? Support your answer with details.

   _____

   _____

   _____

3. How does using this particular narrator help create a surprise ending?

   _____

   _____

   _____

B. DIRECTIONS: *Choose one incident that the narrator reports, and retell it from the first-person point of view of Laurie or Laurie's teacher. Use a separate sheet of paper, if necessary.*

   _____

   _____

   _____

   _____

   _____

   _____

   _____

"**Charles**" by Shirley Jackson
Vocabulary Builder

Word List

cynically   deprived   haggard   insolently   renounced   simultaneously

A. DIRECTIONS: *Answer each question with a sentence that uses one of the Word List words. Each answer must correctly reflect the details in "Charles."*

1. At Laurie's school, do parents go one by one at different times to meet with teachers?

   _____

2. At the end of the story, what does Laurie's teacher report about Laurie's behavior in school?

   _____

3. Why are Charles's blackboard privileges taken away, according to Laurie?

   _____

4. Why does Laurie's mother expect Charles's mother to look worn out?

   _____

5. When Laurie's father hears that Charles has been behaving well, why does he respond with disbelief?

   _____

6. What evidence does Laurie offer to show that Charles behaves disrespectfully toward the teacher?

   _____

B. WORD STUDY: The Latin root -*nounc*-/-*nunc*- means "report." Answer each of the following questions using one of these words containing this root: *pronunciation, announcer, denounce.*

1. What types of messages would a sports *announcer* be delivering during a game?

   _____

2. For what types of activities might the people *denounce* their political leaders?

   _____

3. What message do you convey to speakers of a foreign language when your *pronunciation* of that language is excellent?

   _____

Name _____ Date _____

"**Charles**" by Shirley Jackson
Enrichment: Child Development

Children grow at different rates, but certain patterns of behavior and language development are common to most children. Research in child development helps school counselors determine if a troubled student is behaving typically for his or her age, or if the student needs some special help. The following chart outlines some typical behavior.

Three-Year-Old Child	**Four-Year-Old Child**	**Five-Year-Old Child**
• constantly asks "Why?" • sometimes shares toys • can be reasoned with • listens to general conversation • understands the difference between statements, commands, and questions	• asks complex questions • enjoys playing with others and can share easily • understands right and wrong • speaks in complete sentences • tells long stories, confusing fact and fantasy	• enjoys imaginative and dramatic play • understands the need for rules and fairness • speaks fluently and with the grammar he or she hears spoken to him • enjoys rhymes and telling stories

DIRECTIONS: *Imagine that you are a counselor in Laurie's school. Your job is to decide if Laurie is acting like a typical five-year-old, or if he is acting immaturely. For each example of Laurie's behavior, use the chart to determine if his action is typical or immature for his age. Write your assessment and explain your answer.*

1. Laurie hit his teacher because she tried to make him color with red crayons when he wanted to use green.

   Laurie's behavior is immature even for a three-year-old. At five, he should understand the need for rules and fair play.

2. Laurie says, "I didn't learn nothing" instead of "I didn't learn anything."

   _____

   _____

3. Laurie talks in rhymes, such as "Hi, Pop, y'old dust mop."

   _____

   _____

4. Laurie invents an imaginary classmate rather than admit he was misbehaving himself.

   _____

   _____

"**Flowers for Algernon**" by Daniel Keyes
"**Charles**" by Shirley Jackson

Integrated Language Skills: Grammar

The Present, Past, and Future Tenses

A **verb tense** tells when the action or condition takes place.

- The **present tense** shows an action or a state of being that occurs regularly.
  These inferences **seem** logical.
  Good readers usually **understand** an author's inferences.

- The **past tense** shows actions that have already happened. Regular verbs form the past tense by adding -ed or -d.
  Yesterday, the story **seemed** a lot more difficult to read.

- The **future tense** shows actions that are going to happen. The future tense is usually formed with the helping verb will.
  The lesson **will seem** clearer after you practice the skill.

A. PRACTICE: *On the line after each sentence, identify the underlined verb as present, past, or future. Then, rewrite the sentence in the other two tenses.*

1. The scientists <u>use</u> mice in their experiments. _____

_____

_____

2. Some children <u>will behave</u> badly on the first day of school. _____

_____

_____

3. He <u>visited</u> a psychologist twice a week. _____

_____

_____

B. Writing Application: *Write three sentences about a school subject or field of study that interests you. One sentence should use the past tense, one should use the present tense, and one should use the future tense. Underline the verbs, and label the verb tenses.*

_____

_____

_____

_____

_____

_____

Unit 2 Resources: Short Stories
154

"Flowers for Algernon" by Daniel Keyes
"Charles" by Shirley Jackson

Integrated Language Skills: Support for Writing Dialogue

The dialogue for a movie scene adapted from either "Flowers for Algernon" or "Charles" can start with actual dialogue given in the stories. On the blank lines, write notes for expanding the scene with dialogue that you can imagine. Alternatively, on another sheet of paper, prepare notes for expanding a script that starts with a conversation from elsewhere in one of the stories.

[*Scene: after-dinner conversation between Miss Kinnian and Charlie*]

MISS KINNIAN: I won't go much higher than I am now, but you'll keep climbing up and up, and see more and more, and each step will open new worlds that you never even knew existed. I hope . . . I just hope to God—

CHARLIE: What?

MISS KINNIAN: Never mind, Charles. I just hope I wasn't wrong to advise you to go into this in the first place.

CHARLIE: How could that be? It worked, didn't it? Even Algernon is still smart.

_____

_____

_____

[*Scene: lunchtime after Laurie's first day of kindergarten*]

MOTHER: How *was* school today?

LAURIE: All right.

FATHER: Did you learn anything?

LAURIE: I didn't learn nothing.

MOTHER: Anything. Didn't learn anything.

LAURIE: The teacher spanked a boy, though. For being fresh.

MOTHER: What did he do? Who was it?

LAURIE: It was Charles. He was fresh. The teacher spanked him and made him stand in a corner. He was awfully fresh.

MOTHER: What did he do?

_____

_____

_____

_____

Now, convert your notes into actual dialogue.

"Flowers for Algernon" by Daniel Keyes
"Charles" by Shirley Jackson

Integrated Language Skills: Support for Extend Your Learning

Research and Technology: "Flowers for Algernon"
Use the chart below to record the information from the article you use.

Source	
Main Idea	
Significant Details (at least two)	
Quotation	

Research and Technology: "Charles"
Use the chart below to record the information from the article you use.

Source	
Main Idea	
Significant Details (at least two)	
Quotation	

"Charles" by Shirley Jackson
Open-Book Test

Short Answer *Write your responses to the questions in this section on the lines provided.*

1. The point of view of a story is the perspective from which the story is told. Describe the point of view in "Charles." How early in the story can readers identify it? Explain your answer.

   _____

   _____

2. In the first paragraph of "Charles," the narrator describes Laurie as he leaves for his first day of kindergarten. What can readers infer about Laurie's thoughts about starting kindergarten? Name two details that lead to that inference.

   _____

   _____

3. In "Charles," how do readers learn about Charles? What does your answer to that question show about the story's point of view?

   _____

   _____

   _____

4. In "Charles," Laurie comes home late on Monday. Think about the reason he gives. What does his mother infer about her son from that reason? How is her inference different from the inference that readers make?

   _____

   _____

   _____

5. After a while, Charles almost becomes a part of Laurie's family. What does Laurie's family mean when they say that someone has done "a Charles"? Cite a detail in "Charles" that is an example of that expression.

   _____

   _____

   _____

6. About halfway through "Charles," Laurie's father speaks "cynically" about Charles's improved behavior. How would you describe Laurie's father's attitude? Why does he feel that way? Base your answer on the definition of *cynically.*

   _____

   _____

   _____

7. As "Charles" unfolds, Charles's behavior changes. Complete this chart with details from the story. Then, on the line below, give one possible reason for Charles's behavior *after* the fourth week of kindergarten.

During the . . .	Charles . . .
first day	is fresh.
first Friday	
next Tuesday	
third and fourth weeks	
day of the second PTA meeting	

_____

8. In "Charles," why are Laurie's parents very interested in meeting Charles's mother? Is there more to their interest than they admit to? Explain.

_____

_____

_____

_____

9. Reread the teacher's final words in "Charles." What does the narrator realize at that moment? Why must that realization be called an *inference*?

_____

_____

_____

_____

10. If the teacher in "Charles" were telling the story from her point of view, what important, humorous story element would be missing? What could she add that the existing narrator could not? Explain your answers.

_____

_____

_____

_____

Essay

Write an extended response to the question of your choice or to the question or questions your teacher assigns you.

11. At the end of "Charles," Laurie's mother meets her son's kindergarten teacher. As a result of their conversation, Laurie's mother has an important realization. In your opinion, how does Laurie's mother feel at the end of the story? In an essay, predict how Laurie's mother will feel and behave. Be sure to explain the reasons for your predictions.

12. Write a short essay about the character of Laurie in "Charles." Explain why, in your opinion, he behaves as he does. Be sure to include details from the story to support your ideas. Also, refer to your own experience with young children's behavior.

13. Why do you think Laurie's parents in "Charles" fail to see the true situation earlier? In an essay, explain your ideas and support them with evidence from the story. Consider in particular the many clues that Laurie's parents fail to notice.

14. **Thinking About the Big Question: Can all conflicts be resolved?** Think about Laurie's behavior in kindergarten as it is revealed in "Charles." In an essay, trace Laurie's conflict with his teacher. Support your narrative with details from the story. At the end of your essay, explain why you think the conflict is—or is not—resolved by the end of the story.

Oral Response

15. Go back to question 3, 4, or 5 or to the question your teacher assigns you. Take a few minutes to expand your answer and prepare an oral response. Find additional details in "Charles" that support your points. If necessary, make notes to guide your response.

"Charles" by Shirley Jackson
Selection Test A

Critical Reading *Identify the letter of the choice that best answers the question.*

_____ 1. In the story "Charles," what new experience is Laurie facing?
   A. starting kindergarten
   B. starting third grade
   C. having a new babysitter
   D. moving to a new town

_____ 2. In the beginning of "Charles," how does Laurie behave as he leaves his mother?
   A. He is very sweet to his mother.
   B. He seems less confident than usual.
   C. He seems somewhat bad-mannered.
   D. He seems shy and frightened.

_____ 3. In "Charles," who is *I*, or the narrator?
   A. Laurie
   B. Laurie's mother
   C. the teacher
   D. Charles

_____ 4. What can you infer from this description of Laurie's behavior in "Charles"?
   At lunch he spoke insolently to his father, spilled his baby sister's milk, and
   remarked that his teacher said we were not to take the name of the Lord in vain.

   A. Laurie behaves well at home.
   B. Laurie does not behave well at home.
   C. Laurie behaves well at school.
   D. Laurie is clumsy.

_____ 5. Based on the details that Laurie gives his parents in "Charles," what sort of boy is Charles?
   A. smart but unfriendly
   B. shy and sensitive
   C. adorable
   D. very badly behaved

6. According to "Charles," in what way does Charles become an "institution" in Laurie's house?
   A. The parents think Charles should be put in a mental institution.
   B. Laurie's family wants to help Charles.
   C. Anyone who makes a mess or causes trouble is said to be acting like Charles.
   D. Laurie talks about Charles so much that he seems like part of the family.

7. What can you infer from these details in "Charles"?

   "You know what Charles did today?" Laurie demanded at the lunch table, in a voice slightly awed. "He told a girl to say a word and she said it and the teacher washed her mouth out with soap and Charles laughed."

   A. The little girl is mean.
   B. Charles is mean.
   C. Charles is rude to the teacher, but he is usually kind to his classmates.
   D. The little girl said something about the weather.

8. In "Charles," how does Charles change in the third and fourth weeks of school?
   A. He stops talking.
   B. He agrees to do exercises in gym.
   C. He starts helping the teacher.
   D. He starts wearing his jacket.

9. In "Charles," whom does Laurie's mother look for at the PTA meeting?
   A. Charles
   B. Charles's mother
   C. Laurie's father
   D. the principal

10. At the end of "Charles," when the teacher says that there is no Charles in the kindergarten, what inference can you make?
    A. The teacher does not know some of the students' names.
    B. The teacher is not telling the truth.
    C. Laurie was mixed up.
    D. Laurie is the bad boy who did the things he says Charles did.

11. How does the point of view help create the surprise ending to "Charles"?
    A. The narrator does not know the truth about Charles until the end.
    B. The narrator never gives any hints that Laurie behaves badly.
    C. The author tells many different characters' thoughts and feelings.
    D. Laurie is so mischievous that he tricks the reader.

Vocabulary and Grammar

____ 12. What is the meaning of *simultaneously* in this sentence?

The two students answered *simultaneously*.

A. correctly

B. incorrectly

C. one at a time

D. at the same time

____ 13. What is the opposite of *renounced*?

A. reclaimed

B. whispered

C. finished

D. restated

____ 14. Which sentence uses the past tense?

A. Laurie is starting school on Monday.

B. Charles talks freshly to the teacher.

C. The teacher punished Charles.

D. Will Charles's mother be at the meeting?

____ 15. What is the tense of the underlined verb in this sentence?

Laurie's mother <u>will attend</u> a PTA meeting.

A. past tense

B. present tense

C. future tense

D. no tense

Essay

16. Write a short essay about the surprise ending in "Charles." Tell what Laurie says about Charles as the story goes on, and what he makes his parents and the readers think. Then, tell what we find out at the end of the story about the situation involving Charles.

17. How do you think Laurie's mother feels at the end of "Charles"? What do you think she will do? Make a short prediction about the mother's feelings and behavior. Tell what you base your predictions on.

18. **Thinking About the Big Question: Can all conflicts be resolved?** Think about Laurie's behavior in kindergarten in "Charles." In an essay, trace Laurie's conflict with his teacher. Support your narrative with details from the story. At the end of your essay, explain why you think the conflict is—or is not—resolved by the end of the story.

"Charles" by Shirley Jackson
Selection Test B

Critical Reading *Identify the letter of the choice that best completes the statement or answers the question.*

____ 1. From what point of view is "Charles" told?
A. first person, from Laurie's point of view
B. first person, from Laurie's mother's point of view
C. third person, with thoughts and experiences limited to those of Laurie's mother
D. third person, with thoughts and experiences of many characters

____ 2. In "Charles," what is the mother's impression of Laurie *before* he begins kindergarten?
A. She sees him as a sweet little boy.
B. She sees him as a swaggering, noisy boy.
C. She sees him as a mean, nasty little boy.
D. She sees him as a shy, sensitive little boy.

____ 3. In "Charles," what is the mother's impression of Laurie on the day he starts kindergarten ?
A. He seems less sweet and innocent.
B. He seems less mature.
C. He seems sly and dishonest.
D. He seems shy and frightened.

____ 4. In "Charles," how do readers learn what the person named Charles is like?
A. Laurie, as narrator, tells us about him.
B. Laurie's mother reports what Laurie says about him.
C. Laurie's teacher writes reports about Charles and other students.
D. The narrator tells us Charles's thoughts and feelings.

____ 5. Which phrase best describes the boy Charles through most of "Charles"?
A. class scholar
B. class dunce
C. class leader
D. class troublemaker

____ 6. In "Charles," what does "doing a Charles" mean in Laurie's house?
A. telling a lie
B. inventing a friend
C. falling down
D. doing anything bad

____ 7. In "Charles," why is Laurie's mother interested in meeting Charles's mother?
A. She feels great pity for the woman and wants to help her.
B. She thinks someone with such a bad child would be interesting.
C. She suspects there really is no Charles and wants to prove it.
D. She assumes the woman will be just like her.

____ 8. In "Charles," how does Laurie's mother expect Charles's mother to look?
   A. cheerful
   B. confident
   C. tired
   D. evil

____ 9. What do you think Laurie's mother realizes at the end of "Charles"?
   A. The teacher does not know how to control her class.
   B. Laurie has learned many bad things from Charles.
   C. Laurie was just joking about Charles.
   D. Laurie is the bad boy who did the things he says Charles did.

____ 10. How does the point of view contribute to the surprise ending of "Charles"?
   A. The narrator does not know the truth about Charles, so neither do readers.
   B. The narrator portrays Laurie as angelic, so his bad behavior shocks readers.
   C. The author tells many characters' thoughts, so readers are not as surprised at the end.
   D. The narrator is dishonest, so readers are tricked until the end.

____ 11. Which of these earlier details hints at the surprise ending of "Charles"?
   A. Laurie tells his parents that Charles was fresh.
   B. Laurie tells his parents that Charles hit the teacher.
   C. Laurie tells his father, "Look at my thumb. Gee, you're dumb."
   D. Laurie predicts that they may throw Charles out of school.

____ 12. Earlier in "Charles," Laurie's mother is worried about the bad influence Charles may have on her son. Why is the mother's concern humorous, once you know the story's ending?
   A. Her son is Charles's best friend.
   B. Her son is just as bad as Charles.
   C. Her son is so well behaved that the other children tease him.
   D. Her son is the boy who is misbehaving.

____ 13. In "Charles," why does Laurie say that the whole class had to stay late when the teacher punished the boy Charles?
   A. The teacher always makes everyone stay late to punish one child.
   B. Laurie does not want his parents to know that after school he went somewhere off limits.
   C. Laurie is trying to hide that he alone is the badly behaved child who had to stay late.
   D. Laurie stays late to walk home with his friend Charles.

Vocabulary and Grammar

____ 14. You would be most likely to do things *simultaneously* if you were
   A. tired.
   B. not too bright.
   C. trying to kill time.
   D. multitasking.

_____ 15. To which observation would you most likely respond *incredulously?*
   A. Teachers sometimes punish schoolchildren by making them stay late in class.
   B. In some schools, students wear green uniforms.
   C. The weather forecast is for three days of rain.
   D. A newspaper is reporting that Martians have landed.

_____ 16. What is the tense of the underlined verb in this sentence?
   Will Laurie's mother attend a PTA meeting?

   A. past tense
   B. present tense
   C. future tense
   D. no tense

_____ 17. Based on the verb tense in this sentence, tell the time of the action.
   Charles behaves badly in school.

   A. in the past
   B. in the future
   C. just today
   D. regularly

Essay

18. Write a short essay about the character of Laurie in "Charles." Explain why you think he behaves as he does. Be sure to include details from the story to support your ideas. Also, include details from your own experience with children's behavior.

19. Why do you think Laurie's parents in "Charles" fail to see the true situation earlier? Write a short essay explaining your ideas. Focus especially on the mother and her false impressions of Laurie.

20. **Thinking About the Big Question: Can all conflicts be resolved?** Think about Laurie's behavior in kindergarten as it is revealed in "Charles." In an essay, trace Laurie's conflict with his teacher. Support your narrative with details from the story. At the end of your essay, explain why you think the conflict is—or is not—resolved by the end of the story.

Vocabulary Warm-up Word Lists

Study these words from "Thank You, M'am." Then, apply your knowledge to the activities.

Word List A

blondes [BLAHNDZ] *n.* people with pale yellow hair
　　Many people with dark-colored hair want to be <u>blondes</u>.

cocoa [KOH koh] *n.* hot chocolate drink
　　Nothing tastes as great as a cup of <u>cocoa</u> after a long day of snow skiing.

combined [kuhm BYND] *adj.* joined together
　　The weights of the two suitcases <u>combined</u> tipped the scale over the limit.

contact [KAHN takt] *n.* communication; meeting
　　You often come into <u>contact</u> with others when traveling.

frail [FRAYL] *adj.* thin and weak
　　The boy had grown so tall so quickly that he looked <u>frail</u>.

permit [per MIT] *v.* to allow something to happen
　　We do not <u>permit</u> our animals to get on our furniture.

release [ri LEES] *v.* to stop holding something; let go
　　My little sister would not <u>release</u> my arm during the scary movie.

switched [SWICHT] *v.* turned something electrical on or off
　　We <u>switched</u> off the power strip in the office during any big thunderstorm.

Word List B

brunettes [broo NETS] *n.* people with dark brown hair
　　I'm glad more children's dolls are dark-skinned <u>brunettes</u> these days.

devilish [DE vel ish] *adj.* very bad
　　My older cousin played <u>devilish</u> tricks on us every summer.

good-night [GOOD NYT] *inter.* remark when parting at night or going to sleep
　　At bedtime, our family always tells one another <u>good-night</u>.

icebox [EYES bahks] *n.* refrigerator, or chest with ice for keeping foods cold;
　　When my grandmother was young, she called a refrigerator an <u>icebox</u>.

pocketbook [PAHK it book] *n.* purse or handbag
　　My mom has always wanted a red leather <u>pocketbook</u>.

redheads [RED hedz] *n.* people with red hair
　　Have you noticed that one family often will have several <u>redheads</u> in it?

slung [SLUHNG] *adj.* hung or thrown loosely over something
　　With the backpack <u>slung</u> over my shoulder, I headed out the door.

whereupon [WAIR uh pahn] *conj.* after which
　　I laughed aloud, <u>whereupon</u> the teacher glared at me.

"Thank You, M'am" by Langston Hughes
Vocabulary Warm-up Exercises

Exercise A *Fill in the blanks using each word from Word List A only once.*

Wouldn't it be horrible if everyone you came into [1] _____ with every day were the same? Suppose we were all [2] _____, tall and [3] _____. Then, when you [4] _____ on a light in a darkened room, you'd never be surprised by seeing someone new and different. What if all we liked to drink was [5] _____, and no one would eat anything but chicken, eggs, rice, and peas? Even with all of our talents [6] _____, we still would have no variety! We wouldn't even be able to form a sports team or a musical group. I would ask for people to [7] _____ me from a world like this! If you will [8] _____ me to say so, we should be glad we live in a world with so many different types of people!

Exercise B *Write a complete sentence to answer each question. For each answer, use a word from Word List B to replace each underlined word or group of words without changing its meaning.*

1. The coach yells "go," <u>at which time</u> the runners do what in a race?

   _____

2. Where might you find <u>dark-haired people</u> getting light streaks in their hair and straight-haired <u>people with red hair</u> asking for curls?

   _____

3. When might you say, "<u>See you in the morning</u>!" to your best friend?

   _____

4. What are some things that a cute but <u>very bad</u> puppy might do?

   _____

5. What is the strangest <u>purse</u> you have ever seen?

   _____

6. If you could keep only three things in the <u>refrigerator</u>, what would they be?

   _____

7. Why wouldn't a neat person like it if you <u>loosely hung</u> your wet towel over a chair?

   _____

"Thank You, M'am" by Langston Hughes
Reading Warm-up A

Read the following passage. Pay special attention to the underlined words. Then, read it again, and complete the activities. Use a separate sheet of paper for your written answers.

Before World War II, the boardinghouse was a very important part of American culture. Boardinghouses were the answer to many people's problems.

Often, a single woman owned a boardinghouse. She might be a widow or someone who had never married. Running the house allowed her to keep it. In a world in which they weren't allowed to work at high-paying jobs, these women would have otherwise lost their big family homes. To run a boardinghouse, a woman needed the combined skills of cooking, cleaning, and managing helpers. If she also treated her guests kindly, she would certainly succeed. However, the work was hard. Owners rarely got a day off. Those staying at boardinghouses came into contact with many different types of people. Frail elderly people, traveling salesmen, and workers from the town all might chat briefly each day on their way in or out of the house. Fair-skinned young blondes and dark-haired ladies who were shop girls or teachers often stayed in boardinghouses, too. They were able to move away from home because of the safety that these houses offered.

Especially in the South, a boardinghouse could be found in nearly every town. From their stuffy bedrooms, where no televisions could be switched on, the guests would flee to the porch. Sitting together, sipping iced tea, they would talk and get to know one another. Even in cooler months, the porch was a meeting place. The owner might serve hot drinks such as cocoa, tea, or coffee to her guests in the evenings.

Many stories are told of young men and women who met and fell in love on boardinghouse porches. Their behavior had to be very proper. Boardinghouse owners would not even permit couples to hold hands. When an owner discovered couples with fingers entwined, she would ask them to release them. With so many chances just to talk, a young couple could really get to know each other before marrying.

1. Underline the words naming the combined skills that a boardinghouse owner needed. Then, describe something you have done in which you used **combined** skills.

2. Underline words describing five types of people with whom boarders might come into contact. Then, explain what **contact** means.

3. Write a sentence describing what *frail blondes* might look like.

4. Circle the word naming something that could not be switched on. Then, write about something that had not been invented and could not be **switched** on in a boardinghouse.

5. Underline the word that tells what cocoa is. Tell what you like or don't like about **cocoa**.

6. Circle what owners would not permit. Then, describe something your parents will not **permit**.

7. Circle the words naming what an owner would ask a couple to release. Then, explain what **release** means.

Name _____ Date _____

"Thank You, M'am" by Langston Hughes
Reading Warm-up B

Read the following passage. Pay special attention to the underlined words. Then, read it again, and complete the activities. Use a separate sheet of paper for your written answers.

Shoes protect our feet, but how they look has always seemed to matter as much as their ability to save our feet from cold, injury, and dirt. The first shoes were simply animal skins wrapped around the feet. Around the 1400s, however, shoes were becoming quite fancy.

Men who were rich wore shoes with very long pointed toes. Ribbons tied around the knees held the toes off the ground. After a day of trying to walk in such shoes, the wearers no doubt headed for the <u>icebox</u> for ice to apply to their sore feet!

Workers wore less <u>devilish</u> shoes, often with leather or wood bottoms strapped on to the feet with leather ties. At home, people might have worn soft fabric slippers. They would keep them on even after saying <u>good-night</u> and going to bed. What could feel better than toasty warm feet while you sleep?

In the 1850s, an American shoemaker developed a machine that could sew the upper parts of shoes to their soles. He sold the rights of ownership to the machine to a factory owner, <u>whereupon</u> the first mass-produced shoes could be made. Since then, we have had shoes for every type of activity. We have sports shoes, work shoes, and dress shoes. If you want, you can even find a pair of shoes to match your <u>pocketbook</u>. In fact, our society might be described as shoe crazy. You can see people with one pair of shoes on their feet and another pair <u>slung</u> across their shoulders.

Shoe fashion is big business today. Colors, styles, and materials are offered in huge variety. When you watch the <u>brunettes</u> and <u>redheads</u> on fashion show runways, be sure to look at their feet. These models will be wearing the latest shoe fashions to match their outfits.

1. Underline the words telling why rich men in the Middle Ages might need an <u>icebox</u>. Then, make a list of five things usually kept in an *icebox*.

2. Explain why <u>devilish</u> is a good word to use when describing painful shoes.

3. Circle the words naming where people go after saying <u>good-night</u>. Then, describe your own routine after saying *good-night*.

4. Write a sentence of your own using *whereupon*.

5. Circle the word that names what some people like to match to their <u>pocketbook</u>. Describe what you think is the best type of *pocketbook* for someone to carry.

6. Underline the words naming what some people have <u>slung</u> across their shoulders. Then, explain what *slung* means.

7. Circle the words saying where the <u>brunettes</u> and <u>redheads</u> described can be found. Then, name one *brunette* and one *redhead* you know or admire.

"Thank You, M'am" by Langston Hughes
Writing About the Big Question

 Can all conflicts be resolved?

Big Question Vocabulary

argument	compromise	injury	insecurity	interact
irritate	mislead	negotiate	oppose	reaction
solution	stalemate	victorious	viewpoint	violence

A. *Use one or more words from the list above to complete each sentence.*

1. Using _____ is usually the worst way to deal with a problem.

2. When two people cannot agree, they might have a loud _____ about the topic.

3. People who know how to _____ can often find a _____ to a problem.

4. You show respect to someone else when you listen to his or her _____ even though you disagree.

B. *Follow the directions in responding to each of the items below. Answer in complete sentences.*

1. Write two sentences about a person you trust completely. Tell why you trust him or her.

   _____

   _____

2. Suppose a conflict between you and another person hurt your relationship. How might you fix it? Use at least two of the Big Question vocabulary words.

   _____

   _____

C. *Complete the sentence below. Then, write a short paragraph describing a time when you were successful in earning someone's trust.*

   The best way to earn trust is _____

   _____

   _____

   _____

   _____

Name _____ Date _____

"Thank You, M'am" by Langston Hughes
Reading: Identify the Connections to Make Inferences

An **inference** is a logical assumption that you make about something the writer suggests but does not directly state. You often make inferences by **identifying the connections** between story events and outcomes or between characters' behavior and backgrounds, personalities, or other reasons for the behavior. For example, in "Thank You, M'am," if you connect the detail about the boy's background to his snatching the purse, you can infer that the boy may misbehave because of lack of attention at home.

A young boy snatches a purse.	+	He has a dirty face and no one at home to wash it.	=	The boy misbehaves because of lack of attention at home.

DIRECTIONS: *For each numbered item, connect the two details in order to make the requested inference about a character's behavior or about the outcome of events.*

1. Mrs. Jones lifts Roger by the shirtfront and demands the return of her purse.	+	Roger returns the purse.	=	*Make an inference about why Roger returns the purse:* _____ _____
2. Roger says he has no one at home to wash his face.	+	Mrs. Jones says it will get washed this evening.	=	*Make an inference about how Roger's face will get washed:* _____ _____
3. Roger does not appear to be eating well.	+	Roger snatched the purse to buy blue suede shoes.	=	*Make an inference about the kind of person Roger is:* _____ _____
4. Mrs. Jones leaves her purse out in the open when she prepares food for herself and Roger.	+	Roger sits far away from the purse and does not want to be mistrusted.	=	*Make an inference about how Mrs. Jones has changed Roger's behavior:* _____ _____

"Thank You, M'am" by Langston Hughes
Literary Analysis: Theme

A **theme** is a central idea, insight, or message that a work of literature conveys. It is usually expressed as a generalization about life or people. A theme is sometimes **stated** directly in a work, either by a character or by the narrator. More often, a theme is **unstated.** That is, it is only **implied,** and you must infer the theme from details in the work.

To determine the theme, consider the experiences of the characters and the outcome of events, and think about the general message to which they point. For example, in a story about a young dancer who practices and practices until she finally lands a starring role in a movie musical, the theme might be "Hard work pays off in the end."

DIRECTIONS: *Create word webs listing details about the story's characters, settings, and events. Then, answer the questions below the word webs.*

Roger — **Characters** — Mrs. Jones

street/neighborhood — **Settings** — Mrs. Jones's apartment

purse snatching — **Events** — taking Roger home

1. Based on the details you listed above, what aspect of life do you think the author is asking you to think about when you read this story? _____

_____

_____

2. Based on the details you listed above, what does the story seem to be saying about that aspect of life? _____

_____

_____

"Thank You, M'am" by Langston Hughes
Vocabulary Builder

Word List

barren   contact   frail   mistrusted   presentable   slung

A. DIRECTIONS: *Write a full-sentence answer using each Word List word only once.*

1. Do people comb their hair in order to look neat enough to be seen?

_____

_____

2. Is the frozen sheet of ice near the South Pole an empty part of the world?

_____

_____

3. Can you use e-mail to stay in communication with friends who move away?

_____

_____

4. What kind of weather would prompt you to take off your jacket and wear it just thrown over your shoulder?

_____

_____

5. If you doubted whether it was safe to be friendly to a strange dog, what would you do?

_____

_____

6. What is one way a person with weak muscles could improve his or her strength?

_____

_____

B. WORD STUDY: The prefix *mis-* means "opposite" or "badly, wrongly." Answer the following questions using one of these words containing the prefix *mis-*: *misrepresent, mislead, misuse.*

1. What is one example of how an ad might *mislead* a potential customer?

_____

2. What is one way a politician might *misrepresent* himself or herself to the voters?

_____

3. How might a beginner *misuse* headphones?

_____

"Thank You, M'am" by Langston Hughes
Enrichment: Inflation

Mrs. Jones gave Roger $10 to buy a pair of blue suede shoes. That figure reflects the buying power of the dollar when this story was published in 1958. Today, people can pay more than $100 for a pair of suede shoes. The increase in the price of basic goods and services is called *inflation*. In general, as inflation increases, the number of goods and services you can buy with a dollar decreases.

DIRECTIONS: *The table shows some items and their average prices in 1960 and 2005. For each item, calculate the price increase and the percent of inflation over the forty-five-year period. Write your answers in the spaces provided. The first calculation has been done as an example. At the bottom of this sheet are the math formulas needed to calculate the percent of inflation.*

Item	1960 Price	2005 Price	Price Increase	Inflation*
1. gallon of milk	$ 1.04	$ 2.78	$ 1.74	167%
2. loaf of bread	$ 0.20	$ 2.09		
3. gallon of gas	$ 0.26	$ 2.09		
4. automobile	$ 2,610.00	$ 19,500.00		
5. house	$ 12,675.00	$ 176,000.00		

* To calculate percent of inflation, follow these steps:

Formula
a. 2005 price – 1960 price = price increase
b. percent of inflation = $\frac{\text{increase}}{\text{1960 price}}$ x 100

Example
$2.78 – $1.04 = $1.74
$\frac{1.74}{1.04}$ x 100 = 1.67 x 100 = 167%

Unit 2 Resources: Short Stories
174

Name _____ Date _____

"Thank You, M'am" by Langston Hughes
Open-Book Test

Short Answer *Write your responses to the questions in this section on the lines provided.*

1. At the beginning of "Thank You, M'am," a young man tries to steal the pocketbook that a large woman is carrying. Why does the young man choose that woman as his target? Why is he probably sorry—at first—that he has made this choice?

   _____

   _____

   _____

2. Reread the dialogue at the beginning of "Thank You, M'am," after Mrs. Jones picks the young man up off the ground. What can readers infer from the statement that "you are going to remember Mrs. Luella Bates Washington Jones"? Cite two details from that part of the story that support the inference.

   _____

   _____

   _____

3. In "Thank You, M'am," Mrs. Jones says to Roger, "I were young once. . . . I have done things, too." What is she implying that she has in common with Roger? How can you tell?

   _____

   _____

   _____

4. Halfway through "Thank You, M'am" the narrator describes the kitchen area in Mrs. Jones's apartment. Complete this chart using details from that paragraph. Then, on the lines below, describe an inference about Mrs. Jones or about Roger that readers can make about the trust between the two characters.

Mrs. Jones does . . .	fix a meal for herself and Roger.
Mrs. Jones does not . . .	
Roger does . . .	
Roger does not . . .	

_____

_____

5. While Mrs. Jones is fixing a meal in "Thank You, M'am," the narrator says of Roger, "He did not trust the woman not to trust him." What does the narrator mean? Explain how Roger's decision about where he sits illustrates the statement.

_____

_____

_____

6. Reread what Mrs. Jones says about blue suede shoes near the end of "Thank You, M'am." What does she mean? How do her words relate to a theme of the story?

_____

_____

_____

7. What message about relationships between generations can readers infer from "Thank You, M'am"? Support your answer with a detail from the story.

_____

_____

_____

_____

8. What kinds of contact—physical, intellectual, and/or emotional—do Mrs. Jones and Roger have in "Thank You, M'am"? Base your answer on the meaning of *contact*.

_____

_____

_____

9. At the end of "Thank You, M'am," Roger wants to say something to Mrs. Jones. What inference can readers make about Roger's feelings based on what he actually says—or does not say—to Mrs. Jones?

_____

_____

_____

10. The theme of a story is its central message. What theme about trust does "Thank You, M'am" explore? Describe a detail in the story that illustrates that theme.

_____

_____

_____

_____

Essay

Write an extended response to the question of your choice or to the question or questions your teacher assigns you.

11. Think about the question in "Thank You, M'am" that Roger asks while Mrs. Jones is behind the screen. Write an essay in which you explain why the question is important and what it shows about Roger.

12. In "Thank You, M'am," Mrs. Jones bases her judgments about people on various experiences. In an essay, identify two of those experiences, and explain how they appear to have affected her judgments about people's behavior.

13. Write a short essay about the title "Thank You, M'am." Discuss why you think Langston Hughes chose that title and why you think it is—or is not—effective. Explain, too, why the title is unusual or even ironic. Use evidence from the story to support your ideas.

14. **Thinking About the Big Question: Can all conflicts be resolved?** At the end of "Thank You, M'am," what conflict has been resolved? What conflict may remain? Answer these questions in an essay, and support your ideas with details from the story.

Oral Response

15. Go back to question 4, 5, or 10 or to the question your teacher assigns you. Take a few minutes to expand your answer and prepare an oral response. Find additional details in "Thank You, M'am" that support your points. If necessary, make notes to guide your response.

Name _____   Date _____

"**Thank You, M'am**" by Langston Hughes
Selection Test A

Critical Reading *Identify the letter of the choice that best answers the question.*

____ 1. What happens when Roger tries to steal Mrs. Jones's purse in "Thank You, M'am"?
   A. He changes his mind because he knows stealing is wrong.
   B. He changes his mind because he is frightened by her large size.
   C. The purse is so heavy that he loses his balance and falls.
   D. He runs away but is caught by another person and brought back to Mrs. Jones.

____ 2. What can you infer about Mrs. Jones's first reaction to Roger from this sentence in "Thank You, M'am"?

   The large woman simply turned around and kicked him right square in his blue-jeaned sitter.

   A. She is confused.
   B. She is scared.
   C. She is angry.
   D. She is sad.

____ 3. What can you infer about Roger from this exchange with Mrs. Jones in "Thank You, M'am"?

   "Your face is dirty. I got a great mind to wash your face for you. Ain't you got nobody home to tell you to wash your face?"
   "No'm," said the boy.

   A. He is shy.
   B. He is neglected at home.
   C. He has trouble telling the truth.
   D. He has a good sense of humor.

____ 4. What can you infer about Mrs. Jones from this remark to Roger in "Thank You, M'am"?

   "But you put yourself in contact with me," said the woman. "If you think that that contact is not going to last awhile, you got another thought coming. When I get through with you, sir, you are going to remember Mrs. Luella Bates Washington Jones."

   A. She is shy.
   B. She is easily frightened.
   C. She has trouble expressing herself.
   D. She is bossy.

Unit 2 Resources: Short Stories
178

_____ 5. In "Thank You, M'am," how does Mrs. Jones get Roger to her home?
A. She drags him up the street.
B. She asks the person who caught Roger to drop off the boy.
C. She promises Roger food.
D. She tells him he can have money for blue suede shoes if he comes with her.

_____ 6. In "Thank You, M'am," why is Roger scared at first in Mrs. Jones's home?
A. He is very hungry.
B. Mrs. Jones is a strong, large woman.
C. Mrs. Jones talks so fast that he cannot understand her.
D. He fears that Mrs. Jones will turn him over to the police.

_____ 7. In "Thank You, M'am," why does Roger try to steal the purse?
A. to get money for food
B. to get back at Mrs. Jones for stealing from his father
C. to get money for blue suede shoes
D. to show he is tough

_____ 8. In "Thank You, M'am," how does Mrs. Jones show she trusts Roger?
A. She makes him wash his face.
B. She makes sure neighbors keep their doors open.
C. She leaves her purse near him when she prepares food.
D. She tells him her full name.

_____ 9. Which idea does the theme of "Thank You, M'am" deal with?
A. the value of kindness
B. the value of hard work
C. the value of a dollar
D. the value of city life

_____ 10. How might a reader state the theme of "Thank You, M'am"?
A. Children should respect their elders.
B. A child needs attention from an adult.
C. Do not try to steal in your own backyard.
D. The city streets are dangerous at night.

Vocabulary and Grammar

____ 11. What does *barren* mean in this sentence?

The surface of the moon is dark and *barren*.

A. distant   C. frightening

B. empty   D. full of life

____ 12. For which activity would you most want to look *presentable*?

A. going to sleep   C. cleaning the garage

B. hanging out at a friend's house   D. going to a job interview

____ 13. What is the tense of the underlined verb in this sentence?

The boy <u>has robbed</u> the wrong person.

A. past perfect   C. future perfect

B. present perfect   D. imperfect

Essay

14. Write a short essay about the character of Roger in "Thank You, M'am." Explain why you think he behaves as he does and whether you think he changes over the course of the story. Be sure to include details from the story to support your ideas. Also, include details from your own experience of people's behavior.

15. Do you think that Mrs. Jones in "Thank You, M'am" does Roger a favor by letting him get away with his mistake, or do you think Roger should have been punished? Explain your answer in an essay that uses examples from the story to support your opinion.

16. **Thinking About the Big Question: Can all conflicts be resolved?** By the end of "Thank You, M'am," a major conflict has been resolved. What is that conflict? What conflict may remain? Answer these questions in an essay. Support your ideas with details from the story.

"Thank You, M'am" by Langston Hughes
Selection Test B

Critical Reading *Identify the letter of the choice that best completes the statement or answers the question.*

_____ 1. Why does Roger lose his balance when he tries to steal Mrs. Jones's purse in "Thank You, M'am"?
  A. Mrs. Jones kicks him.
  B. Mrs. Jones is very large.
  C. The purse is very heavy.
  D. Roger is weighed down by guilt.

_____ 2. What is Mrs. Jones's first reaction to Roger's attempt to steal her purse in "Thank You, M'am"?
  A. She is puzzled.
  B. She is frightened.
  C. She is angry.
  D. She is deeply hurt.

_____ 3. In "Thank You, M'am," what does Mrs. Jones do when Roger struggles to get away?
  A. She jerks him in front of her, wrestles him with one arm, and drags him up the street.
  B. She shouts very loudly for help, frightening the boy into staying at her side.
  C. She warns him that she will call the police and that they will track him down.
  D. She hits him over the head with her purse and knocks him to the ground.

_____ 4. In "Thank You, M'am," what can you infer from reading that Roger has no one at home to wash his face?
  A. He is shy.
  B. He is neglected at home.
  C. He has trouble telling the truth.
  D. He has a good sense of humor.

_____ 5. According to Mrs. Jones in "Thank You, M'am," what lesson has Roger not been taught?
  A. why "early to bed and early to rise" is true
  B. how to apologize
  C. how to steal a purse without getting caught
  D. the difference between right and wrong

_____ 6. In "Thank You, M'am," what can you infer about Mrs. Jones from this remark?
  "When I get through with you, sir, you are going to remember Mrs. Luella Bates Washington Jones."

  A. She respects whomever she speaks to.
  B. She is a conceited showoff.
  C. She is a strong-minded person.
  D. She intends to do physical harm to Roger.

___ 7. In "Thank You, M'am," when Mrs. Jones brings Roger home, what does he first fear she will do?
   A. poison him with the food she serves
   B. hit him over the head again
   C. bore him to death with her stories
   D. turn him in to the police

___ 8. In "Thank You, M'am," why does Roger sit on the far side of the room when Mrs. Jones goes behind the screen?
   A. He is frightened that she is phoning the police and wants to see what she is doing.
   B. He does not want to smell the food she is cooking because it will make his stomach growl.
   C. He wants her to see that he is not taking anything from her purse.
   D. He wants to be where she cannot see him so that he can take money from her purse.

___ 9. In "Thank You, M'am," how does Mrs. Jones's admission that she did bad things when young reveal a theme of the story?
   A. She brags about her youthful adventures so that Roger will be humble in her presence.
   B. She is older and lonely and needs to confide in someone younger.
   C. She wants to be the adult whom Roger trusts to understand and help him.
   D. She wants to prove to Roger that all teenagers are delinquents.

___ 10. The author of "Thank You, M'am" calls Mrs. Jones "a large woman." What might *large* apply to besides her size?
   A. her large amount of money
   B. her large number of friends
   C. her large heart
   D. her large temper

___ 11. In "Thank You, M'am," what does Mrs. Jones mean by telling Roger that "shoes come by devilish like that will burn your feet"?
   A. The devil wears hot shoes.
   B. People who buy shoes with stolen money often go to jail.
   C. Shoes that do not fit will pinch your toes.
   D. Get shoes with stolen money, and guilt will burn your feet.

___ 12. In "Thank You, M'am," Mrs. Jones says she would have given Roger money for shoes if he had simply asked. Roger pauses for a long time. What can you infer from that pause?
   A. He is surprised, touched, and confused by her offer.
   B. He is growing more suspicious of Mrs. Jones.
   C. He is not used to washing his face, so he is taking his time.
   D. He is plotting ways to get more money from Mrs. Jones.

____ 13. Which statement is a main theme of "Thank You, M'am"?
   A. Lonely, older people seek company even from those who harm them.
   B. Kindness and goodwill are stronger than fear and mistrust.
   C. If you are going to steal, do not get caught.
   D. City streets are full of dangers for young and old alike.

Vocabulary and Grammar

____ 14. Which place would best be described as *barren*?
   A. a lush garden in summer
   B. an empty beach in winter
   C. a dirty, crowded subway car
   D. a football field during an exciting play

____ 15. In which sentence is *presentable* used correctly?
   A. The past is over, so it is time to focus on what is presentable.
   B. I wore my oldest shirt to be presentable.
   C. At the wedding, the gifts were piled high on the presentable table.
   D. I combed my hair to look more presentable.

____ 16. Which sentence would come first in a story about a lion and a woman at the circus?
   A. The lion has roared for hours.
   B. The woman had entered the tent with a lion.
   C. I have never enjoyed a circus more.
   D. The circus will have departed by tomorrow.

____ 17. Which verb form correctly completes this sentence?

   By tomorrow, the show _____.

   A. had ended
   B. has ended
   C. ended
   D. will have ended

Essay

18. Why do you think Mrs. Jones treats Roger as she does in "Thank You, M'am"? Write a short essay explaining your ideas. Focus on the kind of person Mrs. Jones is and on her behavior in taking Roger home and treating him kindly.

19. Write a short essay about the title "Thank You, M'am." Explain why you think Langston Hughes used this remark, which, in the final paragraph, Roger thinks of but does not voice, as the title for the whole story.

20. **Thinking About the Big Question: Can all conflicts be resolved?** At the end of "Thank You, M'am," what conflict has been resolved? What conflict may remain? Answer these questions in an essay, and support your ideas with details from the story.

Vocabulary Warm-up Word Lists

Study these words from "The Story-Teller." Then, apply your knowledge to the activities that follow.

Word List A

approval [uh PROO vuhl] *n.* good opinion
The mother looked at her son with approval after he cleaned his room.

conduct [KAHN duhkt] *n.* the way a person behaves
The conduct of the students really changed when a substitute teacher was there.

horribly [HAWR uh blee] *adv.* to an awful extent; disagreeably
The book was horribly hard to read as well as boring.

momentarily [moh muhn TER uh lee] *adv.* for a short time
The television screen was momentarily black when the power went off.

promptly [PRAHMPT lee] *adv.* very quickly; immediately
The waiter promptly came to our table to take our order.

retort [ri TAWRT] *n.* quick and clever reply
My sister always seems to have a retort for what I thought were good ideas.

unspeakable [un SPEE kuh buhl] *adj.* so bad that you can't describe it; extremely bad
To make rude comments about Grandma seemed unspeakable to me.

utterly [UHT er lee] *adv.* completely
I knew Dad was utterly lost when he pulled over to study the map.

Word List B

assail [uh SAYL] *v.* to attack, often with words
The curious child would assail his parents daily with questions.

audible [AW duh buhl] *adj.* loud enough to be heard
The radio wasn't audible to the people in the next room.

extraordinarily [ek strawr de NER uh lee] *adv.* in a very special or unusual way
The skater was extraordinarily graceful on the ice.

inevitable [in EV uh tuh buhl] *adj.* sure to happen and impossible to avoid
One famous saying states that only two things in life are inevitable: death and taxes.

novelty [NAHV uhl tee] *n.* something new and different
After a new haircut, I look in the mirror often because of the novelty of it.

persistent [per SIS tuhnt] *adj.* continuing firmly and stubbornly
The bad cold left me with a persistent cough.

repetition [rep uh TISH uhn] *n.* the act of saying or doing something more than once
Children learn best through repetition; they love hearing the same stories over and over.

satisfactory [sat is FAK tuh ree] *adj.* good enough for a certain situation
Our small school band received satisfactory marks from the judges.

"The Story-Teller" by Saki
Vocabulary Warm-up Exercises

Exercise A *Fill in the blanks using each word from Word List A only once.*

The track team's [1] _____ on the bus while going to meets

had become [2] _____. The runners were mean to each other and

[3] _____ rude to the driver. The coach decided she had to take action.

She began the next trip by saying the team would be [4] _____ silent for

the first thirty miles. A runner's snort and scornful [5] _____ to her

words landed him [6] _____ in the back row of the bus, far from anyone

else. After pausing [7] _____ to be sure she had everyone's attention

again, the coach continued to state her plan. After thirty miles, each runner would have

a chance to speak. Each would make a kind statement about the team. Only with the

coach's [8] _____ could talking begin again.

Exercise B *Answer the questions with complete explanations.*

1. Would a person who likes to do things perfectly be happy to hear that his work is
   <u>satisfactory</u>?

   _____

2. Would a shy person be likely to <u>assail</u> a new student with questions?

   _____

3. If something is <u>inevitable</u>, is it likely to happen or is it certain not to occur?

   _____

4. How big would an <u>extraordinarily</u> large house cat be?

   _____

5. Why would early peoples think of a matchbook as a <u>novelty</u>?

   _____

6. Why should the sound of any type of alarm be clearly <u>audible</u>?

   _____

7. When you learn a new skill, is <u>repetition</u> important?

   _____

8. Why might you describe the sound of a flowing stream as <u>persistent</u>?

   _____

Unit 2 Resources: Short Stories
185

"The Story-Teller" by Saki
Reading Warm-up A

Read the following passage. Pay special attention to the underlined words. Then, read it again, and complete the activities. Use a separate sheet of paper for your written answers.

No one should ever be in the <u>horribly</u> sad position of watching a best friend lie motionless in bed, hardly seeming to be alive. The doctors call this awful condition a coma, but I think its name should be <u>unspeakable</u>.

Anyway, I found myself in this position last year. My best friend was in a terrible car crash, and he then went into a coma. It took a few days for me to visit Sam. My desire to visit met with the <u>approval</u> of Sam's parents and doctor. Yet, everyone thought I needed lots of talking to about the proper <u>conduct</u> I should have in the hospital room. Despite the waiting and the talking, I was <u>utterly</u> determined to see my friend.

When I finally entered the room, I was <u>momentarily</u> choked up by what I saw. Sam was very still and very pale. All kinds of tubes and machines were attached to him. I didn't like the sight, the sounds, or the smells of that room. After a few seconds, however, I looked more closely at Sam's face. I <u>promptly</u> snapped out of it. Sam—my buddy since preschool, the source of my best memories—needed me.

I had read that people in comas can hear and understand you. Therefore, I wasn't going to sit silently by Sam's bed. My plan was to tell Sam the story of our lives together. I would start at the beginning. For the one hour I was given each day, I would tell our tale in all its glory. Sam and I would grow up together again through my storytelling. Before too many days had passed, I knew—no, I believed with all my heart—Sam would open his eyes and give a smart <u>retort</u> to some story detail I had managed to mess up.

It was time to begin. "We met the first day of preschool," I said, "when you tried to take the big red truck away from me. . . ." I could see Sam's eyes blink!

1. Underline the words describing a <u>horribly</u> sad position to be in. Then, describe something else that is *horribly* sad.

2. Circle the word that is the <u>unspeakable</u> name of a medical condition. Then, explain what *unspeakable* means.

3. Write a sentence about parents that includes both the words *approval* and *conduct*.

4. Underline the words naming what the author was <u>utterly</u> determined to do. Then, explain what *utterly* means.

5. Circle the words that describe what feelings the author <u>momentarily</u> had upon seeing Sam. Then, explain what *momentarily* means.

6. Underline the words that describe what caused the author to <u>promptly</u> change his mood. Describe what you think he *promptly* did as a result.

7. Circle what the narrator expected Sam to give a <u>retort</u> to. Explain why Sam's ability to give a *retort* would be wonderful news.

"The Story-Teller" by Saki
Reading Warm-up B

Read the following passage. Pay special attention to the underlined words. Then, read it again, and complete the activities. Use a separate sheet of paper for your written answers.

Every fall, more than ten thousand people come from all around the world to a tiny town in Tennessee. They come to the National Storytelling Convention. Here, they listen to masters of the oral tradition tell their tales. As visitors pass by colorful tents, stories on all kinds of topics are <u>audible</u>. Feelings of being connected to history, people, and culture are sure to <u>assail</u> all who come to experience the grand art of storytelling.

A single man began the National Storytelling Convention. Back in 1973, Jimmy Neil Smith, mayor of Jonesborough, heard an <u>extraordinarily</u> well-told tale on the radio. He decided a storytelling festival would allow the <u>repetition</u> of great stories. Then, people visiting from all parts of the world could hear them, and help keep them alive. Smith began the festival in his own town. Judging from its success over the years and the increased interest in storytelling worldwide, Smith's idea was more than just a <u>novelty</u>.

Today, the International Storytelling Center in Jonesborough works in a <u>persistent</u> way to spread its strong beliefs about the power and importance of stories. The center reminds us that having a central place for people to meet was a part of all early societies. At this place, usually a fire pit, people made and ate food. They also celebrated and told stories there. The center believes that feelings of loneliness and mistrust that many people feel today are an <u>inevitable</u> result of losing the place where storytelling could occur.

The center also feels that people might have more <u>satisfactory</u> relationships with one another as a result of sharing stories. So, it encourages us all to pass on our own stories. We should eagerly tell our tales at home, at school, and at work. As we listen to one another and understand our stories, perhaps "we can transform our lives—and the world."

1. Underline the words telling what is <u>audible</u> from tents. Then, explain what *audible* means.

2. Circle the words naming what would <u>assail</u> people who hear the storytellers. Describe a time when your feelings *assail* you.

3. Describe some ways that someone would tell an <u>extraordinarily</u> well-told story.

4. Explain why <u>repetition</u> is important if stories are to be passed down from age to age.

5. Underline the words that indicate that Smith's idea was more than a <u>novelty</u>. Then, explain what *novelty* means.

6. Explain why people would want to be <u>persistent</u> in how they express important ideas.

7. Write a sentence about something that you know is <u>inevitable</u>.

8. Describe what you would call a <u>satisfactory</u> relationship with someone.

Name _____ Date _____

"The Story-Teller" by Saki (H. H. Munro)
Writing About the Big Question

 Can all conflicts be resolved?

Big Question Vocabulary

argument	compromise	injury	insecurity	interact
irritate	mislead	negotiate	oppose	reaction
solution	stalemate	victorious	viewpoint	violence

A. *Use one or more words from the list above to complete each sentence.*

1. In most children's stories, good is _____ over evil.

2. The audience's _____ to the shocking story was a loud gasp.

3. There is little _____ over the idea that _____ in children's stories is best avoided.

4. In some children's stories, human characters _____ with talking animals.

B. *Follow the directions in responding to each of the items below. Answer in complete sentences.*

1. Describe a conflict in one of your favorite children's stories.

_____

_____

2. Why might a parent have inner conflict about allowing a child to view violence on TV? Use at least two of the Big Question vocabulary words.

_____

_____

C. *Complete the sentence below. Then, write a short paragraph in which you comment on the types of conflict commonly found in fairy tales.*

The endings of fairy tales are _____

_____

_____

_____

_____

Name _____   Date _____

"The Story-Teller" by Saki
Reading: Identify Connections to Make Inferences

An **inference** is a logical assumption that you make about something the writer suggests but does not directly state. You often make inferences by **identifying the connections** between story events and outcomes or between characters' behavior and backgrounds, personalities, or other reasons for the behavior. For example, "The Story-Teller" opens with three children cooped up in a hot railway carriage along with their aunt and a bachelor who is a stranger to them. A few sentences later, you read that most of the aunt's remarks seem to begin with "Don't." By connecting these details, you can infer that the children are restless and that the aunt is having trouble controlling them.

Three children are cooped up in a hot railway carriage.	+ Most of the aunt's remarks begin with "Don't."	= The children are restless and the aunt is having trouble controlling them.

DIRECTIONS: *For each numbered item, connect the two details in order to make the requested inference about a character's behavior or the outcome of events.*

1. Cyril is smacking the seat cushions of the railway carriage.	+ The aunt invites Cyril to look out the window.	= *Make an inference about why the aunt tells Cyril to look out the window:* _____ _____
2. Cyril asks questions about what he sees.	+ Cyril is not satisfied with the aunt's answers and asks more questions.	= *Make an inference about the kind of boy Cyril is:* _____ _____ _____
3. The smaller sister recites one line of a poem over and over.	+ The bachelor looks twice at the aunt and once at the train's communication cord.	= *Make an inference about why the bachelor looks at the aunt and the cord:* _____ _____
4. The bachelor tells a story about a good little girl who is eaten by a wolf because of her goodness.	+ The children enjoy the story.	= *Make an inference about why the children enjoy the story:* _____ _____

Unit 2 Resources: Short Stories
189

"The Story-Teller" by Saki
Literary Analysis: Theme

A **theme** is a central idea, insight, or message that a work of literature conveys. It is usually expressed as a generalization about life or people. A theme is sometimes **stated** directly in a work, either by a character or by the narrator. More often, a theme is **unstated.** That is, it is only **implied,** and you must infer the theme from details in the work.

To determine the theme, consider the experiences of the characters and the outcome of events, and think about the general message to which they point. For example, in a story about a jewel thief who risks breaking his neck by scaling a building to steal a bracelet that turns out to be fake, the theme might be "Crime does not pay."

DIRECTIONS: *Create word webs about the story that the bachelor tells the children. Then, answer the questions below the word webs.*

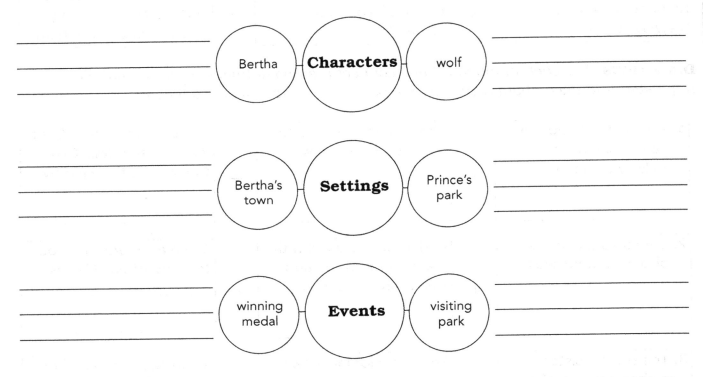

1. Based on the details you listed above, what sort of human behavior do you think the bachelor wants listeners to think about when they hear his story? _____

_____

_____

2. Based on the details you listed above, what does the story seem to be saying about the benefits and drawbacks of that kind of behavior?

_____

_____

"The Story-Teller" by Saki
Vocabulary Builder

Word List

assail   conviction   immensely   inevitable   persistent   suppressed

A. DIRECTIONS: *Write a full-sentence answer that uses each Word List word only once.*

1. How should you speak about a strong belief that you want others to share?

   _____

   _____

2. If you refuse to give up your habit of saving half your allowance for a year, what will be the result?

   _____

   _____

3. How would you react if your young cousin were to attack you with demands for interesting stories every time you met?

   _____

   _____

4. Describe a school event that is certain to happen sometime in the next week.

   _____

   _____

5. What is one accomplishment of yours that makes you feel extremely proud?

   _____

   _____

6. Describe one situation in which you thought it best to hold back your laughter.

   _____

   _____

B. WORD STUDY: The prefix *per-* means "thoroughly" or "throughout." Revise each sentence so that the underlined word containing the prefix *per-* is used logically. Be sure not to change the underlined word.

1. These plants are <u>perennials</u>, so they will definitely die after one season.

   _____

2. The color red is barely <u>perceptible</u> against a yellow background.

   _____

3. Charlotte's <u>perfect</u> performance was filled with mistakes.

   _____

Unit 2 Resources: Short Stories
191

"The Story-Teller" by Saki
Enrichment: Parks

The man in "The Story-Teller" captures the children's interest by telling a story about an imaginary private park filled with pigs, parrots, fish, and a wolf. Parks come in all shapes and sizes. Some, such as Central Park in New York City, are created and designed. Some, such as the Badlands National Park in South Dakota, are wilderness areas. Others, such as Gettysburg National Military Park in Pennsylvania, are created around points of historic interest—in this case, the Battle of Gettysburg during the American Civil War.

In all their forms, parks are places for community. Neighborhood parks provide opportunities for people to gather with friends or family. Wilderness-area parks allow people to enjoy the beauty and power of the natural landscape. Parks of historic interest help people understand and appreciate the national heritage.

DIRECTIONS: *Describe a park you know. Explain how you might spend a day there. Include details about the park's landscape, its natural inhabitants, and the facilities you can use for sports and other activities in the park. Then, explain how spending a day in the park can help give you a sense of community or a deeper appreciation of nature, history, or heritage. Continue your description on a separate sheet of paper, if necessary.*

_____

_____

_____

_____

_____

_____

_____

_____

_____

_____

_____

_____

_____

_____

_____

_____

_____

"Thank You, M'am" by Langston Hughes
"The Story-Teller" by Saki
Integrated Language Skills: Grammar

The Perfect Tenses and the Subjunctive Mood

A **verb tense** tells when the action or state of being takes place. A **perfect tense** describes an action or a state of being that was or will be completed at a certain time. It uses a form of the helping verb *have* and the past participle of the main verb, which in regular verbs ends in *-ed*.

- The **present perfect tense** shows a past action or condition that continues into the present. Example: The gas gauge **has indicated** an empty tank for some time now.
- The **past perfect tense** shows a past action or condition that was completed before another began. Example: Dad **had filled** the tank before we started our vacation.
- The **future perfect tense** shows a future action or condition that will have ended at a certain time. Example: By this time next week, our trip **will have ended.**

The **subjunctive mood** is used to express a wish or a condition contrary to fact, as in this example: If he *were* a dog-owner, he would understand dogs better.

A. PRACTICE: *Complete each sentence with the verb form requested in parentheses.*

1. The teacher _____ our short-answer test papers, and now we are waiting for the class bell to ring. (*collect* in the present perfect)

2. The teacher _____ an essay for us to write before she scheduled this test. (*assign* in the past perfect)

3. By five o'clock, the teacher _____ all our short-answer tests. (*reviewed* in the future perfect)

4. If our teacher _____ any faster, she would set a record. (*be* in the subjunctive mood)

B. Writing Application: *Write four sentences about your education and future plans. One sentence should use the past perfect tense, one should use the present perfect tense, one should use the future perfect tense, and one should use the subjunctive mood. Underline the verbs, and label the verb tenses.*

_____

_____

_____

_____

"Thank You, M'am" by Langston Hughes
"The Story-Teller" by Saki

Integrated Language Skills: Support for Writing a Personal Essay

Use this sheet to do the suggested prewriting for your personal essay. At the top of the graphic, state in your own words what you believe to be the theme of the story. In the boxes below the statement of theme, note thoughts that occur to you as you brainstorm about your own past experiences that relate to this theme. You do not need to fill in all the boxes, but try to examine at least two different experiences. If you cannot think of experiences in your own past, you might consider events and reactions you have heard about through your family or in the local news.

Theme:	
Notes on Experience 1 Relating to Theme:	Notes on Experience 2 Relating to Theme:
Notes on Experience 3 Relating to Theme:	Notes on Experience 4 Relating to Theme:

Now, use your notes to draft your personal essay.

Unit 2 Resources: Short Stories

"Thank You, M'am" by Langston Hughes
"The Story-Teller" by Saki

Integrated Language Skills: Support for Extend Your Learning

Listening and Speaking: "Thank You M'am"

In the box below, check off your opinion, and list the support you find for your opinion as you review the story.

Opinion

☐ Mrs Jones did the right thing.
☐ Mrs. Jones did not do the right thing.

Support

1. _____
2. _____
3. _____
4. _____
5. _____
6. _____
7. _____

Listening and Speaking: "The Story-Teller"

In the box below, check off your opinion, and list the support you find for your opinion as you review the story.

Opinion

☐ The bachelor should have told the gruesome story.
☐ The bachelor should not have told the gruesome story.

Support

1. _____
2. _____
3. _____
4. _____
5. _____

Unit 2 Resources: Short Stories
195

"The Story-Teller" by Saki (H. H. Munro)
Open-Book Test

Short Answer *Write your responses to the questions in this section on the lines provided.*

1. The first paragraph of "The Story-Teller" describes a group of people sitting together on a railroad car. There is a woman, her two nieces and her nephew, and a bachelor. What evidence helps readers infer that the aunt is having trouble keeping the children under control?

   _____

   _____

   _____

2. As "The Story-Teller" opens, why are the children so persistent with their questions? Base your answer on the definition of *persistent*.

   _____

   _____

3. At the beginning of "The Story-Teller," the children do not know the bachelor at all. Why, then, do they misbehave so freely in his presence?

   _____

   _____

   _____

4. At the end of her aunt's story in "The Story-Teller," the older girl asks whether the girl in the story would have been rescued even if she had not been good. What does she seem to think is the theme of her aunt's story? What detail in the aunt's story leads her to think so?

   _____

   _____

   _____

5. In "The Story-Teller," the children respond enthusiastically when the bachelor describes Bertha as "horribly good." What do they understand about Bertha? Why are they enthusiastic about the description?

   _____

   _____

   _____

Name _____ Date _____

6. Complete this chart with information about the bachelor in "The Story-Teller."
   Then, on the line below, write an inference that readers can make about the
   bachelor based on this information.

The Bachelor Observes	The Bachelor Thinks or Knows
The children ask their aunt, "Why?"	The children are irritating.

_____

_____

_____

7. In "The Story-Teller," the children interrupt the bachelor's story with questions.
   What can readers infer about the children from this behavior? What can readers
   infer about the bachelor from his response?

_____

_____

_____

_____

8. When the central message of a literary work is not directly stated, it is said to be an
   implied theme. In "The Story-Teller," what is one implied theme of the bachelor's
   story? How can you tell?

_____

_____

_____

9. In "The Story-Teller," in what two ways are the stories that the children hear
   similar? What is it about the bachelor's story that they prefer to their aunt's
   story?

_____

_____

_____

_____

10. Suppose that "The Story-Teller" had ended before the bachelor spoke up. How would the theme of the story have been different from the theme of the story you read? Explain.

_____

_____

_____

_____

Essay

Write an extended response to the question of your choice or to the question or questions your teacher assigns you.

11. The aunt in "The Story-Teller" calls the bachelor's story "most improper." In an essay, describe how that judgment fits with what readers know about her. Use details or examples from the story to show what she is like.

12. Based on "The Story-Teller," write a definition of a good story-teller. Refer to the story as you explain what Saki seems to think good story-telling is all about.

13. "The Story-Teller" can be described as three stories—the two short stories that are told during the course of the longer story of what happens in the railroad car. All three stories have a message about children's behavior. In an essay, identify the three messages. Which message do you think readers will find most memorable, and why?

14. **Thinking About the Big Question: Can all conflicts be resolved?** In "The Story-Teller," the bachelor resolves his conflict with the three children. In an essay, explain what the aunt might have learned from him. Then, explain why you think that she would—or would not—follow his example in future conflicts with the children. Support your ideas with evidence from the story.

Oral Response

15. Go back to question 1, 5, or 9 or to the question your teacher assigns you. Take a few minutes to expand your answer and prepare an oral response. Find additional details in "The Story-Teller" that will support your points. If necessary, make notes to guide your response.

Unit 2 Resources: Short Stories
198

"The Story-Teller" by Saki
Selection Test A

Critical Reading *Identify the letter of the choice that best answers the question.*

—— 1. Where does "The Story-Teller" take place?
   A. on a train
   B. on a ship
   C. on a plane
   D. in a country house

—— 2. What is the relationship of the bachelor in "The Story-Teller" to the other characters?
   A. He is the children's uncle.
   B. He is the aunt's boyfriend.
   C. He is a neighbor traveling to work.
   D. He is a stranger.

—— 3. What can you infer about the aunt from this sentence in "The Story-Teller"?
   "Don't, Cyril, don't," exclaimed the aunt, as the small boy began smacking the cushions of the seat. . . .
   A. The aunt is easily scared.
   B. The aunt is good at handling Cyril.
   C. The aunt is a positive person.
   D. The aunt wants Cyril to behave.

—— 4. Which statement best describes Cyril in "The Story-Teller"?
   A. He likes to tell stories.
   B. He is bored by everything.
   C. He is lazy.
   D. He is curious and asks lots of questions.

—— 5. What can you infer about the bachelor from this sentence in "The Story-Teller"?
   The frown on the bachelor's face was deepening to a scowl.
   A. He is amused by the children.
   B. He wants to learn more about the children.
   C. He is annoyed by the children.
   D. He is bored by the scenery.

___ 6. In "The Story-Teller," what do the children think of the aunt's story?
   A. They enjoy it.
   B. They do not understand it.
   C. They find it boring and silly.
   D. They find it comforting and familiar.

___ 7. In "The Story-Teller," what do the children think of the bachelor's story?
   A. They enjoy it.
   B. They do not understand it.
   C. They find it boring and stupid.
   D. They find it comforting and familiar.

___ 8. In "The Story-Teller," the bachelor says that Bertha was "horribly good." What do you think this term means?
   A. She is so good that she deserves three medals.
   B. She is horrible-looking but is very well behaved.
   C. Being good is a horrible quality.
   D. She is so good that other people find her a little awful.

___ 9. According to the bachelor in "The Story-Teller," what happens to Bertha at the end of his story?
   A. She gets lost in the woods.
   B. She is eaten by a wolf.
   C. She makes the wild animals her friends.
   D. none of the above

___ 10. What is the main theme of the story the bachelor tells in "The Story-Teller"?
   A. Good children win many medals.
   B. Parks are beautiful places.
   C. Too much goodness can be bad.
   D. Good people do something bad eventually.

___ 11. In "The Story-Teller," why does the aunt think the bachelor's story is improper?
   A. The aunt's name is also Bertha.
   B. It is a long way to Templecombe.
   C. It makes the unrealistic suggestion that virtue is always rewarded.
   D. It makes fun of children who are very good.

Unit 2 Resources: Short Stories
200

___ 12. Which statement is a main theme of "The Story-Teller"?
   A. Long train trips make everyone restless regardless of age.
   B. Children do not know right from wrong.
   C. Children do not like being taught good behavior all the time.
   D. People learn a lot when they travel.

Vocabulary and Grammar

___ 13. What does *conviction* mean in this sentence?
   His voice rang with great *conviction* as he told us his ideas.
   A. anger   C. confusion
   B. certainty   D. sorrow

___ 14. Which word is a synonym for *resolute*?
   A. weak   C. dishonest
   B. stubborn   D. unclear

___ 15. What is the tense of the underlined verb in this sentence?
   The bachelor <u>had looked</u> twice at her and once at the communication cord.
   A. present perfect   C. future perfect
   B. past perfect   D. imperfect

Essay

16. In a short essay, describe the children in "The Story-Teller." Explain what they are like, how they behave, and why you think they behave that way.

17. In a short essay, explain what the children like about the bachelor's story and what they don't like about the aunt's story. Be sure to include details from the stories to support what you say about them.

18. **Thinking About the Big Question: Can all conflicts be resolved?** In "The Story-Teller," the bachelor resolves his conflict with the three children. In an essay, explain what the aunt might have learned from him. Support your ideas with examples from the story.

"The Story-Teller" by Saki
Selection Test B

Critical Reading *Identify the letter of the choice that best completes the statement or answers the question.*

_____ 1. What is the setting for "The Story-Teller"?
   A. on a public railway carriage made uncomfortable by the heat
   B. on a crowded subway in New York City
   C. in the carriage of an old-fashioned horse-drawn stagecoach
   D. on an elegant private train where every comfort is assured

_____ 2. What is the relationship among the bachelor, the aunt, and the three children in "The Story-Teller"?
   A. He is the children's uncle and the aunt's brother-in-law.
   B. He is engaged to marry the aunt but has never met the children before.
   C. He is someone the other characters see on the train all the time but do not know well.
   D. He is a complete stranger to the other characters.

_____ 3. What can you infer from this sentence near the start of "The Story-Teller"?
   Most of the aunt's remarks seemed to begin with "Don't," and nearly all of the children's remarks began with "Why?"
   A. It is a long trip to Templecombe.
   B. The aunt is extremely clever about handling the children.
   C. The children are pleasant and well-behaved.
   D. The aunt is having trouble keeping the children under control.

_____ 4. While Cyril is smacking the seat cushions, his aunt invites him to look out the window. What can you infer from these two details in "The Story-Teller"?
   A. The aunt is trying to distract Cyril and get him to behave.
   B. The aunt is punishing Cyril for his bad behavior.
   C. The aunt is not aware of what Cyril is doing but wants to teach him about cows.
   D. The aunt is trying to anticipate Cyril's loss of interest in the seat cushions.

_____ 5. After Cyril looks out the window and asks questions about the sheep, the aunt starts talking about cows. What can you infer from these two details in "The Story-Teller"?
   A. The aunt prefers cows to sheep.
   B. The aunt, unaware of Cyril's interest, brings up an entirely new subject.
   C. The aunt is trying to stop Cyril from asking so many questions.
   D. The aunt has attention deficit disorder.

_____ 6. In "The Story-Teller," what does Cyril's constant questioning suggest about him?
   A. He is foolish and ignorant.
   B. He is nervous and worried.
   C. He is timid and shy.
   D. He is curious and mischievous.

_____ 7. In "The Story-Teller," what is the bachelor's reaction toward the children at first?
   A. amusement
   B. curiosity
   C. annoyance
   D. delight

_____ 8. In "The Story-Teller," what can you infer about the children's reaction to the aunt's story?
   A. They enjoy the story.
   B. They are puzzled by the story.
   C. They find the story boring and stupid.
   D. They only pretend to like the story.

_____ 9. In "The Story-Teller," what can you infer about the bachelor from the answers he gives when the children interrupt his story with questions?
   A. He is impatient.
   B. He does not understand what others say.
   C. He does not know what children like.
   D. He has a good imagination.

_____ 10. In "The Story-Teller," which statement best expresses a theme of the story about Bertha?
   A. Violence never solves anything.
   B. It is important to protect the environment.
   C. Goodness is eventually rewarded.
   D. If you are too proud of being good, you are not really so good.

_____ 11. What does the aunt in "The Story-Teller" find improper about the bachelor's story?
   A. It makes fun of Bertha's goodness.
   B. It has too many fantasy elements.
   C. It unrealistically suggests that virtue is always rewarded.
   D. The bachelor tells it without invitation, interrupting the aunt's story to do so.

_____ 12. Which statement best expresses a central theme of "The Story-Teller"?
   A. People with no children to care for are usually better at handling children.
   B. It is important to instruct children about right and wrong at all times.
   C. The best way for adults to deal with children is to appeal to their imagination.
   D. Traveling and visiting new places can be very uncomfortable.

_____ 13. Who is "The Story-Teller" of the title?
   A. Saki
   B. the bachelor
   C. Cyril
   D. none of the above

Vocabulary and Grammar

___ 14. Who would best be described as *resolute*?
    A. people who cannot make up their minds
    B. people who are timid and shy
    C. people who stick to their principles
    D. people who talk with their hands

___ 15. What does *conviction* mean in this sentence?
    His voice rang with great *conviction* as he told us his ideas.

    A. anger
    B. certainty
    C. confusion
    D. illegality

___ 16. Which sentence tells about the earliest of the four activities?
    A. By now, my aunt has journeyed by plane all over the world.
    B. My aunt had originally feared airplanes.
    C. I have enjoyed looking at my aunt's photographs of Chile.
    D. At the end of next year, my aunt will have visited three more countries.

___ 17. Which verb form correctly completes this sentence?
    By tomorrow, the train _____ Templecombe.

    A. had reached
    B. has reached
    C. have reached
    D. will have reached

Essay

18. In an essay, state what you feel is the main theme of "The Story-Teller." Then, show how details in the story point to that theme.

19. Based on "The Story-Teller," write a definition of a good storyteller. Explain what Saki seems to think good storytelling is all about.

20. **Thinking About the Big Question: Can all conflicts be resolved?** In "The Story-Teller," the bachelor resolves his conflict with the three children. In an essay, explain what the aunt might have learned from him. Then, explain why you think that she would—or would not—follow his example in future conflicts with the children. Support your ideas with evidence from the story.

Unit 2 Resources: Short Stories
204

Vocabulary Warm-up Word Lists

Study these words from the selections. Then, apply your knowledge to the activities that follow.

Word List A

assigned [uh SYND] *v.* given as a duty or task
No one could believe our teacher <u>assigned</u> homework over the holidays.

consideration [kuhn sid uh RAY shuhn] *n.* thoughtfulness about other people's needs
We showed <u>consideration</u> for others who were trying to sleep by keeping our voices low.

despair [di SPAIR] *n.* feeling of no hope
The homeless man's eyes were filled with <u>despair</u> as he asked for help.

fatigue [fuh TEEG] *n.* extreme tiredness
My <u>fatigue</u> from staying up all night at the sleepover lasted for three days.

filthy [FIL thee] *adj.* very dirty
After playing in the mud, the children were <u>filthy</u> but happy.

reluctantly [ri LUHK tuhnt lee] *adv.* unwillingly
My sister <u>reluctantly</u> helped me do the dishes.

sacred [SAY krid] *adj.* holy; deserving great respect
My most <u>sacred</u> possession is my great-grandfather's pocket watch.

wrung [RUHNG] *v.* twisted with a squeezing motion
Each taking an end of the blanket, we <u>wrung</u> out the last of the water.

Word List B

convertible [kuhn VER tuh buhl] *n.* car with a roof that can be folded back
The mayor rode in a <u>convertible</u> during the parade.

embarrassment [em BAR uhs muhnt] *n.* feeling of shame or lack of ease in a situation
Can you feel your face getting hot during times of <u>embarrassment</u>?

fringed [FRINJD] *adj.* having an edge decorated with hanging threads or cords
The <u>fringed</u> scarf matched her hat and mittens.

glamorous [GLAM er us] *adj.* excitingly attractive
The <u>glamorous</u> movie star was actually a very unhappy person.

guidance [GY duhns] *n.* helpful advice or direction
When you start high school, you might look to older students for <u>guidance</u>.

radiant [RAY dee uhnt] *adj.* glowing; showing happiness or love
The couple looked <u>radiant</u> on the day they were married.

stately [STAYT lee] *adj.* grand in size or style
They tore down <u>stately</u> houses and put up ugly apartment buildings.

unreliable [un ri LY uh buhl] *adj.* not to be depended on or trusted
It's disappointing when a friend you counted on becomes <u>unreliable</u>.

"The White Umbrella" by Gish Jen
"The Medicine Bag" by Virginia Driving Hawk Sneve
Vocabulary Warm-up Exercises

Exercise A *Fill in the blanks using each word from Word List A only once.*

As future teachers, we were [1] _____ a class of students to help

educate for three months. I was stunned when I saw my school. It was in a

[2] _____ area of downtown. The school was clean and nice, but

some of the students seemed to be filled with sadness and [3] _____.

Perhaps from lack of sleep, [4] _____ showed in their eyes. I

[5] _____ walked to Room 4, my classroom. Imagine my happiness when

all the students stood up to greet me! Their [6] _____ for me was won-

derful. Right away, I could see why this room must be a [7] _____ place

for them. The teacher was great, and the kids were eager to learn. Later, at home, I cried

so hard that I [8] _____ tears out of my handkerchief.

Exercise B *Revise each sentence so that the underlined vocabulary word is used in a logical way. Be sure to keep the vocabulary word in your revision.*

1. Because she wanted a plain look, she chose a <u>fringed</u> scarf.

   _____

2. Since it was stormy outside, Franco took the <u>convertible</u> and put down the top.

   _____

3. Long hours and having to fire people are two <u>glamorous</u> things about some jobs.

   _____

4. Young people do not need <u>guidance</u> from their elders.

   _____

5. I could tell from her red face that she felt no <u>embarrassment</u>.

   _____

6. The scraggly bushes made the long brick driveway look <u>stately</u>.

   _____

7. Many famous scientists had approved the report because of its <u>unreliable</u> nature.

   _____

8. Her face was <u>radiant</u> as she tearfully placed a rose on the grave.

   _____

"**The White Umbrella**" by Gish Jen
"**The Medicine Bag**" by Virginia Driving Hawk Sneve
Reading Warm-up A

Read the following passage. Pay special attention to the underlined words. Then, read it again, and complete the activities. Use a separate sheet of paper for your written answers.

Long ago, Plains Indians lived as hunters and farmers. The wide-open plains were theirs to roam freely. Men, women, and children were all <u>assigned</u> jobs that kept the cultures strong and the people rich in food, shelter, and clothing.

You can imagine the <u>despair</u> of the Plains Indians upon losing their land and way of life. Beginning in the 1860s, the federal government forced the nations onto land called reservations. Officials had little <u>consideration</u> for the Plains Indians' needs. The land was generally hard to farm. The buffalo herds, which were central to their cultures, were steadily wiped out as well.

In response to the horrible things they experienced, Plains Indians often fought back. <u>Fatigue</u> and disease made the battles harder and harder for the Plains Indians, however. At the same time, the government acted more and more harshly. Through it all, the Plains Indians kept their faith in a <u>sacred</u> power. Many began taking part in Ghost Dances. They came together and prayed to the Great Spirit, asking for the white settlers to leave and the buffalo to return. They prayed to be released from the reservations, which often could become <u>filthy</u> from dust storms. They asked to be reunited with their lost loved ones. The Sioux Indians, led by Chief Sitting Bull, were particularly strong in this tradition.

Seeing the number of Ghost Dancers grow, the government grew afraid. Officials decided to arrest Sitting Bull in 1890. A bloody battle followed. Two weeks later, more than two hundred Sioux were killed as they <u>reluctantly</u> gave up their weapons near Wounded Knee Creek.

People throughout the United States were outraged to learn of this attack. Tears were <u>wrung</u> out of handkerchiefs belonging to Indians and non-Indians alike. Many people demanded that all military actions against Indians be stopped. Still, the golden age of the Plains Indians was gone forever.

1. Underline the word that names what Plains Indians were <u>assigned</u>. Then, write a sentence about a chore that has been **assigned** to you.

2. Circle the words describing what led the Indians to feel <u>despair</u>. Then, explain what **despair** means.

3. Rewrite the sentence with <u>consideration</u>, using a synonym for the word. What might officials have done differently if they had had **consideration**?

4. Underline the word naming what, besides <u>fatigue</u>, hurt the Plains Indians. Then, explain what effects **fatigue** can have on a person.

5. Circle the name of the power that was <u>sacred</u> to the Plains Indians. Explain what **sacred** means.

6. Circle the words that tell what caused the reservations to become <u>filthy</u>. Tell what **filthy** means.

7. Underline the words describing what the Sioux did <u>reluctantly</u>. Then, write about something else the Plains Indians might have done **reluctantly**.

8. Describe something that can be **wrung**.

"The White Umbrella" by Gish Jen
"The Medicine Bag" by Virginia Driving Hawk Sneve
Reading Warm-up B

Read the following passage. Pay special attention to the underlined words. Then, read it again, and complete the activities. Use a separate sheet of paper for your written answers.

My <u>embarrassment</u> over having hippies as parents reached its height during my eighth-grade year. That's the same year when my admiration for my parents also peaked. It's amazing how conflicting emotions can come together at a single moment in time.

It all happened at the graduation ceremony during my last week of middle school. That's the day when eighth graders are officially promoted to high school. It is always a <u>stately</u> affair in our town, complete with band music, honored speakers, and plenty of pomp.

I had carefully planned my outfit, managing to create a <u>glamorous</u> yet classy look. Mom and Dad, on the other hand, gave no thought to how they would dress. I wasn't surprised when I turned around to see them entering the auditorium in their usual jeans and tie-dyed shirts. My mom had added a <u>fringed</u> shawl in some weird color, and I think my dad had actually trimmed his beard. I felt like melting into my seat.

Meanwhile, my best friend Robin kept craning her neck, looking for her dad. I knew he would arrive in his <u>convertible</u>, dressed in some totally cool, professional outfit. That is, if he arrived at all. I also knew Robin's dad had a way of being very <u>unreliable</u> when it came to picking up Robin, attending important events, or remembering her birthday.

The ceremony went on and on. When I finally got my certificate and walked up the aisle to return to my seat, I saw my mom and dad. Their faces were both <u>radiant</u>, and I felt proud and loved and lucky to be their daughter.

On that day, my parents had showed up early, in all their glory, yet I had felt shame upon seeing them. On that day, I realized that my parents *always* showed up. They were a constant in my life, offering support and quiet <u>guidance</u>. On that day, as Robin hid a lonely face wet with tears, I felt great joy in being part of my reliable, hippie family.

1. Underline a word in the next sentence that is in contrast to <u>embarrassment</u>. Then, use both words in your own sentence.

2. Circle the descriptions that help define the graduation as <u>stately</u>. Then, define **stately** in your own words.

3. Write a description of what you think a <u>glamorous</u> outfit would be.

4. Circle the word naming a <u>fringed</u> item. Then, describe something you have seen that was **fringed**.

5. Write a sentence describing the <u>convertible</u> Robin's father would drive.

6. Underline the words listing the ways in which Robin's dad is <u>unreliable</u>. Choose the one that you think is the worst, and explain why.

7. Write a sentence describing something or someone <u>radiant</u>.

8. Describe the <u>guidance</u> that eighth graders like to receive from their parents.

Name _____ Date _____

"The White Umbrella" by Gish Jen
"The Medicine Bag" by Virginia Driving Hawk Sneve
Writing About the Big Question
Can all conflicts be resolved?

Big Question Vocabulary

argument	compromise	injury	insecurity	interact
irritate	mislead	negotiate	oppose	reaction
solution	stalemate	victorious	viewpoint	violence

A. *Use a word from the list above to complete each sentence.*

1. A show-off can really _____ other people by the way he or she acts.

2. The student's _____ to her teacher's praise was to smile broadly.

3. Do not let another person's shabby appearance _____ you about his or her character.

4. The _____ done to the Native Americans took place in a shameful period of history.

B. *Follow the directions in responding to each of the items below. Answer in complete sentences.*

1. List two times when you had to negotiate for something you wanted.

   _____

   _____

2. For one of those times, what was the conflict between you and the person with whom you negotiated? Use at least two of the Big Question vocabulary words.

   _____

   _____

C. *Both of these stories involve characters who struggle with feelings of embarrassment. Complete the sentence below. Then, write a short paragraph in which you connect this sentence to the Big Question.*

People are most likely to react with embarrassment when they _____

_____

_____

_____

_____

"The White Umbrella" by Gish Jen
"The Medicine Bag" by Virginia Driving Hawk Sneve
Literary Analysis: Comparing Symbols

A **symbol** is a person, place, or thing that represents something beyond its literal meaning. For example, a national flag is more than just a colorful rectangle of fabric—it represents a country. Similarly, doves usually symbolize peace. **Symbolism** can add meaning to a literary work. Authors can use symbols in two ways:

- Using existing cultural symbols—such as a dove or a flag—that have commonly understood meanings
- Creating their own symbols and developing their meaning through the descriptions, actions, and events of a story

Appreciating a story's symbolism helps you grasp its main message, or theme.

DIRECTIONS: *Answer the following questions about symbolism in "The White Umbrella" and "The Medicine Bag."*

1. When does the narrator of "The White Umbrella" first see the umbrella?

   _____

   _____

2. What feelings does the white umbrella provoke in the narrator early in the story?

   _____

   _____

3. What significance does the umbrella have in the development of the story?

   _____

   _____

4. At the outset of "The Medicine Bag," whom does the bag belong to? How does Martin feel about this person when he first comes to Martin's house?

   _____

   _____

5. What feelings does the medicine bag provoke in Martin early in the story?

   _____

   _____

6. What significance does the medicine bag have in the development of the story?

   _____

   _____

Unit 2 Resources: Short Stories
210

"The White Umbrella" by Gish Jen
"The Medicine Bag" by Virginia Driving Hawk Sneve
Vocabulary Builder

Word List

authentic   credibility   discreet   procession   revelation   unseemly

A. DIRECTIONS: *Write a complete sentence to answer each question using a Word List word in place of the underlined word.*

1. What is something you could do that would hurt your <u>believability</u>?

   _____

2. At what kind of event have you seen <u>a group moving forward together</u>?

   _____

3. What could you tell others about yourself that would be <u>something that surprises them</u>?

   _____

4. What do you own that is <u>genuine</u>, or real?

   _____

5. What is something that used to be <u>inappropriate</u> but is now considered normal?

   _____

6. In what situation should you be <u>careful about what you say or do</u>?

   _____

B. DIRECTIONS: *Circle the letter of the word or phrase that is most* opposite *in meaning to the word in CAPITAL LETTERS.*

1. UNSEEMLY
   A. improper
   B. prim
   C. sewn well
   D. secretive

2. DISCREET
   A. careless
   B. safe
   C. plain
   D. conservative

3. CREDIBILITY
   A. possibility
   B. lunacy
   C. trustworthiness
   D. improbability

4. AUTHENTIC
   A. dependable
   B. false
   C. real
   D. unfavorable

Name _____ Date _____

"The White Umbrella" by Gish Jen
"The Medicine Bag" by Virginia Driving Hawk Sneve

Integrated Language Skills:
Support for Writing to Compare Symbols

Before you write your essay that compares the symbols in "The White Umbrella" and "The Medicine Bag," use the graphic organizer below to write ideas about the symbols in each story.

Questions to Answer	"The White Umbrella"	"The Medicine Bag"
What are the main symbols used in the story?		
Does the author use any existing cultural symbols in the story? Name them.		
Do any of the symbols have cultural meanings outside of the story?		
Does the author create her own symbols?		
How does the author develop the meanings of the symbols?		
What does the change in each narrator's attitude toward the symbol tell you?		
What message do the symbols help the story convey?		
Which symbol is more effective and therefore easier for you to understand?		

Now, use your notes to help you write an essay that compares and contrasts these symbols.

"The White Umbrella" by Gish Jen
"The Medicine Bag" by Virginia Driving Hawk Sneve
Open-Book Test

Short Answer *Write your responses to the questions in this section on the lines provided.*

1. At the beginning of "The White Umbrella," the sisters talk about the job their mother has taken. When the narrator suggests that she might be delivering flowers, Mona says, "She would've hit something by now." What does that statement reveal about the girls' mother?

   _____

2. When the sisters wait for their mother after their piano lessons, the narrator of "The White Umbrella" refuses to go back into Miss Crosman's house to get out of the rain. Why is she afraid to go back inside?

   _____
   _____
   _____

3. The sisters in "The White Umbrella" wait in the rain for their mother to pick them up after their piano lessons. While they are waiting, Miss Crosman gives the narrator her umbrella. Why does the piano teacher give the white umbrella away?

   _____
   _____
   _____

4. The narrator of "The Medicine Bag" tells his friends about Grandpa, but he never shows them his picture. Why does he avoid showing his friends his great-grandfather's picture?

   _____
   _____
   _____

5. According to the narrator of "The Medicine Bag," a show of affection between adults is "unseemly." Does that mean that such a show of affection is a good thing or a bad thing? Explain your answer based on the definition of *unseemly*.

   _____

6. In "The Medicine Bag," what does Martin learn from his friends' reaction to Grandpa when they finally meet him?

   _____
   _____

7. Both "The White Umbrella" and "The Medicine Bag" focus on a single symbol. Complete this chart by explaining the meaning of each story's symbol. Then, on the line below, describe one way in which the two symbols are alike or one way in which they are different.

Symbol	Meaning
White umbrella	
Medicine bag	

_____

8. The narrator of "The White Umbrella" is embarrassed by her mother, and the narrator of "The Medicine Bag" is embarrassed by his great-grandfather. What larger group or idea do both adults symbolize?

_____

_____

_____

9. At the end of "The White Umbrella," the narrator throws the umbrella down a sewer. At the end of "The Medicine Bag," Martin stands to receive the medicine bag. Both actions are symbolic. What do they have in common?

_____

_____

10. The narrators of both "The White Umbrella" and "The Medicine Bag" come to a realization. As a result, the narrator of "The White Umbrella" views her mother differently, and Martin views Grandpa differently. What does each narrator realize?

_____

_____

Essay

Write an extended response to the question of your choice or to the question or questions your teacher assigns you.

11. Both the narrator of "The White Umbrella" and the narrator of "The Medicine Bag" feel embarrassment. Choose one of these stories, and in a brief essay, describe the circumstances of the narrator's embarrassment. Cite at least two details from the story to support your point.

12. Both the narrator of "The White Umbrella" and the narrator of "The Medicine Bag" experience a change in their feelings about an older relative and a loved or hated object. In a brief essay, compare and contrast the feelings the two narrators have for their relative and for the central symbol in each story. Then, compare and contrast the changes in the narrators' attitudes. Cite at least two details from each story to support your ideas.

13. The authors of "The White Umbrella" and "The Medicine Bag" use symbolism to add depth and power to their stories. In an essay, explain how they do this. Be sure to identify objects and actions that are symbolic, tell what each symbol represents, and note whether the meaning of each symbol changes over time.

14. **Thinking About the Big Question: Can all conflicts be resolved?** The narrators of "The White Umbrella" and "The Medicine Bag" have conflicting feelings about people they love. In your view, is each conflict fully resolved by the end of the story? Answer this question in a short essay. Cite at least one detail from each story to support your points.

Oral Response

15. Go back to question 2, 7, or 8 or to the question your teacher assigns you. Take a few minutes to expand your answer and prepare an oral response. Find additional details in the relevant story or stories that support your points. If necessary, make notes to guide your oral response.

"**The White Umbrella**" by Gish Jen
"**The Medicine Bag**" by Virginia Driving Hawk Sneve
Selection Test A

Critical Reading *Identify the letter of the choice that best answers the question.*

_____ 1. Why does the narrator in "The White Umbrella" lie about her mother?
  A. She is trying to impress Eugenie Roberts's mother.
  B. She does not know she is lying; she really believes what she says.
  C. She is embarrassed that her mother works.
  D. She is playing a trick on Miss Crosman.

_____ 2. How does the narrator of "The White Umbrella" first feel about the umbrella?
  A. She wants one of her own.
  B. She thinks it is ridiculous.
  C. She does not want Eugenie to have it.
  D. She wants to buy one with her allowance.

_____ 3. What does the umbrella first represent to the narrator in "The White Umbrella"?
  A. It represents what American girls have.
  B. It represents her love for her mother.
  C. It represents her piano lessons.
  D. It represents her love for Miss Crosman.

_____ 4. When the narrator learns who the true owner of the umbrella is, what does she say that makes her immediately feel bad?
  A. She says to Miss Crosman, "Thank you, but I can't accept it."
  B. She says to Miss Crosman, "I wish you were my mother."
  C. She says to Miss Crosman, "I don't need an umbrella. I have a raincoat."
  D. She says to Eugenie, "Thank you, but I can't accept it."

_____ 5. What job does the narrator of "The White Umbrella" learn that her mother has?
  A. check-out clerk at the A&P
  B. florist delivering roses
  C. perfume salesperson at a store
  D. recipe tester for the newspaper

_____ 6. In "The Medicine Bag," which statement should you infer from Martin's embarrassment about his grandfather?
  A. Martin is a cruel and insensitive person.
  B. Grandpa's behavior is out of control.
  C. Martin is overly sensitive to what his friends think.
  D. Martin once had a bad experience with his grandfather.

____ 7. In "The Medicine Bag," why does Grandpa collapse after arriving at the house?
 A. He is having a heart attack.
 B. He has heat exhaustion.
 C. He is shocked by life in the suburbs.
 D. He is overcome with emotion.

____ 8. In "The Medicine Bag," how does Cheryl's reaction to Grandpa's visit differ from Martin's?
 A. Cheryl is not ashamed for her friends to see Grandpa.
 B. Cheryl is jealous because she will not get a medicine bag.
 C. Cheryl wishes Grandpa had never come.
 D. Cheryl is afraid of Grandpa and tries to hide from him.

____ 9. What does Martin do at the end of "The Medicine Bag" to show that his feelings for his grandfather and the medicine bag have changed?
 A. He wears the medicine bag to school.
 B. He buries the medicine bag with his grandfather on the prairie.
 C. He puts the medicine bag away so that no harm will come to it.
 D. He puts sacred sage from the prairie in his medicine bag.

____ 10. What does the medicine bag represent to Martin at the end of "The Medicine Bag"?
 A. his dislike for his Sioux heritage
 B. his feelings of embarrassment for Grandpa
 C. his desire to please his Grandpa
 D. his grandfather and his Sioux heritage

Vocabulary

____ 11. Which word is most *similar* in meaning to *discreet*?
 A. foolish   C. cautious
 B. controlled   D. fierce

____ 12. What is the meaning of the word *authentic* in this sentence?
 We always had some *authentic* Sioux article to show our listeners.
 A. genuine   C. questionable
 B. convincing   D. mechanical

Essay

13. In "The White Umbrella" and "The Medicine Bag," the feelings of the narrator are central to each story. Write an essay that compares the feelings of the narrator in "The White Umbrella" with the feelings of the narrator in "The Medicine Bag" by answering these questions: How do the feelings of the narrator of "The White Umbrella" change during the story? How do the feelings of the narrator of "The Medicine Bag" change during the story? How are the ways the two narrators' feelings change alike or different?

14. In an essay, compare the symbolism in "The White Umbrella" with the symbolism in "The Medicine Bag" by answering these questions:
"The White Umbrella"
What item is symbolic?
At first, how does the narrator feel about it?
What does the item represent to the narrator?
What does the narrator do with the item at the end? Why does she do this?
"The Medicine Bag"
What item is symbolic?
At first, how does Martin feel about it?
How do his feelings change?
What does this item come to represent to Martin at the end of the story?

15. **Thinking About the Big Question: Can all conflicts be resolved?** The narrators of "The White Umbrella" and "The Medicine Bag" have conflicting feelings about people they love. In your view, is each conflict resolved by the end of the story? Answer this question in a short essay. Cite at least one detail from each story to support your points.

"The White Umbrella" by Gish Jen
"The Medicine Bag" by Virginia Driving Hawk Sneve

Selection Test B

Critical Reading *Identify the letter of the choice that best completes the statement or answers the question.*

_____ 1. The narrator of "The White Umbrella" refuses to go into Miss Crosman's house to get out of the rain because she
   A. does not mind the rain.
   B. is trying to be loyal to her mother.
   C. feels unwelcome in the house.
   D. does not want to see the white umbrella.

_____ 2. Why does the narrator of "The White Umbrella" hide Miss Crosman's gift to her?
   A. She is afraid that her mother will take away the umbrella from her.
   B. She plans to give the gift back to Miss Crosman.
   C. She does not want to distract her mother from driving the car.
   D. She feels guilty about wishing that Miss Crosman were her mother.

_____ 3. Which two statements are true about the narrator of "The White Umbrella"?
   I.   She enjoys telling lies all the time.
   II. She cares about what others think of her and her family.
   III. She cannot easily say what is on her mind.
   IV. She is very close to her mother.
   A. I and II
   B. II and III
   C. I and IV
   D. III and IV

_____ 4. What does the white umbrella come to represent to the narrator of "The White Umbrella" at the end of the story?
   A. her desire to live as an American girl rather than as a Chinese girl
   B. her sense that her mother's job means her mother is rejecting her
   C. her desire to be friends with Eugenie Roberts
   D. her guilt for feeling embarrassed about her mother

_____ 5. In "The Medicine Bag," what is the main reason given by Grandpa for his surprise visit to the family?
   A. He wants to see Cheryl.
   B. He feels that death is near and he wants to pass on the medicine bag to Martin.
   C. He wants to see what life is like in the city.
   D. He wants to discuss the resentment he feels toward his family.

_____ 6. In "The Medicine Bag," what can the reader infer about Grandpa when he dresses in fancy clothes on the day he expects a visit from Martin's friends?
   A. He is losing his wits.
   B. He is vain.
   C. He is sensitive to Martin's insecurities.
   D. He has bad taste in clothes.

____ **7.** The medicine bag is passed along through the tribe's generations of
    A. chiefs only.
    B. males only.
    C. females only.
    D. males and females.

____ **8.** In "The Medicine Bag," how do Martin's feelings about Grandpa relate to his feelings about wearing the medicine bag?
    A. Martin feels he has no place in his life for Grandpa or for the medicine bag.
    B. From the time Grandpa arrives, Martin is always proud of him and his medicine bag.
    C. Martin likes Grandpa but never sees the point of the medicine bag.
    D. Martin feels embarrassment and pride about both Grandpa and the medicine bag.

____ **9.** In "The Medicine Bag," the medicine bag comes to represent Martin's
    A. decision to go and live on the reservation.
    B. family heritage and his pride in his grandfather.
    C. desire to reject his Sioux heritage.
    D. love for the Sioux way of life and for the prairie.

____ **10.** When authors create their own symbols, how do they develop the meanings of the symbols?
    A. They use symbols that are commonly understood.
    B. They use the description, actions, and events in a story to develop the symbol.
    C. They tell the reader directly what the symbol is and what it means.
    D. They give footnotes that explain the symbols.

____ **11.** What similar feelings do the narrator in "The White Umbrella" and the narrator in "The Medicine Bag" experience?
    A. concern about the health of someone
    B. dislike for the other kids in the story
    C. embarrassment about a family member
    D. worry about what their parents think

____ **12.** How do both the narrator of "The White Umbrella" and the narrator in "The Medicine Bag" change during the story?
    A. They are both proud of their families after the death of a loved one.
    B. They both think that their friends will tease them about the umbrella or the medicine bag.
    C. They both want to please their family members.
    D. They both realize that their feelings of shame for their relatives are wrong.

____ **13.** What message do the symbols of "The White Umbrella" and "The Medicine Bag" help convey?
    A. Be proud of who you are, and do not worry about what others think.
    B. Trust your friends, and do not fear that they will tease you.
    C. Listen to your elders, and do what they say at all times.
    D. Never lie to people because you fear them.

Unit 2 Resources: Short Stories
220

Vocabulary

____ 14. Which word is most nearly *opposite* in meaning to *discreet*?
   A. insensitive
   B. cautious
   C. controlled
   D. fierce

____ 15. Which word best completes the following sentence?
   John lost all _____ with the teacher when he showed up in the gym after saying that he was going to the office.
   A. procession
   B. revelation
   C. credibility
   D. authentic

____ 16. Which word is most nearly *opposite* in meaning to *authentic*?
   A. convincing
   B. questionable
   C. genuine
   D. mechanical

____ 17. In earlier days, dating without a chaperone was considered
   A. discreet.
   B. authentic.
   C. procession.
   D. unseemly.

Essay

18. In an essay, explain how the authors of "The White Umbrella" and "The Medicine Bag" use symbolism to add depth to their literary works. Be sure to tell which item is a symbol in each story and how the meaning of the symbol changes over time.

19. In "The White Umbrella" and "The Medicine Bag," both narrators have conflicting feelings. In an essay, discuss the conflicting feelings experienced by both narrators. How are their feelings similar? How do their feelings affect the events in the story? What can you infer about their characters based on their feelings? How do the characters resolve their conflicting feelings?

20. **Thinking About the Big Question: Can all conflicts be resolved?** The narrators of "The White Umbrella" and "The Medicine Bag" have conflicting feelings about people they love. In your view, is each conflict fully resolved by the end of the story? Answer this question in a short essay. Cite at least one detail from each story to support your points.

Name _____ Date _____

Prewriting: Gathering Details

Answer the questions below to clarify the problem you want to develop in your story.

What is the problem or conflict in your story?	
How will the problem reveal itself?	
How will the problem intensify?	
How will each of the characters react to the problem?	
How will the problem reach resolution or be solved?	

Drafting: Building to a Climax

Use the plot diagram below to help you construct and organize the events of your story.

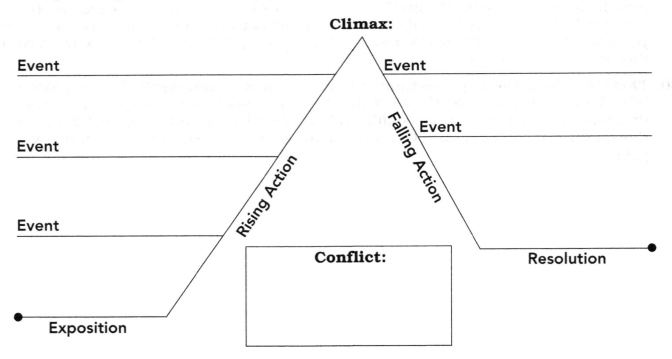

Writing Workshop—Unit 2, Part 2
Short Story: Integrating Grammar Skills

Revising for Subject/Verb Agreement

A verb must agree with its subject in number. Only nouns, pronouns, and verbs have number. Singular subjects need singular verbs, and plural subjects need plural verbs. Verbs with -s or -es added are singular. See the examples in the chart.

	Singular	**Plural**
Nouns and Pronouns	soldier, bus, child, goose, I, you, he, she, it	soldiers, buses, children, geese, we, us, you, they, them
Verbs	runs, reads, sleeps, writes	run, read, sleep, write

To fix problems with subject/verb agreement, first identify the subject. Then, make the verb agree. Refer to the examples below.

Singular: The <u>child</u> *goes* to sleep at eight o'clock.

Plural: The <u>children</u> *go* to sleep at eight o'clock.

Compound, Plural: <u>George and Martha</u> *agree* to get married.

Inverted, Singular: *Waiting* for Martha at the altar *was* George.

A. DIRECTIONS: *Circle the verb that agrees with the subject in each sentence.*

1. The characters in this cartoon (act, acts) too silly.
2. One Oscar (go, goes) to the best film of the year.
3. Another (is awarded, are awarded) to the best director.
4. The stars usually (wear, wears) stunning outfits.

B. DIRECTIONS: *Rewrite these sentences so that the verbs agree with their subjects.*

1. My favorite artist do vivid oil paintings.

   _____

2. Kayla and Nichole prefers watercolors.

   _____

3. When I grow up, I wants to study to be an architect.

   _____

4. Here is three good paintings by Picasso.

   _____

Unit 2 Vocabulary Workshop—1
Latin Root Words

Many words that we use every day come from Latin. Familiarity with Latin roots can help you define unfamiliar words.

Latin Root	**Definition**
-scrib-, -script-	to write
-gress-	to walk, to step
-tract-	to pull
-port-	to carry
-trans-	across, over

DIRECTIONS: *Select the appropriate word to complete each sentence below. Use the roots given above to help you define the words. If necessary, you may consult a dictionary.*

digress	portfolio	progress	subscribe
subscript	traction	transcend	transport

1. I have made a lot of _____ toward my goal of raising $100.
2. Did you _____ to that magazine?
3. The doctors put her leg in _____, which will pull on the muscle to relieve pressure.
4. When you write a chemical formula, the style describing numbers written below the line is called _____.
5. Instead of moving forward with her presentation, it seems as though she has _____ed.
6. Tom quickly put his drawings into his _____ to take them to the meeting.
7. The film was so meaningful that it _____ed all my expectations.
8. The driver continued on for three days without pause in order to _____ the goods cross country.

Unit 2 Vocabulary Workshop—2
Greek Roots

With knowledge of root words, it is often possible to figure out the meanings of words you have never heard before.

Greek Root	Meaning
-phil(e)-	loving; having a fondness for
-biblio-	Bible; book
-sophos-	wise; clever
-anthropos-	human being

DIRECTIONS: *Match the following words to their descriptions. Use the Greek roots above to help you.*

____ 1. philanthropist

____ 2. bibliophile

____ 3. philosopher

____ 4. anthropologist

    A. a person who studies human beings

    B. a collector of books

    C. a person who studies the principles underlying conduct, thought, knowledge, and the nature of the universe

    D. an altruistic person who is concerned with human welfare and advancement

Choose the person listed above who is most like you. Explain. Your explanation should show that you understand the definition of the word you choose.

_____

_____

Name _____ Date _____

Conducting Interviews

After choosing a person to interview, fill out the following chart to complete the interview and gather the information you need.

Topic of interview: _____

What kind of information do you want to obtain from this interview?
What basic research have you done to prepare for the interview?
What questions have you created for the interview?
What follow-up questions might there be?

Unit 2: Short Stories
Benchmark Test 4

MULTIPLE CHOICE

Reading Skill: Making Inferences

1. What is an inference?
   A. a logical assumption about something an author leaves unstated
   B. a reader's appreciation of an author's skills or techniques
   C. a conversation in which characters have to read between the lines
   D. the central idea or insight expressed in a literary work

2. Which of these steps is basic to making inferences?
   A. focusing on the main ideas
   B. connecting several details
   C. separating fact from opinion
   D. restating in simpler words

Read this selection. Then, answer the questions.

Marlena wheeled her cart down the aisle and paused in front of the cold cereals. She took a box of bran flakes from the shelf without comparing prices as she usually did. Her mind was elsewhere—on the science test her teacher had announced a few hours before. Marlena always got high grades in school, but she still worried about tests. She was worrying now as she went into the bread aisle and absently dropped a package of regular English muffins into her cart, even though she and her parents preferred the whole wheat muffins. As she approached the checkout area, Marlena hoped the lines were not too long, because she wanted to get home and study before supper.

3. From the details in the selection, what inference can you make about Marlena's location?
   A. She is in a supermarket.
   B. She is at a drug store.
   C. She is in a department store.
   D. She is on her way to school.

4. Which details in the selection help you infer that the events take place on a weekday afternoon?
   A. "as she went into the bread aisle" and "as she approached the checkout area"
   B. "wheeled her cart down the aisle" and "absently dropped a package"
   C. "her teacher had announced a few hours before" and "study before supper"
   D. "was worrying now" and "get home and study before supper"

5. Based on details in the selection, what inference can you draw about Marlena?
   A. She is smart but lazy.
   B. She is foolish and impulsive.
   C. She is selfish and unkind.
   D. She is studious but anxious.

6. What do the details about Marlena's purchases suggest about her and her family?
   A. They eat wholesome food.
   B. They love sweets.
   C. They eat a lot of red meat.
   D. They pay little attention to cost.

Reading Skill: Evaluate Persuasive Appeals

7. Which of the following strategies can help you evaluate persuasive appeals?
   A. Do not believe any claims that are made in an advertisement.
   B. Look for celebrity endorsements and expert testimonials.
   C. Separate arguments that appeal to the emotions from those that appeal to the mind.
   D. Focus on the pictures in an advertisement rather than on the words.

8. Which answer choice contains an example of loaded language?
   A. Green Turtle Cove is the vacation destination of the stars.
   B. Everyone loves Green Turtle Cove!
   C. Isn't it time you planned your trip to Green Turtle Cove?
   D. Green Turtle Cove is a magical paradise for the entire family.

9. Why are pictures used extensively in advertising?
   A. because visual appeals are often more persuasive than verbal appeals
   B. because visuals make the advertisements cheaper to produce
   C. because customers respond to factual information
   D. because they generate a more thoughtful response from the viewer

Literary Analysis: Point of View

10. What is narrative point of view in a story?
    A. the author's attitude toward his or her subject or audience
    B. the perspective from which the story is told
    C. the customs of the period or society in which the work takes place
    D. the central idea, insight, or message that the story conveys

Read this selection. Then, answer the question that follows.

"The New House"

Arlen was impressed by the new house. He especially liked the high gables on the second floor and the large porch that ran along the whole front of the house. "I'd love to live in a house like that," he thought to himself.

Eva considered the house an awful monstrosity, way too big for the small plot of land on which it stood. "It's like an elephant on a postage stamp," she told herself, although she did not share her thoughts with Arlen.

11. Which is the point of view of the selection "The New House"?
   A. first person, narrated by Arlen
   B. third person, limited to the thoughts and impressions of the character telling the story
   C. first person, narrated by Eva
   D. third person omniscient, providing the thoughts and impressions of more than one character

Read this selection. Then, answer the questions that follow.

"Our Farm"

Our farm was on Stone Church Road near the parkway. I was very upset when my parents sold it, but Dad said the buyers made him an offer he couldn't refuse. Mom agreed with the decision. "We're not getting any younger, Johnny," she told me. "And the price they offered was a good one."

12. What is the point of view of the selection "Our Farm"?
   A. third person omniscient, providing the thoughts and impressions of more than one character
   B. first person, narrated by Johnny
   C. third person, limited to the thoughts and impressions of only one character
   D. first person, narrated by the father

13. Which pronouns in the selection "Our Farm" help indicate the point of view?
   A. *my, him,* and *he*   C. *our, I,* and *me*
   B. *our, we,* and *they*   D. *him, he,* and *we*

Literary Analysis: Theme

14. Which of these statements about theme is true?
   A. There is usually just one correct interpretation of the theme of a literary work.
   B. The theme of a literary work is usually directly stated at the end.
   C. The theme of a literary work is never directly stated but is always implied.
   D. The theme of a literary work is often a generalization about life or people.

15. If an author were to use the symbol of a dove in a novel about war what would the dove most likely represent?

    A. the officer corps   C. more deadly weaponry

    B. better times   D. peace

Read this selection. Then, answer the questions that follow.

Once a lion captured a mouse and was about to eat it. "Spare me!" cried the mouse. "I am but a small mouthful to you, yet my family needs and loves me. If you let me go, I will help you in return." The lion did not think that anything so small could ever help him, but he was touched by the tiny creature's plight and amused by the bold claim of future aid, so he decided to let the mouse go. Years later, the lion was captured by some men. He was tied up in a cage when the mouse came by and saw him. When the men went to sleep, the mouse slipped into the cage and gnawed through the ropes. Later, when the men opened the cage to feed him, the lion was able to escape. The mouse had saved the creature who had spared him, thereby proving that kindness will be rewarded.

16. What is the stated theme of this selection?

    A. My family needs and loves me.   C. He decided to show compassion.

    B. I will help you in return.   D. Kindness will be rewarded.

17. Which of these is an additional theme of the selection?

    A. Do not judge capability based only on appearances.

    B. Those who love their families will show compassion to others.

    C. Do not let great changes catch you sleeping.

    D. Human beings are stronger and more clever than the strongest beast.

18. What does the mouse in the selection seem to symbolize, or represent?

    A. wisdom   C. boastfulness

    B. cleverness   D. compassion

19. What does the lion in the selection seem to symbolize, or represent?

    A. size and ambition   C. strength and power

    B. cruelty and greed   D. endangered species

Vocabulary: Roots and Prefixes

20. Which of the following words has the same root as *introspective*?

    A. entrenched   C. astronomy

    B. triumph   D. spectacle

21. Using your knowledge of the root -*nunc*-, what is the definition of *enunciated* in the following sentence?

During his graduation speech, Carlos enunciated clearly.

    A. spoke   C. questioned

    B. shouted   D. interpreted

22. Which of the following sentences uses the word *mistrusted* correctly?
    A. Jackson mistrusted Smith, believing everything he said.
    B. After being lied to, Jackson always mistrusted Smith.
    C. Jackson mistrusted Smith, knowing Smith would never lie to him.
    D. After being lied to, Jackson never mistrusted Smith.

23. What is the meaning of the prefix *per-* in the word *persistent*?
    A. not
    B. outside of
    C. throughout
    D. the same

24. Which sentence correctly uses the word *spectator*?
    A. One of many spectators in the stadium, Tanya played her best game yesterday.
    B. The spectators bowed as the audience cheered them.
    C. Tanya's performance impressed every spectator in the crowded stadium.
    D. In the sport of baseball, each team has nine spectators.

25. What is the meaning of *denounced* in the following sentence?

    Holding the proof in his hand, Greg rose and angrily denounced the traitor in the room.

    A. accused
    B. defended
    C. introduced
    D. interviewed

Grammar

26. Which of the following sentences has the correct verb?
    A. Yesterday Denise hikes to the top of the mountain.
    B. Yesterday Denise hiked to the top of the mountain.
    C. Yesterday Denise hiking to the top of the mountain.
    D. Yesterday Denise will hike to the top of the mountain.

27. How do you form perfect tenses of verbs?
    A. Use the helping verb *will* and the base form of the verb.
    B. Use a form of the helping verb *be* and the past participle of the verb.
    C. Use a form of the helping verb *have* and the present participle of the verb.
    D. Use a form of the helping verb *have* and the past participle of the verb.

28. Which of the following sentences has the correct verb?
    A. By next week, I will have finished taking my final exams.
    B. By next week, I will had finished taking my final exams.
    C. By next week, I will have finish taking my final exams.
    D. By next week, I will had finish taking my final exams.

29. Which of the following sentences is correct?
    A. Andy walk home with Beth every afternoon.
    B. Andy will walking home with Beth every afternoon.
    C. Andy walking home with Beth every afternoon.
    D. Andy walks home with Beth every afternoon.

30. Which of the following sentences contains a verb that is correctly formed in the perfect tense?
    A. Susan have speaked at our club before.
    B. Beverly has wanted to be a singer for years.
    C. Desmond has love swimming in the ocean.
    D. Jake have painted his room three times.

31. Which of the following sentences is correct?
    A. Many boys were in the gym.
    B. Many boys was in the gym.
    C. Many boys is in the gym.
    D. Many boys has been in the gym.

32. Which of the following sentences is correct?
    A. Geese have flied south for the winter.
    B. Geese flies south for the winter.
    C. Geese has flown south for the winter.
    D. Geese fly south for the winter.

WRITING

33. Sometimes people avoid saying exactly how they feel. On your paper, write a brief dialogue between two people who are trying to hide their feelings. Try to make the characters' feelings clear to the reader without having either character express those feelings directly.

34. Recall a fictional book, film, or TV drama that taught a life lesson that you think applied to your own experiences in the real world. On a separate sheet, explain how the theme or lesson of that work applied to your own experience.

35. Think of a value you hold dear or an observation you have made about life or human behavior. How could you convey that value or observation by telling a story? On your paper, jot down ideas for a short story that conveys your value or observation as its main theme.

Vocabulary in Context

Identify the answer choice that best completes the statement.

1. The space center is going to send a new _____ in orbit around the moon.
   A. galaxy
   B. orbit
   C. satellite
   D. universe

2. Whether he is guilty of the crime will be decided by the _____ .
   A. jury
   B. legal
   C. republic
   D. counsel

3. We are studying about fish and other _____ life.
   A. solar
   B. marine
   C. mutation
   D. landscape

4. It was a clear night, and the stars shone _____ against the dark sky.
   A. context
   B. equally
   C. numerous
   D. brilliantly

5. This truck will run for a long time because it is _____ .
   A. registered
   B. durable
   C. thorough
   D. taut

6. After I graduate, a career in the armed forces is what I would like to _____ .
   A. enlist
   B. pursue
   C. compel
   D. guarantee

7. The agreement was signed by both parties after one more _____ was added.
   A. narrative
   B. biography
   C. moral
   D. clause

8. The chairs in the unused room were protected by _____ .
   A. tethers
   B. shrouds
   C. boosters
   D. segments

9. She served in the U.S. Army and is a proud _____ .
   A. entitled
   B. astronomer
   C. veteran
   D. administration

10. He was out of breath and quickly inhaling and _____ .
    A. exhaling
    B. desolate
    C. isolating
    D. circulating

11. A best-selling book was written based on her daydreams and _____ .
    A. booklets
    B. imaginative
    C. pledges
    D. fantasies

12. For safety's sake, our town needs to hire more _____ .
    A. institutions
    B. capitalists
    C. republicans
    D. firefighters

13. Our mission has specific goals and _____ to meet.
    A. objectives
    B. fragments
    C. highlights
    D. developments

14. With the beginning of the building project, many new jobs were being _____ .
    A. confirmed
    B. generated
    C. revealed
    D. confronted

15. The road seemed to stretch in front of us_____ .
   A. virtually
   B. stately
   C. endlessly
   D. vividly

16. We will raise money for a very needy and_____ cause.
   A. fashionable
   B. unreasonable
   C. mightily
   D. worthwhile

17. It seemed that every time I was running late, the bus would_____ be early.
   A. invariably
   B. reportedly
   C. skeptically
   D. elaborately

18. My learning style was the topic of my conversation with the school_____ .
   A. congressman
   B. associate`
   C. commissioner
   D. psychologist

19. For old animals, this farm has become a shelter and_____ .
   A. agricultural
   B. establishment
   C. haven
   D. historic

20. The time when young children believe in fairy tales is a time of_____ for them.
   A. separation
   B. enchantment
   C. immunity
   D. discrimination

Diagnostic Tests and Vocabulary in Context
Use and Interpretation

The Diagnostic Tests and Vocabulary in Context were developed to assist teachers in making the most appropriate assignment of *Prentice Hall Literature* program selections to students. The purpose of these assessments is to indicate the degree of difficulty that students are likely to have in reading/comprehending the selections presented in the *following* unit of instruction. Tests are provided at six separate times in each in each grade level—a *Diagnostic Test* (to be used prior to beginning the year's instruction) and a *Vocabulary in Context,* the final segment of the Benchmark Test appearing at the end of each of the first five units of instruction. Note that the tests are intended for use not as summative assessments for the prior unit, but as guidance for assigning literature selections in the upcoming unit of instruction.

The structure of all Diagnostic Tests and Vocabulary in Context in this series is the same. All test items are four-option, multiple-choice items. The format is established to assess a student's ability to construct sufficient meaning from the context sentence to choose the only provided word that fits both the semantics (meaning) and syntax (structure) of the context sentence. All words in the context sentences are chosen to be "below-level" words that students reading at this grade level should know. All answer choices fit *either* the meaning or structure of the context sentence, but only the correct choice fits *both* semantics and syntax. All answer choices—both correct answers and incorrect options—are key words chosen from specifically taught words that will occur in the subsequent unit of program instruction. This careful restriction of the assessed words permits a sound diagnosis of students' current reading achievement and prediction of the most appropriate level of readings to assign in the upcoming unit of instruction.

The assessment of vocabulary in context skill has consistently been shown in reading research studies to correlate very highly with "reading comprehension." This is not surprising as the format essentially assesses comprehension, albeit in sentence-length "chunks." Decades of research demonstrate that vocabulary assessment provides a strong, reliable prediction of comprehension achievement— the purpose of these tests. Further, because this format demands very little testing time, these diagnoses can be made efficiently, permitting teachers to move forward with critical instructional tasks rather than devoting excessive time to assessment.

It is important to stress that while the Diagnostic and Vocabulary in Context were carefully developed and will yield sound assignment decisions, they were designed to *reinforce*, not supplant, teacher judgment as to the most appropriate instructional placement for individual students. Teacher judgment should always prevail in making placement—or indeed other important instructional—decisions concerning students.

Diagnostic Tests and Vocabulary in Context Branching Suggestions

These tests are designed to provide maximum flexibility for teachers. Your *Unit Resources* books contain the 40-question **Diagnostic Test** and 20-question **Vocabulary in Context** tests. At *PHLitOnline*, you can access the Diagnostic Test and complete 40-question Vocabulary in Context tests. Procedures for administering the tests are described below. Choose the procedure based on the time you wish to devote to the activity and your comfort with the assignment decisions relative to the individual students. Remember that your judgment of a student's reading level should always take precedence over the results of a single written test.

Feel free to use different procedures at different times of the year. For example, for early units, you may wish to be more confident in the assignments you make—thus, using the "two-stage" process below. Later, you may choose the quicker diagnosis, confirming the results with your observations of the students' performance built up throughout the year.

The **Diagnostic Test** is composed of a single 40-item assessment. Based on the results of this assessment, make the following assignment of students to the reading selections in Unit 1:

Diagnostic Test Score	Selection to Use
If the student's score is 0–25	more accessible
If the student's score is 26–40	more challenging

Outlined below are the three basic options for administering **Vocabulary in Context** and basing selection assignments on the results of these assessments.

1. For a one-stage, quicker diagnosis using the *20-item* test in the *Unit Resources:*

Vocabulary in Context Test Score	Selection to Use
If the student's score is 0–13	more accessible
If the student's score is 14–20	more challenging

2. If you wish to confirm your assignment decisions with a *two-stage* diagnosis:

Stage 1: Administer the 20-item test in the *Unit Resources*	
Vocabulary in Context Test Score	Selection to Use
If the student's score is 0–9	more accessible
If the student's score is 10–15	(Go to Stage 2.)
If the student's score is 16–20	more challenging

Stage 2: Administer items 21–40 from *PHLitOnline*	
Vocabulary in Context Test Score	Selection to Use
If the student's score is 0–12	more accessible
If the student's score is 13–20	more challenging

3. If you base your assignment decisions on the full 40-item **Vocabulary in Context** from *PHLitOnline:*

Vocabulary in Context Test Score	Selection to Use
If the student's score is 0–25	more accessible
If the student's score is 26–40	more challenging

Name _____ Date _____

Grade 8—Benchmark Test 3
Interpretation Guide

For remediation of specific skills, you may assign students the relevant Reading Kit Practice and Assess pages indicated in the far-right column of this chart. You will find rubrics for evaluating writing samples in the last section of your Professional Development Guidebook.

Skill Objective	Test Items	Number Correct	Reading Kit
Reading Skill			
Compare and Contrast	1, 2, 3, 4, 5, 6		pp. 52, 53
Compare an Original to a Summary	7, 8, 9		pp. 54, 55
Literary Analysis			
Setting	10, 11, 12		pp. 56, 57
Character Traits	13, 14, 15		pp. 58, 59
Comparing Types of Narratives	16, 17, 18		pp. 60, 61
Vocabulary			
Prefixes and Suffixes *de-, -ee, -ity*	19, 20, 21, 22, 23, 24		pp. 62, 63
Grammar			
Action and Linking Verbs	25, 26, 27		pp. 64, 65
Principal Parts of Regular Verbs	28, 29, 30		pp. 66, 67
Revising Irregular Verbs	31, 32, 33		pp. 68, 69
Writing			
Description of a Setting	34	Use rubric	pp. 70, 71
Character Profile	35	Use rubric	pp. 72, 73
Critical Review	36	Use rubric	pp. 74, 75

Name _____ Date _____

Grade 8—Benchmark Test 4
Interpretation Guide

For remediation of specific skills, you may assign students the relevant Reading Kit Practice and Assess pages indicated in the far-right column of this chart. You will find rubrics for evaluating writing samples in the last section of your Professional Development Guidebook.

Skill Objective	Test Items	Number Correct	Reading Kit
Reading Skill			
Make Inferences	1, 2, 3, 4, 5, 6		pp. 76, 77
Evaluate Persuasive Appeals	7, 8, 9		pp. 78, 79
Literary Analysis			
Point of View	10, 11, 12, 13		pp. 80, 81
Theme	14, 15, 16, 17		pp. 82, 83
Comparing Symbols	18, 19		pp. 84, 85
Vocabulary			
Roots and Prefixes -spec-, -nounc-, mis-, per-	20, 21, 22, 23, 24, 25		pp. 86, 87
Grammar			
Simple Tenses	26, 28, 29		pp. 88, 89
Perfect Tenses	27, 30		pp. 90, 91
Subject-Verb Agreement	31, 32		pp. 92, 93
Writing			
Dialogue	33	Use rubric	pp. 96, 97
Personal Essay	34	Use rubric	pp. 98, 99
Short Story	35	Use rubric	pp. 100, 101

ANSWERS

Big Question Vocabulary—1, p. 1

Sample Answers

1. "You really *irritate* me when you *oppose* my *viewpoint*."
2. "Okay, what's the *argument* all about? Can I help you settle this problem?"
3. "I want you to stop the *argument*, share your *viewpoints*, and try to reach a *compromise*."
4. They agreed to a *compromise* in which some of each girl's ideas were used.

Big Question Vocabulary—2, p. 2

Sample Answers

A. 1. insecurity
   2. mislead
   3. injury
   4. interact
   5. solution

B. 1. interact
   2. injury
   3. insecurity
   4. solution
   5. mislead

Big Question Vocabulary—3, p. 3

Sample Answers

A.

1. Violence causes harm, and can be avoided by a calm use of negotiation and compromise.
2. I might negotiate a compromise.
3. winning a race or getting an A on a test
4. the ability to listen carefully, to speak clearly, and to remain calm
5. Why do you disagree? Tell me your ideas.

B. Dialogues will vary, but should focus on the assignment and include Thematic Vocabulary words.

"An Hour With Abuelo" by Judith Ortiz Cofer

Vocabulary Warm-up Exercises, p. 8

A. 1. adults
   2. dictionary
   3. ignorant
   4. drafted
   5. graduated
   6. wheelchairs
   7. poetry
   8. obvious

B. Sample Answers

1. *Maturity* involves trying to handle things in an effective way, but pouting definitely does not help anyone be effective.

2. A low-cost motel would not draw the type of traveler who would rent a *suite*, so it probably wouldn't offer one.
3. Since real *parchment* is made from animal skin, I don't think animal lovers who do not support killing animals even for food would choose to use it.
4. Because *ammonia* is a strong gas that can make you sick, you need to have fresh air when using it.
5. I don't think my *grandchildren* will find space travel amazing, since by then it will have been around for a long time.
6. I think a *principal* needs patience, good leadership skills, a sense of humor, and a love for kids.
7. This saying must mean that even the hardest *labor* feels easy when you like doing it.
8. My favorite reading *material* is a news magazine I get every week.

Reading Warm-up A, p. 9

Sample Answers

1. (defines); The writer used a *dictionary* to look up the meaning of the word *battalion*.
2. vote in United States elections, be drafted for service; Voting was an optional right for *adults*, but being *drafted* was not something most men could avoid.
3. (Korean War); *Obvious* means "easy to see and understand."
4. (Artworks), (music); Since *poetry* is pleasing to the ear and packed with meaning, it makes a good choice for writing in praise of something.
5. Someone who has *graduated* is around eighteen years old; a Korean War veteran might be more than seventy years old; Young people who have just *graduated* can learn from their elders, and older people often enjoy the energy and ideas of younger folks.
6. (elderly war veterans); They might use *wheelchairs* because they were injured in the war, or because they may have trouble walking.
7. (unaware); Puerto Ricans can keep their children from growing up *ignorant* by talking to them about the sacrifices made for democracy.

Reading Warm-up B, p. 10

Sample Answers

1. A good high-school *principal* knows as much as possible about the colleges to which his or her students are applying.
2. cleaned windows, weeded gardens, and scrubbed floors; The hardest *labor* I've done is shoveling the snow from our driveway in the winter.
3. Because *ammonia* is a gas with a very strong smell, it can cause people to feel unwell.
4. (magazines), (books); The best reading *material* for me is a good novel.

5. (the residents); Since the home is for elderly people, it makes sense that their children might bring the *grandchildren* there for visits.

6. (wide brushes), (little pots of paint); Because Lily was looking for a heavy, fancy type of paper that would work for her art project, she chose *parchment*.

7. The *suite* of guidance offices would probably consist of a few rooms connected by a hallway.

8. (unselfish); A high-school student acts with *maturity* whenever he or she thinks about people besides him- or herself and makes wise decisions.

Judith Ortiz Cofer

Listening and Viewing, p. 11

Sample Answers and Guidelines for Evaluation

Segment 1. As a child, she learned that whoever was telling a story in her house had a captive audience and was powerful. Her awareness of the power of words influenced her to become a writer. Students may say that stories bring ideas and universal experiences to a larger audience and help people to connect and understand others.

Segment 2. You find out who truly, and ironically, possesses the wisdom in the story. The themes in "An Hour with Abuelo" tell us that it is important to spend time with our elders and hear their stories because they can teach us about our world and what is important in life.

Segment 3. Judith Ortiz Cofer wakes up at 5:00 A.M. daily in order to be able to write without interruption. Students may suggest that choosing a particular time and place to write helps a writer become disciplined about his or her work.

Segment 4. Judith Ortiz Cofer's goal is to provide a bridge between reader and writer and to show that, despite physical differences, all people are the same on the inside. Students may answer that exploring literature can help them learn more about their ancestry, interests, and emotions.

Learning About Short Stories, p. 12

A. 1. B; 2. A; 3. A; 4. C; 5. C

B. Sample Answers

Title: Cinderella

Main Characters: Cinderella, her stepmother and stepsisters, Prince Charming

Setting: a kingdom long ago

Conflict: Cinderella versus her stepmother and stepsisters

Theme: Virtue will be rewarded.

"An Hour With Abuelo" by Judith Ortiz Cofer

Model Selection: Short Story, p. 13

Sample Answers

1. He is torn between doing what his mother wants him to do and his reluctance to visit Abuelo because he has reading to do, he hates the senior home, and he does not feel close to his grandfather.

2. He is hard-working, but self-centered. He is motivated by his ambition to do well in school and succeed in life. He dislikes the idea that individuals cannot control their own destiny and have to accept whatever life throws at them.

3. It recounts events from an earlier time in Abuelo's life. It is told in the first person by Abuelo. It helps me understand the hardships he has faced in life, the importance he always placed on education, and the times in which he lived.

4. Young Arturo has seen his grandfather as something of a loser who could not take charge of his life, but in fact, grandfather is respected by his friends and is enjoying his life. Young Arturo expected to be bored by his visit, but he was very interested. It was Abuelo, not Arturo, who cut the visit short.

Open-Book Test, p. 14

Short Answer

1. The *a-ha* moment in a story happens when both a character and the reader suddenly make a discovery, or have an insight into a universal truth.

   Difficulty: *Average*   **Objective:** *Literary Analysis*

2. His main conflict is internal. The decision involves a struggle in the character's mind.

   Difficulty: *Easy*   **Objective:** *Literary Analysis*

3. I am reading the rising action, the part in which the conflict is introduced. That is the part that deals with the conflict. It comes before the climax, the point where it is clear how the story will turn out.

   Difficulty: *Challenging*   **Objective:** *Literary Analysis*

4. The narrator is not part of the story, so he or she is telling the story from a third-person point of view. The narrator does not know everything about the characters, so he or she is limited.

   Difficulty: *Easy*   **Objective:** *Literary Analysis*

5. He is offering a lot of excuses because he feels guilty about not visiting his grandfather more often.

   Difficulty: *Average*   **Objective:** *Interpretation*

6. Abuelo's conflict was with society and the demands of his family. After the war Abuelo could not work as a teacher because teachers had to have a college education. He had to work to take care of his parents. He responded by working as a farmer. He adopted the attitude that "así es la vida" ("that's the way life is").

   Difficulty: *Challenging*   **Objective:** *Literary Analysis*

7. Arturo strongly disagrees with the expression. When his mother uses it, he says, "Not for me. I go after what I want." When Abuelo says that it is the title of his autobiography, Arturo thinks that Abuelo did not try hard enough to find a way to keep his job as a teacher.

   Difficulty: *Easy*   **Objective:** *Interpretation*

8. Abuelo spends his time with the books that he is writing: the autobiography ("Así es la vida") and a book of poems ("Poemas de Arturo").

   Difficulty: *Average*   **Objective:** *Interpretation*

9. Arturo's attitude is disrespectful: He calls her "an old lady in hot pink running shoes" and "the world's oldest marathoner."
   Difficulty: *Average*   **Objective:** *Interpretation*

10. Arturo expects to hate his visit with Abuelo. He also believes that the people in the home lead dull lives (they play "old people's games"; they are lined up in their wheelchairs for no reason). Instead, Arturo is not bored, and Abuelo's life is interesting: He is writing "books," he has a poetry reading to attend, and he has a lively woman friend who pushes his wheelchair "a little too fast."
    Difficulty: *Challenging*   **Objective:** *Literary Analysis*

Essay

11. At the beginning of the story Arturo is ambitious but self-centered: He does not want to take time away from his summer reading to visit his grandfather even though his mother says that his grandfather is dying. He is also sure that he is different from people who accept what happens to them instead of fighting for what they want. By the end of the story, Arturo realizes that the idea of accepting life for what it is might be more complicated than he had thought. He also has gained some respect for his grandfather.
    Difficulty: *Easy*   **Objective:** *Essay*

12. Themes of "An Hour With Abuelo" include the following: (1) It is important to make time for family; (2) you can learn things from older people that you cannot learn from books; and (3) life can be fulfilling even if you cannot make all your dreams come true. Students should cite evidence from the story to support whichever message they believe is most central to the story.
    Difficulty: *Average*   **Objective:** *Essay*

13. Students should recognize that the autobiography is a flashback. It presents Abuelo's life story from Abuelo's point of view, not Arturo's. They should recognize some of the ideas that the flashback reveals: Abuelo's lifelong love of learning, his youthful efforts to do what he wanted to do and improve his life, his willingness to accept life's disappointments, and his ability to lead a fulfilling life despite those disappointments. Students should connect (some of) that information with an idea in the story, such as the idea that one can learn from life as well as from books or that one can lead a fulfilling life in spite of personal disappointments.
    Difficulty: *Challenging*   **Objective:** *Essay*

14. Some students may think that Arturo considers Abuelo's conflict unresolved because Abuelo still feels the disappointment of losing his job as a teacher. Arturo also may consider the conflict unresolved because he believes that if he were in such a situation, he would keep fighting for what he wants. Other students may say that Arturo understands that Abuelo settled the conflict long ago but strongly disagrees with the way that Abuelo has done so—that is, by accepting the disappointment and moving on with his life.
    Difficulty: *Average*   **Objective:** *Essay*

Oral Response

15. Oral responses should be clear, well organized, and well supported by appropriate examples in the selection.
    Difficulty: *Average*   **Objective:** *Oral Interpretation*

Selection Test A, p. 17

Critical Reading

1. ANS: A	DIF: Easy	OBJ: Comprehension
2. ANS: C	DIF: Easy	OBJ: Interpretation
3. ANS: A	DIF: Easy	OBJ: Interpretation
4. ANS: B	DIF: Easy	OBJ: Interpretation
5. ANS: A	DIF: Easy	OBJ: Point of View
6. ANS: D	DIF: Easy	OBJ: Setting
7. ANS: C	DIF: Easy	OBJ: Comprehension
8. ANS: C	DIF: Easy	OBJ: Plot
9. ANS: B	DIF: Easy	OBJ: Comprehension
10. ANS: D	DIF: Easy	OBJ: Character
11. ANS: C	DIF: Average	OBJ: Comprehension
12. ANS: B	DIF: Easy	OBJ: Comprehension
13. ANS: B	DIF: Easy	OBJ: Irony and Plot
14. ANS: A	DIF: Easy	OBJ: Conflict
15. ANS: C	DIF: Easy	OBJ: Interpretation

Essay

16. Students should recognize that Arturo at the start is a good student who is very ambitious to do well in school. He is also self-centered, absorbed with his own plans and dreams, and reluctant to give time to his grandfather even after his mother tells him that his grandfather does not have long to live. They should recognize Arturo's low opinion of the attitude that older people in his family seem to have about accepting whatever happens and not being in control of their own lives. They should note that by the end of the story, Arturo is interested in his grandfather's life and respects him much more.
    Difficulty: *Easy*
    Objective: *Essay*

17. Students should discuss some or all of these ironies in the story: Arturo jokes about Abuelo's writing his autobiography, never expecting that his grandfather is doing so. Arturo thinks the nursing home is a terrible place, never expecting his grandfather to enjoy socializing there. Abuelo proves to be sharp in mind, even though he is frail in body. Arturo at first thinks his grandfather has failed in life by failing to control his destiny, never expecting his grandfather to enjoy the respect of others and feel fulfilled in life. Arturo plans to give his grandfather only an hour and to time his visit, not realizing his grandfather is giving Arturo only a hour and is timing *his* visit.
    Difficulty: *Average*
    Objective: *Essay*

18. Some students may argue that Arturo believes that Abuelo has an unresolved conflict. Abuelo still feels disappointed over losing his job as a teacher. Arturo believes that if he were in such a situation, he would keep fighting for what he wants. Other students may say that Arturo understands that Abuelo settled the conflict long ago but strongly disagrees with the way that Abuelo has done so—that is, by accepting the disappointment and moving on with his life.

Difficulty: *Average*
Objective: *Essay*

Selection Test B, p. 20

Critical Reading

1. ANS: D	DIF: Average	OBJ: Interpretation
2. ANS: D	DIF: Average	OBJ: Comprehension
3. ANS: A	DIF: Average	OBJ: Interpretation
4. ANS: A	DIF: Average	OBJ: Interpretation
5. ANS: B	DIF: Average	OBJ: Interpretation
6. ANS: B	DIF: Challenging	OBJ: Interpretation
7. ANS: A	DIF: Challenging	OBJ: Interpretation
8. ANS: C	DIF: Challenging	OBJ: Irony
9. ANS: B	DIF: Average	OBJ: Interpretation
10. ANS: A	DIF: Average	OBJ: Comprehension
11. ANS: C	DIF: Average	OBJ: Interpretation
12. ANS: C	DIF: Average	OBJ: Point of View
13. ANS: D	DIF: Average	OBJ: Conflict
14. ANS: A	DIF: Average	OBJ: Interpretation
15. ANS: D	DIF: Challenging	OBJ: Interpretation
16. ANS: D	DIF: Average	OBJ: Interpretation
17. ANS: B	DIF: Challenging	OBJ: Interpretation
18. ANS: A	DIF: Challenging	OBJ: Plot and Irony

Essay

19. Students should state a theme that focuses on a lesson Arturo learns or a key perception the reader makes. Make sure they support the theme by referring to details in the story. Here are some possible statements of theme: It is important to make time for family. You can learn things from older people that you cannot learn in books. Life can be fulfilling even if we do not get all we dream about when young. No one can completely control his or her own destiny.

Difficulty: *Average*
Objective: *Essay*

20. Students' essays should address all three of the topics: traits, motivation, and attitudes. **Traits:** Students may note that both Arturo and his grandfather enjoy literature and learning, but that Arturo is more ambitious about his schoolwork. They may mention that the grandfather represents a much earlier generation, is steeped in Puerto Rican heritage, and is more

comfortable using Spanish; Arturo, in contrast, is a modern American boy. **Motivation:** They may note that Arturo is at the beginning of his life, full of hope and confidence; the grandfather is at the end of his, looking back on successes and failures, but still leading as fulfilling a life as he can. **Attitudes:** Arturo feels confident that working hard will mean success and that he will have the ability to control his future, whereas Abuelo's philosophy, born of experience, is that one must accept what life offers and then make the best of it, finding fulfillment where one can.

Difficulty: *Average*
Objective: *Essay*

21. Students should recognize that the autobiography serves as a flashback, telling the reader Abuelo's life story from his own point of view. They should recognize that it reveals the grandfather's lifelong love of learning, his youthful efforts to fight the system and do good work in life, and his ability to accept life's disappointments, yet go on to lead a fulfilling life. They should connect those insights, and the title of the autobiography, with one or more themes of the story: That one can lead a fulfilling life despite life's disappointments, for example, or that some learning is not found in books.

Difficulty: *Challenging*
Objective: *Essay*

22. Some students may think that Arturo considers Abuelo's conflict unresolved because Abuelo still feels the disappointment of losing his job as a teacher. Arturo also may consider the conflict unresolved because he believes that if he were in such a situation, he would keep fighting for what he wants. Other students may say that Arturo understands that Abuelo settled the conflict long ago but strongly disagrees with the way that Abuelo has done so—that is, by accepting the disappointment and moving on with his life.

Difficulty: *Average*
Objective: *Essay*

"Who Can Replace a Man?" by Brian W. Aldiss

Vocabulary Warm-up Exercises, p. 24

A. 1. complex
2. momentarily
3. communicate
4. superior
5. quantity
6. babble
7. plainly
8. activity

B. Sample Answers
1. It is to our *mutual* benefit to strike a deal at the bargaining table.
2. The doctor made the *deduction* that her patient had gone *berserk* from grief.

3. On weekday mornings, Martha's *routines* keep her from walking around *aimlessly*.

4. After George regained the use of his legs, he was happy to be *mobile*.

5. The machine runs *continuously* for twelve hours, so it doesn't stop.

6. There is a *distinction* between apples and oranges.

Reading Warm-up A, p. 25

Sample Answers

1. (told), (say); To "*communicate* better than the average teenager" means "to express oneself more clearly than the way teenagers usually do."

2. (simple), (primitive); This *complex* stereo system requires a detailed manual.

3. (primitive); Fritz has greater abilities than the simpler robots; therefore, he is *superior*.

4. clear; I see *plainly* that you prefer to spend your time with your new friends.

5. When something flickers, it moves quickly for just a short time, and momentarily means "for a short time."

6. number; I ate a large *quantity* of grapes for dessert.

7. body language, verbal language; My neighborhood is jumping with *activity*, especially on Saturdays, when people wash their cars, run to the grocery store, and play outside with their kids.

8. (Fritz said nothing meaningful); It's not good for Fritz to speak *babble* because that means he is not speaking intelligently, as he is supposed to.

Reading Warm-up B, p. 26

Sample Answers

1. robots that roam about, rovers; The school bus is something *mobile* that I use every day.

2. (don't show signs of stopping); The light in front of the train station shines *continuously*.

3. A robot that wandered *aimlessly* would be walking without any purpose; and therefore, it would not be performing any tasks.

4. (lost control); With sparks flying out of it, the robot gone *berserk* destroys whatever it meets until it finally falls over in a heap.

5. piece together evidence; When I saw the dog sitting on the porch with all the lights out in the house, I made the *deduction* that someone had mistakenly left the dog outside.

6. *Routines* are methods or ways of doing things, and the robots use these to accomplish the work that the scientists program them to do.

7. A *distinction* between one area today and that area a long time ago is that it was once wet and now it is dry.

8. (Each group gets something from the other.); Running errands was of *mutual* benefit to my neighbor and me because she got her errands all done and I got some money to put toward my new bike.

Writing About the Big Question, p. 27

A. 1. injury

2. interact

3. negotiate

4. solution

B. Sample Answers

1. Once, my sister and I had a conflict over sharing computer time. Another time, I had a conflict inside myself over whether to spend money on a new cell phone.

2. I explained my viewpoint to my sister, telling her that we should have equal time. Her reaction was to agree with me, and we have not had a problem since.

C. Sample Answer

When people are not sure what to do, they often turn to someone whose opinion they value. They ask that person to advise them about what to do. If the other person usually gives good advice, he or she can help others solve their conflicts.

Reading: Ask Questions to Compare and Contrast, p. 28

Sample Answers

1. They vary in size, from thirty feet tall to the size of a toaster. One has fifty arms with keys on the end of each. They seem to be made of metal.

   A. Like humans, they are different sizes and shapes; they have limbs.

   B. Their shapes and sizes vary to a greater extent than do those of humans.

2. They have voices and use speech. They also hoot and shout.

   A. Like humans, they use speech and other sounds. They use logic.

   B. Their speech patterns are more limited and programmed, based on brain level.

3. They do different jobs, such as fieldwork, repair work, sorting work, and office work.

   A. Humans also have different kinds of jobs.

   B. Unlike humans, the machines are limited to doing the one thing they do for work and seem to have no other purpose or skill.

Literary Analysis: Setting, p. 29

Sample Answers

A. Farm in the Country: large, gray fields, dry and lifeless with over-cropping; populated only by machines

City: humans dead of starvation; machines fighting; some cities burning

Badlands: large; bomb craters; soil erosion and crevices; foothills and mountains; caves; a stream

B. Both the farm, at the beginning, and the Badlands, at the end, are dry, dusty, barren, and lifeless except for machines. Although there are a few humans alive at the end, in caves in the Badlands, they are dying of starvation. The Badlands have not been cultivated, and there has been fighting there, so they are filled with craters and crevices.

Vocabulary Builder, p. 30

Sample Answers

A. 1. A
2. C
3. A
4. B
5. D
6. A

B. 1. Having a *debate* can lead to a peaceful settlement of differences.
2. A *decrease* in strength would lessen one's ability to run fast.
3. The ability to *decode* unfamiliar words helps one unlock meaning.

Enrichment: Planning a Screenplay, p. 31

Sample Answers

Field Landscape: large field of gray ground, worn and dry with overuse; smoggy air; only the field-minder in sight

Agricultural Station: same dry, gray ground; same smoggy atmosphere; large, forbidding machines, a few fighting or going in circles, others not moving, some shouting or hooting; a large, nondescript warehouse with a large machine at the roll-up door

Badlands Landscape: past a burning city; large, endless horizons; bomb craters; soil erosion; dusty, gray, lifeless; dark mountains in the distance

Field-minder: thirty feet tall; deliberate and heavy; notices surroundings; calm and logical

Unlocker: machine with fifty arms, each ending with several keyed fingers; arms rotate continually; limited intelligence

Open-Book Test, p. 32

Short Answer

1. Time/Place: morning; Evidence: "Morning filtered into the sky. . . ."

   Time/Place: the future; Evidence: Intelligent machines are busy.

   Time/Place: a farm; Evidence: The field-minder has just "finished turning the topsoil of a three-thousand-acre field"; the Agricultural Station

   The fact that the story is set in a future in which robots are very active proves that it is science fiction.

   Difficulty: *Average*   **Objective:** *Literary Analysis*

2. Both machines have been built with Class Three brains. That feature makes them superior to other machines in the story, which are expected to follow their leadership. The one exception is the radio operator, which has a

Class Two brain. When that machine enters the story, even the penner and the field-minder follow its leadership.

   Difficulty: *Easy*   **Objective:** *Reading*

3. The reaction is confused noise-making, aimless movement, and overall disruption. Readers can conclude that the machines depend upon orders—orders that originate with humans. That conclusion sets up the ending of the story, where the machines immediately surrender their independence when they receive an order from the first human they meet.

   Difficulty: *Challenging*   **Objective:** *Interpretation*

4. The radio operator reports that "a diet deficiency killed them"; in other words, mass starvation killed almost every human. The other machines were not built to be as intelligent as the radio operator. The main reason that they don't understand, however, is that they do not depend upon a diet of food to survive, as humans do.

   Difficulty: *Average*   **Objective:** *Interpretation*

5. The machines want to rescue the radio operator because the radio operator has ordered them to do so. They are used to taking orders from it, for it has a superior brain. The other machines value that difference; the penner tells the radio operator, "I admire the way you Class Twos can reason ahead." The other machines look to the radio operator for leadership.

   Difficulty: *Average*   **Objective:** *Reading*

6. The machines decide that the safest place to go is the place with the fewest machines—the Badlands. Traveling there, however, means crossing rugged land and hills that are hard to climb. Eventually, the penner breaks down there and is left behind.

   Difficulty: *Easy*   **Objective:** *Literary Analysis*

7. The author says that "[a]ncient bomb craters" can be seen in the eroded Badlands. It seems that war, too, has killed many people. The author also says that the region is the product of "man's talent for war, coupled with his inability to manage forested land." Taken together, these reasons suggest that humans are aggressive, foolish beings, who care only about satisfying their desires of the moment without considering the future.

   Difficulty: *Challenging*   **Objective:** *Literary Analysis*

8. The machines plan to start a city in the Badlands. When they arrive in the foothills, they see a man. They abandon their plans when he orders them to get him food, for they were built to follow the commands of humans.

   Difficulty: *Easy*   **Objective:** *Interpretation*

9. The human in the story is naked and starving—barely alive. The people who built the machines probably had no serious physical needs. The human in the story (or his ancestors) may have been much like them at one time. The machines react to him with immediate obedience, however, because humans have programmed them to do so.

   Difficulty: *Challenging*   **Objective:** *Reading*

10. *Deficiency* means "a lack of something that is necessary." The world of this story has a deficiency of natural resources, especially farmable land. As a terrible result, most of humanity has died of starvation. The lack of people, especially in comparison to the number of robots, is also terrible, as are the conditions that the surviving humans face.

Difficulty: *Average* **Objective:** *Vocabulary*

Essay

11. Students should discuss the condition of the land. For example, they should note the dry, dusty, overused fields; the eroded Badlands; and the loss of the forests. Students may suggest that humans could have kept the soil fertile by rotating crops. In addition, humans could have recycled and replanted instead of stripping the forests. They also might have avoided the devastation of war through negotiation.

Difficulty: *Easy* **Objective:** *Essay*

12. Students might point out that, like the machines, people in our society have differing jobs and intellectual strengths. Unlike the machines, however, people have some choice about what they do; they do not have to do the same job forever, as these machines seem to do. In addition, people in leadership positions usually reach those positions as a result of personality, drive, and so on instead of merely as a result of intelligence, as is the case of the machines.

Difficulty: *Average* **Objective:** *Essay*

13. Students should compare and contrast the machines' size and other physical characteristics, as well as the machines' function and brain class. For example, the field-minder is tall, has a Class Three brain, moves at a slow but steady pace, and has limbs that can plant seeds. The unlocker has fifty rotating arms with fingers and keys at the ends, has a Class Five brain, and unlocks storage rooms. Both machines, however, use logic and speak at a level matching their brain class.

Difficulty: *Average* **Objective:** *Essay*

14. Students should understand that when the penner makes this "revolutionary statement," it believes that all people are dead. If the penner is correct, then the tension between humans and machines has been resolved. Just the same, the comment suggests some uncertainty—or, at least, some hope that the conflict has been resolved. Students should realize that if the penner believes that the conflict is over, then the end of the story, in which a human again controls the machines, proves the penner wrong. If the penner believes that there still is some chance for conflict, then the end of the story proves the penner right.

Difficulty: *Average* **Objective:** *Essay*

Oral Response

15. Students should give oral explanations in response to the questions they choose or that are assigned to them.

Difficulty: *Average* **Objective:** *Oral Interpretation*

Selection Test A, p. 35

Critical Reading

1. ANS: C	DIF: Easy	OBJ: Literary Analysis
2. ANS: A	DIF: Easy	OBJ: Comprehension
3. ANS: D	DIF: Easy	OBJ: Reading
4. ANS: B	DIF: Easy	OBJ: Comprehension
5. ANS: A	DIF: Easy	OBJ: Interpretation
6. ANS: B	DIF: Easy	OBJ: Comprehension
7. ANS: D	DIF: Easy	OBJ: Interpretation
8. ANS: C	DIF: Easy	OBJ: Literary Analysis
9. ANS: C	DIF: Easy	OBJ: Interpretation
10. ANS: B	DIF: Easy	OBJ: Comprehension
11. ANS: A	DIF: Easy	OBJ: Comprehension

Vocabulary and Grammar

12. ANS: D	DIF: Easy	OBJ: Grammar
13. ANS: C	DIF: Easy	OBJ: Vocabulary
14. ANS: D	DIF: Easy	OBJ: Vocabulary
15. ANS: A	DIF: Easy	OBJ: Grammar

Essay

16. Students could compare and contrast the machines' appearance by referring to their size and other physical characteristics. Students should also tell how the machines' jobs and the machines' brain levels compare and contrast. For example, the field-minder is tall, moves at a slow but steady pace, and has limbs that can plant seeds. The unlocker has fifty rotating arms with fingers and keys at the ends of each; it uses the keys to unlock storage rooms. The pen-propeller is as small as a toaster, has ten retractable arms, and moves quickly by rolling; it does clerical work. The quarrier has twelve wheels and a scoop; it does heavy work. The radio operator looks like a filing cabinet with tentacles; it communicates with the city center. The radio operator has the highest-level brain, a Class Two, among the machines that have not received their orders. The field-minder and the penner have Class Three brains, and the unlocker and the quarrier have Class Five brains. Each machine uses logic and speaks at a level that matches its brain class.

Difficulty: *Easy*

Objective: *Essay*

17. In the form of a journal entry, students should describe the condition of the land in the story. They might refer to the dry, dusty fields that have been overused and are no longer able to nourish crops. They could mention the cracked and eroded land beyond the Agricultural Station and the loss of the forests. They could have kept the soil fertile by rotating crops. People could have planned ways to harvest and support forested areas so that trees could have kept growing

and prevented erosion. Bomb craters could have been avoided by not going to war over international problems.

Difficulty: *Easy*

Objective: *Essay*

18. Students might note that when the penner makes his "revolutionary statement," it believes that all people are dead. If the penner is correct, then the tension between humans and machines has been resolved. Even so, the comment suggests that the penner is not sure—or at least that there is some hope that the conflict has been resolved.

Difficulty: *Challenging*

Objective: *Essay*

Selection Test B, p. 38

Critical Reading

1. ANS: B	DIF: Average	OBJ: Literary Analysis
2. ANS: C	DIF: Challenging	OBJ: Interpretation
3. ANS: B	DIF: Average	OBJ: Comprehension
4. ANS: D	DIF: Average	OBJ: Interpretation
5. ANS: C	DIF: Challenging	OBJ: Interpretation
6. ANS: A	DIF: Average	OBJ: Reading
7. ANS: C	DIF: Average	OBJ: Comprehension
8. ANS: B	DIF: Challenging	OBJ: Reading
9. ANS: A	DIF: Challenging	OBJ: Comprehension
10. ANS: C	DIF: Challenging	OBJ: Literary Analysis
11. ANS: A	DIF: Average	OBJ: Interpretation
12. ANS: B	DIF: Average	OBJ: Literary Analysis
13. ANS: D	DIF: Average	OBJ: Comprehension
14. ANS: B	DIF: Average	OBJ: Comprehension
15. ANS: D	DIF: Average	OBJ: Reading

Vocabulary and Grammar

16. ANS: C	DIF: Average	OBJ: Vocabulary
17. ANS: A	DIF: Challenging	OBJ: Grammar
18. ANS: C	DIF: Average	OBJ: Grammar

Essay

19. Students might point out that people in our society, like the machines in the story, have different jobs that require different levels of skills. In addition, people in our society have varying levels of intellectual abilities. Unlike the machines, however, most people in our society have choices about what work they do; they are not handed one job to do forever, as have these machines. Students also might discuss similarities and differences regarding leadership roles taken on by the machines in the story and people in our society. For example, certain machines, as a result of their brain class, take charge of the situation and make decisions. In our society, such tendencies may or may not be a result of intelligence but rather a function of personality, confidence, drive, and so on.

Difficulty: *Average*

Objective: *Essay*

20. Students should point out that up to the beginning of the story the machines have been operating according to instructions from humans. They have been doing so with no objection, apparently, until the day the orders fail to come. Since some of their brains are able to think more logically than others, these machines become aware that they can make decisions on their own. This ability is a new idea for the penner, which seems to realize that making one's own choices and plans is more pleasant than following orders. The penner is coming up with this idea for the first time, so it can be seen as revolutionary.

Difficulty: *Challenging*

Objective: *Essay*

21. Students should understand that when the penner makes this "revolutionary statement," it believes that all people are dead. If the penner is correct, then the tension between humans and machines has been resolved. Just the same, the comment suggests some uncertainty—or, at least, some hope that the conflict has been resolved. Students should realize that if the penner believes that the conflict is over, then the end of the story, in which a human again controls the machines, proves the penner wrong. If the penner believes that there still is some chance for conflict, then the end of the story proves the penner right.

Difficulty: *Challenging*

Objective: *Essay*

"Tears of Autumn" by Yoshiko Uchida

Vocabulary Warm-up Exercises, p. 42

A. 1. officials
2. anxiety
3. suitable
4. devoting
5. ventured
6. latitude
7. leaden
8. spirited

B. Sample Answers

1. F; During summer you should wear *protective* items like a hat as well as sunscreen.
2. F; A healthy child should have rosy, not *sallow*, skin after exercising outdoors.
3. T; Your *homeland* can be different from that of your grandparents if your family has moved.
4. T; Since *tuberculosis* usually affects the lungs, a person with this disease would have trouble breathing.

5. F; During an *investigation* every detail is examined carefully, and this usually takes time.

6. T; Test scores usually reflect the *varying* ability levels of students.

7. T; The tide is *relentless* because it never stops.

8. T; A family resemblance would help provide some *recognition* of an unknown relative.

Reading Warm-up A, p. 43

Sample Answers

1. his place in society, his personality; *Suitable* means "appropriate; proper; right."

2. (traveling to a new country to be with a husband she had never met); I felt *anxiety* about my mom having another baby.

3. Just think of the *lively* discussions they must have had!

4. her future husband was the most handsome; *Ventured* means "expressed in spite of possible criticism."

5. the wealth to be found in America; I have been *devoting* my time to homework, hoping to bring up some of my grades.

6. Immigration *officials* would know because they worked in positions that gave them information about the women and because they knew about life in the new land.

7. (freedom); Having *latitude* meant that the picture brides had the freedom to start a new life.

8. (unpleasant emotions); The picture brides must have had heavy hearts as they thought about possibly never returning to their homeland.

Reading Warm-up B, p. 44

Sample Answers

1. The new *homeland* is the United States, where San Francisco is located. In the United States, my *homeland*, people have freedom as long as they obey the laws of the land.

2. contagious illness; *Tuberculosis* is an awful disease that affects the lungs.

3. (it was a great place to hunt and fish); *Investigation* means "an official attempt to find out information."

4. The Miwoks would have needed *protective* shelters to keep themselves safe from wild animals and severe weather.

5. Like all early peoples who lived by hunting and gathering, the Miwok had *differing* levels of success. One reason is that animals can be scarce, especially in bad weather.

6. poor diets; Poor health, disease, or even fear can make a person's skin look *sallow*.

7. The Miwoks would have some *recognition* of natural elements on and around Angel Island, including plant and animal life.

8. A *relentless* wind at a place like Angel Island might cause waves to pound against the shore. *Relentless* means "nonstop."

Writing About the Big Question, p. 45

A. 1. negotiate
2. mislead
3. oppose
4. argument

B. Sample Answers

1. Two years ago, my family moved a thousand miles away from our former home. This caused great inner conflict for me because I did not want to leave my friends.

2. I knew that my inner conflict was a normal reaction to such a big change. I began to interact with other kids and made many new friends.

C. Sample Answer

Making a big change in one's life can cause conflicts because it is not easy to get used to new routines. The good thing about big changes is that they often improve our lives. This is true about changes for the better in our health habits. Sometimes, however, we make changes that do not improve our lives. When we realize our mistakes, we should try to change back.

Reading: Ask Questions to Compare and Contrast, p. 46

Sample Answers

A. Hana: does not want to live the conventional life of her sisters; has more radical ideas than her sisters

Hana's Sisters: one married sister and her husband living with Hana and Hana's mother; two married to merchants and living in cities; obedient

Taro: immigrated to America on his own; now thirty-one; hardworking; conscientious; owns his own business

B. Hana is like her sisters and Taro in that she has been raised with similar expectations to have an arranged marriage and stay nearby. Unlike her sisters, she is more outspoken about her ideas. Like Taro, she is interested in change and willing to take risks.

Literary Analysis: Setting, p. 47

Sample Answers

A. Japan: persimmon trees of Oka village; thatched roofs; fields of golden rice; mountains; maple trees; sleeping on a *tatami* mat; death of father, creating loss of financial security; at twenty-one, must find husband

Ship: turbulent November sea; damp salt air; smell of fish on lower decks; hard, narrow bunk

Japanese American Community: Oakland, urban area with many people; immigrant from Japan seeks bride from homeland; immigrant's shop is successful, rents rooms upstairs, has Japanese friends for Hana to stay with

B. In Japan as well as in the Japanese American community in California, there are Japanese people with backgrounds like Hana's. However, the city of Oakland is more populated than Hana's village. The ship is not like either Japan or the Japanese American community.

Vocabulary Builder, p. 48

A. Sample Answers

1. Some people enjoy the added buying power, opportunities for travel, and ability to contribute to charitable causes that more money brings.

2. Some people with a lot of education and experience in a professional career might consider washing dishes in a restaurant a less-than-desirable occupation.

3. One political party may be very conservative, and the other party may be very liberal in what it wants for the country.

4. Turbulent weather is unpredictable, and the pilot might have trouble controlling the plane.

5. A man might recoil at the sight of a rattlesnake because he knows the snake is dangerous, and he wants to stay away from it.

6. A child might be relentless in his requests for a new toy because he is hoping to wear down his parents and persuade them to buy it.

B. 1. If you *despise* the actions of another person, you look down on them.

2. If you agree to the *destruction* of an old building, you agree that it should come down.

3. If the money of a country is suddenly *devalued*, your buying power goes down; you can buy less with it.

Enrichment: Documentary Film, p. 49

Sample Answers

1. Documentary films can reveal personal mannerisms and speaking styles more vividly than written accounts can.

2. Written accounts are easily portable, so they can be read anywhere, whereas viewing films requires more equipment. Encyclopedias and textbooks usually provide information in a straightforward way, often summarizing ideas for the reader. Although documentary films usually include a narrator, the viewer is often left to draw conclusions for himself or herself.

3. A. teenager arriving in America: How do you feel about leaving your friends in your homeland? What do you expect to find in America? Are you excited, regretful, or both?

   B. Americans watching new immigrants' arrival: How long ago did *your* family arrive in America? Are you curious about the immigrants' homelands? Do you feel inclined to help the newcomers or to let them find their own way?

4. It would depend on the filmmaker's point of view and what images and sources he or she chose to include. Most immigrants probably had mixed feelings about the decision to leave their homelands. Viewers would likely see and hear anxiety as well as anticipation in images

and firsthand accounts. Most viewers, however, would probably appreciate having some visual knowledge about their destination.

"Who Can Replace a Man?" by Brian Aldiss
"Tears of Autumn" by Yoshiko Uchida

Integrated Language Skills: Grammar, p. 50

Words that students are to circle appear in parentheses.

A. 1. LV, (has been)
2. AV, (played)
3. LV, (is)
4. LV, (sounded)
5. AV, (sounded)
6. AV, (stared)
7. LV, (are)
8. LV, (will become)
9. AV, (walked)
10. AV, (will eat)

B. Sample Answers

1. One such craft <u>looked</u> all over Mars some years ago.

2. Mars <u>looks</u> a little like the desert in America's Southwest.

3. The little Mars explorer <u>photographed</u> the surface for many weeks.

Open-Book Test, p. 53

Short Answer

1. Hana is on the ship during much of the story, but the important events are revealed in a flashback that takes place in Japan. The last part of the story takes place at Angel Island, in San Francisco, and on a ferry to Oakland.

   Difficulty: *Average*   **Objective:** *Literary Analysis*

2. The reference to thatched roofs and the absence of references to machinery suggest that the story takes place in the past. Details like "fields of golden rice" and "plum white mushrooms" suggest that Hana comes from an agricultural community. Descriptions like "bright," "golden," and "flaming colors" suggest that the place is beautiful.

   Difficulty: *Easy*   **Objective:** *Literary Analysis*

3. Hana feels homesick ("she longed with childlike intensity to be home again") and regretful ("why did I ever leave Japan? she wondered bitterly").

   Difficulty: *Average*   **Objective:** *Interpretation*

4. The main difference is that Taro lives outside Japan.

   Difficulty: *Easy*   **Objective:** *Reading*

5. Hana appears to think that women should receive a high-school education and hold opinions of their own and not just accept the opinions of the men in their

family. It seems, therefore, that Hana favors a change in the social structure.

Difficulty: *Average* **Objective:** *Vocabulary*

6. Hana "understood" that it would not be proper for him to reveal his feelings to her; she "would have recoiled from a man who bared his intimate thoughts to her so soon."

Difficulty: *Easy* **Objective:** *Interpretation*

7. Hana thinks the marriage will help her escape from her village and her family, which she finds "smothering." Just before arriving in California, Hana hopes that her apartment there will be "luxuriously furnished" and that she will have a servant.

Difficulty: *Challenging* **Objective:** *Interpretation*

8. The questions would be personal, and the examinations would require physical contact. Hana probably thinks such intimacy is improper and, therefore, insulting and even dishonorable.

Difficulty: *Average* **Objective:** *Vocabulary*

9. Hana is anxious about getting sea sick on the ferry ride from San Francisco to Oakland. Taro and Hana laugh and the tension and awkwardness between them eases. In particular, Hana does not seem unhappy when she remembers that Taro is the man she will marry. The future seems bright.

Difficulty: *Challenging* **Objective:** *Literary Analysis*

10. Sample answers:
Hana: is twenty-one years old; would like to be a teacher
Hana and Taro: are Japanese; laugh at Hana's idea that the ferry ride to Oakland will be as long and difficult as the voyage from Japan
Taro: is thirty-one years old; runs a small shop
Their shared background means that they probably share values and customs.

Difficulty: *Average* **Objective:** *Reading*

Essay

11. Students should mention these points: Oka Village is a place where Hana has felt "smothered," but she recalls its natural beauty with longing; the ship is unpleasant because the lower deck smells of fish and Hana is seasick, homesick, and uncertain about the future; and California is completely foreign and unknown to her.

Difficulty: *Easy* **Objective:** *Essay*

12. Students should understand that Hana has a positive, adventuresome outlook. They may describe some of her challenges—for example, she is marrying a man whom she does not know well and who looks older than she expected, and she will be living in an urban environment surrounded by a foreign culture about which she apparently knows very little. Students may also point out that Hana sought these challenges because she wanted a way of life that was different from what was available to her in Japan. Her determination, along with the kindness Taro shows, suggests that she will have the resources to overcome the challenges.

Difficulty: *Average* **Objective:** *Essay*

13. Hana expects Taro to look younger (she is surprised that he is "already turning bald") and to have formal manners (because he grew up in Japan); she hopes (and perhaps expects) that he is wealthy (with a "luxuriously furnished" apartment and perhaps a servant). Taro may expect Hana to be young, shy, and ignorant of American culture because that is probably what the other Japanese brides in arranged marriages to Japanese men in American have been like. He knows from his correspondence that she is from a good family. Like Hana's brother-in-law, he may expect that a wife should be obedient and should not express radical ideas.

Difficulty: *Challenging* **Objective:** *Essay*

14. Students will probably conclude that Hana's decision resolves the conflicts with her family. First, Hana has been in conflict with her mother because her mother has been eager for her to marry. The marriage to Taro eliminates that conflict. Second, by leaving Japan to marry, she is eliminating the conflict with her sister's husband, who dislikes her "radical" ideas and, Hana believes, "would be pleased to be rid of her."

Difficulty: *Average* **Objective:** *Essay*

Oral Response

15. Oral responses should be clear, well organized, and well supported by appropriate examples from the selection.

Difficulty: *Average* **Objective:** *Oral Interpretation*

"Tears of Autumn" by Yoshiko Uchida

Selection Test A, p. 56

Critical Reading

1. ANS: C	DIF: Easy	OBJ: Literary Analysis
2. ANS: D	DIF: Easy	OBJ: Comprehension
3. ANS: B	DIF: Easy	OBJ: Interpretation
4. ANS: C	DIF: Easy	OBJ: Interpretation
5. ANS: A	DIF: Easy	OBJ: Comprehension
6. ANS: A	DIF: Easy	OBJ: Reading
7. ANS: C	DIF: Easy	OBJ: Comprehension
8. ANS: B	DIF: Easy	OBJ: Reading
9. ANS: D	DIF: Easy	OBJ: Literary Analysis
10. ANS: A	DIF: Easy	OBJ: Interpretation
11. ANS: D	DIF: Easy	OBJ: Interpretation

Vocabulary and Grammar

12. ANS: B	DIF: Easy	OBJ: Grammar
13. ANS: B	DIF: Easy	OBJ: Vocabulary
14. ANS: D	DIF: Easy	OBJ: Grammar
15. ANS: C	DIF: Easy	OBJ: Vocabulary

Essay

16. Students might write: Dear Mother, My trip across the ocean was very difficult, and I was ill for much of it. When I arrived in America, I had to wait for a few days before meeting Taro so that the authorities could make sure I was healthy enough to enter the country. Taro does not look like the picture we saw of him, but he is not bad-looking. I have grown fond of him and of this new country. I am learning about Taro's business and hope to help him in it as I learn more. The city is busy, and there are many more people than in our village. The Americans are friendly, and I have even learned a little English. I hope you and my sisters are well. Your daughter, Hana

Difficulty: *Easy*

Objective: *Essay*

17. Students might choose to discuss the setting of Hana's village in Japan, the ship on which she travels to California, and the town of Oakland where Taro lives. Hana's father was a large landowner who employed servants and field hands. Since his death, however, Hana has lived a less privileged life in the country. She enjoys the beauty of her surroundings, and she thinks longingly of the rice fields and maple trees as she travels uncomfortably on the ship. The town of Oakland is bigger than Hana's village, and more urban. Taro owns a business and lives in rooms above it. This living arrangement will probably be more cramped and noisy than what Hana is used to.

Difficulty: *Easy*

Objective: *Essay*

18. Students will probably conclude that Hana's decision resolves the conflicts with her family. First, Hana has been in conflict with her mother because her mother has been eager for her to marry. The marriage to Taro eliminates that conflict. Second, by leaving Japan to marry, she resolves the conflict with her sister's husband, who dislikes her "radical" ideas and, Hana believes, "would be pleased to be rid of her."

Difficulty: *Average*

Objective: *Essay*

Selection Test B, p. 59

Critical Reading

1. ANS: C DIF: Average OBJ: Literary Analysis
2. ANS: A DIF: Challenging OBJ: Comprehension
3. ANS: D DIF: Challenging OBJ: Interpretation
4. ANS: B DIF: Challenging OBJ: Interpretation
5. ANS: D DIF: Average OBJ: Comprehension
6. ANS: C DIF: Average OBJ: Interpretation
7. ANS: C DIF: Average OBJ: Comprehension
8. ANS: A DIF: Average OBJ: Interpretation
9. ANS: B DIF: Average OBJ: Literary Analysis

10. ANS: D DIF: Average OBJ: Reading
11. ANS: B DIF: Average OBJ: Interpretation
12. ANS: A DIF: Average OBJ: Reading
13. ANS: C DIF: Average OBJ: Literary Analysis
14. ANS: B DIF: Challenging OBJ: Reading
15. ANS: B DIF: Average OBJ: Literary Analysis

Vocabulary and Grammar

16. ANS: C DIF: Challenging OBJ: Vocabulary
17. ANS: B DIF: Average OBJ: Vocabulary
18. ANS: A DIF: Average OBJ: Vocabulary
19. ANS: A DIF: Average OBJ: Grammar

Essay

20. Hana, indeed, faces a challenging adjustment in moving from Japan to America. She is an educated young woman who wants to escape the narrow horizons of life on the family farm, and to do so, she sails halfway around the world to marry a man she has never met. At first, she is seasick and overcome with worry, and she misses her home. She is surprised to see that Taro looks older than she expected. However, when she experiences his warmth and humor, her hope is restored. Hana is the kind of person whose positive and adventuresome attitude will help her overcome her doubts and fears.

Difficulty: *Average*

Objective: *Essay*

21. Here is one set of responses students might provide: Hana expects Taro to look younger than he does. Since he was raised in Japan, she expects him to be formal in his behavior. Because he owns his own business, she might expect him to be wealthy (she wonders about brocades and lacquers). She probably expects him to know English. Taro probably expects a woman who has the courage and independence to travel a long way to try life in a new country. He probably also expects her to be somewhat nervous and shy.

Difficulty: *Challenging*

Objective: *Essay*

22. Students will probably conclude that Hana's decision resolves the conflicts with her family. First, Hana has been in conflict with her mother because her mother has been eager for her to marry. The marriage to Taro eliminates that conflict. Second, by leaving Japan to marry, she is eliminating the conflict with her sister's husband, who dislikes her "radical" ideas and, Hana believes, "would be pleased to be rid of her."

Difficulty: *Average*

Objective: *Essay*

"Hamadi" by Naomi Shihab Nye

Vocabulary Warm-up Exercises, p. 63

A. 1. local
2. available
3. international
4. crates
5. contagious
6. particularly
7. occasionally
8. purified

B. Sample Answers

1. A person riding a roller coaster for the first time would feel *giddy* because the ride is so exciting.
2. Just last week I had a *significant* moment with my brother when he asked my advice about his girlfriend.
3. Great movies begin and end *dramatically* so that you will become emotionally involved and remember them.
4. While riding in a *rickety* car, I might hear clanking and sputtering sounds.
5. I would describe my haircut in a *wry* way because I think using humor helps you feel better.
6. A young child usually does not have enough life experiences to be called *worldly*.
7. If I were *focusing* on *carolers* and their songs, I would probably feel joy and delight.

Reading Warm-up A, p. 64

Sample Answers

1. air; *Purified* means "made pure or clean."
2. (area nearby); Our most popular *local* food has to be the apples that bring visitors here every fall.
3. (from around the world); Palestine is a foreign land, and an *international* restaurant specializes in foreign foods.
4. (nuts); I have *occasionally* seen cheese served on top of salads.
5. Roasted lamb; A meal that is *particularly* special to me is the turkey and stuffing we eat every Thanksgiving.
6. (artichokes); I've mostly seen fruits and vegetables *available* in *crates*.
7. (The love for these ingredients); *Contagious* means "spread quickly from person to person."

Reading Warm-up B, p. 65

Sample Answers

1. I am lucky that I can afford to live in such a place; You might say something with a lot of feeling when you say it *dramatically*.
2. The writer might be *wry* because she is not too pleased about being in the retirement home, but she expresses her feelings with humor.

3. (thinking), (ability to function); The word *significant* is important in this sentence because it seems the writer might have some problems in this area, even if she doesn't consider them to be important.
4. If I had a *rickety* body, I might have problems walking and making any quick actions.
5. The writer is *focusing* on getting her stiff fingers to work as she buttons her coat.
6. sing holiday tunes; I think it would be fun to join the *carolers*, as they bring joy to the residents of the retirement home.
7. (laughing), (carefree); Someone who is *giddy* is excited about something.
8. A person who is *worldly* has probably had so many different life experiences that nothing seems too interesting anymore.

Writing About the Big Question, p. 66

A. 1. stalemate
2. injury
3. argument, violence
4. reaction

B. Sample Answers

1. One year, I wanted to invite a friend's family to share our Thanksgiving. This caused a big argument at home because my sister did not like to interact with that family.
2. We solved the conflict by agreeing to a compromise. My mom suggested that we invite the family over just for dessert.

C. Sample Answer

Resolving emotional conflicts can be difficult because sometimes we cannot apply logic to our emotions. Our hearts and feelings get in the way of making good decisions. Some wise advice is to make a list of pros and cons for any difficult decision. The longer list can make the right choice clear.

Reading: Compare and Contrast, p. 67

Sample Answers

1. Susan's father visits his relatives in Jerusalem once a year.
2. Hamadi says he meets with his cousins every day by remembering them.
3. Susan visits Hamadi and includes him in outings.
4. Susan's father thinks inviting Hamadi to go caroling is "ridiculous" because Hamadi's English is not good, and he does not know the words to the songs.
5. Hamadi is "thrilled" to be invited and arrives right on time, with dates in his pocket for everyone.
6. Susan invites Hamadi because she enjoys his company and is tired of being with the same people all the time.

Literary Analysis: Character Traits, p. 68

Sample Answers

A. Detail: lives in a run-down hotel with few furnishings; Trait Revealed: does not value material things

Detail: reads a lot; Trait Revealed: has a good imagination; lives in his mind; enjoys solitude

Detail: enjoys looking closely at interesting postage stamps; Trait Revealed: notices details and enjoys beauty

Detail: visits his relatives in Lebanon by thinking about them; Trait Revealed: values memories of important people in his past

Detail: formally expresses good manners; brings dates to share; Trait Revealed: acts kindly toward others

Detail: notices Tracy's pain and comforts her; Trait Revealed: shows sensitivity to others

Detail: says he is "thrilled" to go caroling; Trait Revealed: is open to experimentation

B. Hamadi is a caring person who appreciates family and friends. He values learning through reading and having new experiences.

Vocabulary Builder, p. 69

Answers

A. 1. F; Refugees do not choose to leave their homeland; usually they leave because they are in danger there.

2. T; Having a good friend move away is sad.

3. F: Most people do not look forward to tedious tasks because such tasks are repetitive and boring.

4. T: An expansive person has a free, open, and generous nature.

5. T: Orphaned baby animals need mother figures to nurture them and teach them how to behave; a surrogate mother is a substitute for a real mother.

6. F: An obscure fact is one that few people know or care about.

B. 1. The *absentee* list included the names of all those who did not come to the meeting.

2. The *payee* received a check that took care of the bill.

3. The *employee* benefits apply only to those who work here.

Enrichment: Using an Encyclopedia as a Resource, p. 70

Sample Answers

Geography: country in western Asia, on the eastern coast of the Mediterranean Sea; capital is Beirut; two mountain ranges with a fertile river valley in between; warm summers and mild, rainy winters; valley is rich farm region: oranges, olives

People: mostly Arabs; official language is Arabic; diverse religious community; more than half the people are Muslim; high population density; $^9/_{10}$ urban; excellent educational system; jobs mainly in the service industries

History: was a major shipping port and banking center of the Middle East; in late twentieth century had civil war and foreign occupation; reconstruction in progress

Open-Book Test, p. 71

Short Answer

1. It is unimportant to Hamadi that the hotel room is "spartan." He says that all he needs to be "home" is a white handkerchief spread over a tabletop and an extra pair of shoes. Hamadi is more interested in books, ideas, and people than in having a nice home filled with possessions.

   Difficulty: *Average*   **Objective:** *Interpretation*

2. Hamadi says that the stamps help him focus on the word *love*. At the end of the story, he shows his belief in love by comforting Tracy and offering his thoughts about life.

   Difficulty: *Average*   **Objective:** *Literary Analysis*

3. Unlike Tracy, Susan is not interested in having a boyfriend. The narrator states that "Susan didn't want a boyfriend."

   Difficulty: *Easy*   **Objective:** *Reading*

4. Tracy's words are probably not meant as a compliment. Tracy does not like what Susan has said—that Tracy wants to own Eddie and not truly to love him—and probably feels that Susan is "preaching" to her.

   Difficulty: *Challenging*   **Objective:** *Interpretation*

5. Hamadi is "thrilled" by the invitation. His eagerness reflects a love for new experiences. Hamadi also believes in sharing things (such as an orange or a bag of dates), so he is probably glad that Susan wants to share this experience with him.

   Difficulty: *Easy*   **Objective:** *Interpretation*

6. Susan wants an active life. Her bond with Hamadi, who tells her that "anything can happen," shows this trait. Her desire to expand the view of her English Club by inviting Hamadi to go Christmas caroling with them is further evidence. Alternatively, students may say that Susan can be opinionated. She also shows that trait when lecturing Tracy about her feelings for Eddie.

   Difficulty: *Challenging*   **Objective:** *Literary Analysis*

7. Hamadi is playing a role in her life that her grandmother once played. He and her grandmother have the same cultural background, may be of the same generation, and appear to hold old-fashioned values (the grandmother bakes bread in an old outdoor oven; Hamadi does not watch television).

   Difficulty: *Average*   **Objective:** *Reading*

8. Yes, Tracy is a flat character. All that readers see is that she wants Eddie to show an interest in her. Susan tries to change Tracy's thinking, but Tracy does not change.

   Difficulty: *Easy*   **Objective:** *Literary Analysis*

9. Possible answers:

   Similarities: Both are open to new experiences; Hamadi does not marry, and Susan does not want a boyfriend.

   Differences: Hamadi lives alone, whereas Susan lives with her parents; Hamadi does not want to remember his mother in Palestine, but Susan enjoys remembering her grandmother outside Jerusalem; Hamadi does not know the words to the Christmas carols, but Susan does.

The similarities are more important because they involve the things or people they care for.

Difficulty: *Average*   **Objective:** *Reading*

10. *Melancholy* means "sad or depressed." Hamadi is not at all a melancholy character; he is content with his life, and he loves being with people and having new experiences.

Difficulty: *Average*   **Objective:** *Vocabulary*

Essay

11. A *round character* is a complex character, one with several character traits. Hamadi's advice shows that he is complex. He cares about simple, everyday matters. He is also thoughtful and cares about people and the meaning of life.

Difficulty: *Easy*   **Objective:** *Essay*

12. Students should explain that Hamadi's "spartan" room shows that he thinks little of possessions; he is more interested in reading and learning. Students should also recognize that Hamadi is friendly and outgoing, as his eagerness to go caroling demonstrates. He has sympathy for Tracy, too, but he urges her to move beyond her sadness.

Difficulty: *Average*   **Objective:** *Essay*

13. Students may make any of these points: As a teenager, Susan is old enough to ask a lot of questions, and Hamadi likes to think about the kinds of questions Susan asks. Susan realizes that her grandmother never seemed to rush. She now recognizes that Hamadi, too, takes his time, noticing things and enjoying life. Susan is old enough to be reading the work of Kahlil Gibran, whose ideas are new to her. She is attracted by Hamadi's connection to Gibran.

Difficulty: *Challenging*   **Objective:** *Essay*

14. Because Hamadi is practical, he would most likely say that it is impossible to resolve all conflicts. His advice to Tracy suggests that he believes that when a person cannot resolve a conflict, he or she should keep going instead of giving up. Hamadi probably feels a conflict about his separation from his homeland. He may have resolved it by not speaking the language that reminds him of his mother yet not adopting American customs the way Susan's uncles have. In other words, he has given up certain parts of his past without filling the void with something else. His decision not to marry may also reflect a conflict. By staying single he has not had to earn more money to support a family, and therefore he has not risked doing something that might compromise his principles.

Difficulty: *Average*   **Objective:** *Essay*

Oral Response

15. Oral responses should be clear, well organized, and well supported by appropriate examples from the selection.

Difficulty: *Average*   **Objective:** *Oral Interpretation*

Selection Test A, p. 74

Critical Reading

1. ANS: A	DIF: Easy	OBJ: Comprehension
2. ANS: C	DIF: Easy	OBJ: Reading
3. ANS: B	DIF: Easy	OBJ: Comprehension
4. ANS: A	DIF: Easy	OBJ: Literary Analysis
5. ANS: D	DIF: Easy	OBJ: Literary Analysis
6. ANS: A	DIF: Easy	OBJ: Literary Analysis
7. ANS: C	DIF: Easy	OBJ: Interpretation
8. ANS: A	DIF: Easy	OBJ: Comprehension
9. ANS: B	DIF: Easy	OBJ: Literary Analysis
10. ANS: C	DIF: Easy	OBJ: Interpretation
11. ANS: A	DIF: Easy	OBJ: Comprehension

Vocabulary and Grammar

12. ANS: A	DIF: Easy	OBJ: Grammar
13. ANS: D	DIF: Easy	OBJ: Vocabulary
14. ANS: C	DIF: Easy	OBJ: Grammar
15. ANS: C	DIF: Easy	OBJ: Vocabulary

Essay

16. Students might identify with Susan because she likes to read and is interested more in ideas than in having a boyfriend. They might feel a kinship with her because she is working on figuring out answers to questions about how people live fulfilling lives. They might admire her for building a friendship with Hamadi and for including him in her circle of friends. They might also mention that they like the way she supports her friend Tracy. Students might identify more with Tracy because she is more interested in a romantic attachment and more involved in the social side of high school. She is also interested in books and ideas, and she is open to Susan's ideas.

Difficulty: *Easy*

Objective: *Essay*

17. Students should describe Hamadi's room, which illustrates his lack of interest in having many possessions or living in a more modern building. They might note that he enjoys reading and learning. He has learned some Spanish and takes great pleasure in it. He notices details, as indicated in his interest in the stamps he has brought home to look at. He remembers his relatives and his homeland, but has no interest in visiting them in person. He would rather use his imagination to remember them. Hamadi is friendly and outgoing, as shown by his enthusiastic response to Susan's invitation to go caroling. He shows sympathy toward Tracy in her sadness, but he focuses on moving on beyond sadness. He has a positive, open attitude toward life.

Difficulty: *Easy*

Objective: *Essay*

18. Hamadi is practical, so he would probably say that it is impossible to resolve all conflicts. His advice to Tracy suggests that he believes that when a person cannot resolve a conflict, he or she should keep going instead of giving up. Hamadi probably feels a conflict about his separation from his homeland. He may have resolved it by not speaking the language that reminds him of his mother. Yet, he does not adopt American customs the way Susan's uncles have.

Difficulty: *Average*

Objective: *Essay*

Selection Test B, p. 77

Critical Reading

1. ANS: B	DIF: Average	OBJ: Literary Analysis
2. ANS: D	DIF: Average	OBJ: Comprehension
3. ANS: C	DIF: Average	OBJ: Comprehension
4. ANS: C	DIF: Challenging	OBJ: Interpretation
5. ANS: C	DIF: Average	OBJ: Literary Analysis
6. ANS: A	DIF: Average	OBJ: Interpretation
7. ANS: D	DIF: Average	OBJ: Reading
8. ANS: B	DIF: Average	OBJ: Literary Analysis
9. ANS: B	DIF: Average	OBJ: Interpretation
10. ANS: D	DIF: Challenging	OBJ: Literary Analysis
11. ANS: B	DIF: Average	OBJ: Interpretation
12. ANS: C	DIF: Challenging	OBJ: Literary Analysis
13. ANS: A	DIF: Challenging	OBJ: Reading
14. ANS: B	DIF: Average	OBJ: Literary Analysis

Vocabulary and Grammar

15. ANS: C	DIF: Average	OBJ: Vocabulary
16. ANS: B	DIF: Average	OBJ: Grammar
17. ANS: C	DIF: Challenging	OBJ: Grammar

Essay

18. Students might describe Susan as a typical high school student who spends time with friends like Tracy and participates in school activities like the literary magazine. She is beginning to think beyond her life at school, however, by branching out into books of her own choosing and getting to know Hamadi, a family friend. She is more interested in Hamadi's simple approach to life and stress on imagination than in having a boyfriend. Students might describe Hamadi as an older person who has lived by himself after emigrating from Lebanon to America. He has pursued a life of the mind more than one that includes many people and possessions. He is open to new experiences and is a compassionate person, as seen in his interest in Susan and his response to Tracy's tears.

Difficulty: *Average*

Objective: *Essay*

19. Students might note that Susan is finally old enough to ask herself the questions that Hamadi has spent his life asking. Further, at this point in her life, Susan has pleasant memories of her years with her grandmother near Jerusalem, remembers that her grandmother never seemed to rush, and now notes that Hamadi seems to have the same approach to life—that is, to take time to notice and enjoy it. Susan is reading the work of Kahlil Gibran, a writer who has ideas new to her. Therefore, she is fascinated that Hamadi, also interested in Gibran's writing, claims to have been Gibran's roommate. Susan likes Hamadi's ideas about using memory and imagination fully in order to experience life to its fullest.

Difficulty: *Average*

Objective: *Essay*

20. Students should point out that Hamadi's advice probably helps Tracy at the time of the story because Hamadi shows her that he takes her pain seriously, even as he gives her tools to help her through it. Susan would recall this advice in the future whenever feeling sad, even after college. Remembering his words would help her get through the disappointments that are bound to happen in everyone's life.

Difficulty: *Challenging*

Objective: *Essay*

21. Because Hamadi is practical, he would most likely say that it is impossible to resolve all conflicts. His advice to Tracy suggests that he believes that when a person cannot resolve a conflict, he or she should keep going instead of giving up. Hamadi probably feels a conflict about his separation from his homeland. He may have resolved it by not speaking the language that reminds him of his mother, yet not adopting American customs the way Susan's uncles have. In other words, he has given up certain parts of his past without filling the void with something else. His decision not to marry may also reflect a conflict. By staying single he has not had to earn more money to support a family, and therefore he has not risked doing something that might compromise his principles.

Difficulty: *Average*

Objective: *Essay*

"The Tell-Tale Heart" by Edgar Allan Poe

Vocabulary Warm-up Exercises, p. 81

A. 1. instinct
2. chatted
3. enthusiasm
4. hideous
5. distinct
6. boldly
7. undid
8. grief

B. Sample Answers

1. With difficulty, I *detected* the lizard in the grass because it had changed its color to green.

2. The police officer's *suspicion* lessened as the clues all proved false.

3. As the woman tossed and turned, you could see the *agony* of her constant back pain.

4. I became very upset that my friend *continually* walked home after school without me.

5. The angry man *raved* about waiting so long for his meal.

6. My grandmother loved watching us since we rarely *vexed* her.

7. As the whale *arises* from the depths of the ocean, it gets ready to blow.

8. A *wary* driver regularly checks the rearview mirror.

Reading Warm-up A, p. 82

Sample Answers

1. her eyes were like magnets, drawn to the sparkling rhinestones and metal studs; boldly reached out her hand to touch the jacket

2. That went against our strict "hands off my stuff" rule; I heard a *distinct* sound that scared me, but I *boldly* entered the room anyway.

3. (losing my jacket); Whereas *grief* involves great sadness, *enthusiasm* usually includes feelings of joy.

4. Since *chatted* means "talked in a friendly, informal fashion," it seems natural that *casually* could be used to describe this type of talking.

5. for doubting my sister's innocence; I find it *hideous* when a person says one thing and then does another.

6. lid; When the actor in the mystery play *undid* the curtains, the audience gasped.

7. (found the hidden key); I can find my way from place to place by *instinct* and don't need to use a map.

Reading Warm-up B, p. 83

Sample Answers

1. Not knowing the facts about mental illness; *Agony* means "great suffering."

2. (psychosis); Day turns into night *continually* in the world.

3. A person with psychosis is *vexed* at imaginary things he or she has *detected*, or the person has *raved* about strange topics.

4. that someone could harm them; A *suspicion* is an idea, or feeling, that something is wrong.

5. Someone might be *wary*, or especially cautious, because he or she fears something bad might happen.

6. (whatever . . . may be upsetting the person); *Arises* means "comes up."

Writing About the Big Question, p. 84

A. 1. irritate
2. argument
3. viewpoint
4. insecurity

B. Sample Answers

1. I find it irritating when other people crack their knuckles. I also find it irritating when someone borrows something from me and doesn't return it.

2. When someone borrows something and doesn't return it, my solution is to ask for it back. Then, next time they want to borrow something, my reaction is to say no.

C. Sample Answer

When torn between doing right and wrong, a person may foolishly make the wrong choice and regret it forever. When you are faced with such a choice, do not think twice! Always pick the right way, the way your conscience guides you. Otherwise, you might not be able to make it up to the people you hurt.

Reading: Identify Characters' Perspectives, p. 85

Sample Answers

1. The narrator feels nervous, but he proceeds with great caution.

2. The old man is startled at the noise, sits up in bed, and asks, "Who's there?"

3. The narrator grows furious upon seeing the eye, and he starts to hear a heart beating.

4. The old man has been awake, eyes open, his fear growing. He finally groans in terror.

5. The old man shrieks once.

6. The narrator smiles happily. He continues to hear a heart beating.

Literary Analysis: Character Traits, p. 86

Sample Answers

A. Detail: watches the old man asleep every night for seven days; Trait Revealed: patient, cautious, detail-oriented, logical

Detail: imagines with pleasure the terror the old man must be feeling; Trait Revealed: intuitive, emotional, sadistic

Detail: grows furious at seeing the eye; Trait Revealed: quick to anger

Detail: worries about the beating heart; Trait Revealed: tense, anxious

Detail: is first calm, then agitated, with police; Trait Revealed: unstable emotionally

Open-Book Test, p. 109

Short Answer

1. Realistic details include the place names (the Stewart River, the Yukon, Dawson) and the description of the way of life (the tent, the trip to get the mail, the dog sleds, and the scarcity of firewood).
   Difficulty: *Average* **Objective:** *Literary Analysis*

2. The slide is too steep and slippery to allow Dilham to descend. He thinks that if he goes up to the crest of the cliff, he will find an easier way down.
   Difficulty: *Average* **Objective:** *Interpretation*

3. Swanson is probably relieved that Dilham is safe. Swanson goes out to the mountain to wait for Dilham. This act suggests that Swanson was worried.
   Difficulty: *Average* **Objective:** *Interpretation*

4. Young dogs cannot sustain a long run because they are not strong enough to keep up.
   Difficulty: *Average* **Objective:** *Vocabulary*

5. The dogs are afraid of the glow. The fact that they stop running even though they are not tired is evidence of their fear.
   Difficulty: *Easy* **Objective:** *Interpretation*

6. The source of the glow must be a real event. It probably has a scientific explanation.
   Difficulty: *Challenging* **Objective:** *Literary Analysis*

7. The reader does not know who the narrator of "Up the Slide" is. He does not identify himself, so he seems to be Jack London, the author of the story. The narrator of "A Glow in the Dark" is Gary Paulsen, the author of the story. He uses the word *I* to identify himself in the story.
   Difficulty: *Challenging* **Objective:** *Literary Analysis*

8. Sled dogs are more important in "A Glow in the Dark." The most important part of the narrative is the description of a mysterious light and the dog's reaction to it. The most important part of "Up the Slide" is a description of Dilham's struggle to get off the mountain.
   Difficulty: *Easy* **Objective:** *Literary Analysis*

9. The plot and the characters in "Up the Slide" are made up, but the events and the characters in "A Glow in the Dark" are real.
   Difficulty: *Average* **Objective:** *Literary Analysis*

10. *Similarities:* tough outdoorsmen; *Evidence:* Both men are accustomed to harsh conditions in a cold climate and travel by dogsled.
    Similarities: possibly overconfident; *Evidence:* Dilham climbs up a steep ice-covered mountain; Paulsen runs his dogsled in the dark without a head lamp.
    Difficulty: *Average* **Objective:** *Literary Analysis*

Essay

11. The author of a fictional narrative may invent the story's characters, plot, and setting. In "Up the Slide," Jack London invented the character Clay Dilham and the things that happened to him. However, London included realistic details, such as the Yukon and the town of Dawson. The author of a nonfiction narrative must tell only about real people and real events. Paulsen describes something that actually happened to him.
    Difficulty: *Easy* **Objective:** *Essay*

12. Both characters display a mix of courage and foolhardiness. Dilham does so by climbing up the cliff. Paulsen does so by running with the dogs in the dark without a light. As Dilham faces the challenges of the climb, he proves that he is courageous and intelligent. As Paulsen interacts with his dogs, he shows good-natured affection. Both men also overcome fears and show that they are highly attuned to nature.
    Difficulty: *Average* **Objective:** *Essay*

13. Students may recognize that either kind of work has the potential to be exciting and that the amount of excitement conveyed depends on the writer's ability to convey it. Nonetheless, some students may prefer fictional works, probably because the author has the freedom to invent exciting events. Students who prefer nonfictional works are likely to say that the imagination cannot produce anything scarier than a real-life event. If students base their judgments on the two selections, they will most likely say that Jack London does a better job at creating excitement than Gary Paulsen does. They might note that London puts his character in a life-or-death situation, whereas Paulsen is never in great danger.
    Difficulty: *Challenging* **Objective:** *Essay*

14. Students should point out that both characters face fear. Clay loses his nerve after he falls in the avalanche. He must overcome his terror and climb upward again before he freezes to death. The narrator of "A Glow in the Dark" is terrified of what he imagines is a ghost. He only gets over his fear when the dogs show him it is a stump. Students may note that both characters overcome their fear by facing it directly.
    Difficulty: *Average* **Objective:** *Essay*

Oral Response

15. Oral responses should be clear, well organized, and well supported by appropriate examples from the selections.
    Difficulty: *Average* **Objective:** *Oral Interpretation*

Selection Test A, p. 112

Critical Reading

1. ANS: B	DIF: Easy	OBJ: Interpretation
2. ANS: C	DIF: Easy	OBJ: Interpretation
3. ANS: A	DIF: Easy	OBJ: Literary Analysis
4. ANS: D	DIF: Easy	OBJ: Comprehension
5. ANS: B	DIF: Easy	OBJ: Comprehension
6. ANS: C	DIF: Easy	OBJ: Comprehension
7. ANS: A	DIF: Easy	OBJ: Interpretation
8. ANS: D	DIF: Easy	OBJ: Comprehension
9. ANS: D	DIF: Easy	OBJ: Literary Analysis
10. ANS: B	DIF: Easy	OBJ: Interpretation

11. ANS: C   DIF: Easy   OBJ: Comprehension
12. ANS: A   DIF: Easy   OBJ: Literary Analysis
13. ANS: C   DIF: Easy   OBJ: Literary Analysis

Vocabulary

14. ANS: D   DIF: Easy   OBJ: Vocabulary
15. ANS: B   DIF: Easy   OBJ: Vocabulary

Essay

16. In "Up the Slide," Clay Dilham's decision to take the journey in thirty minutes shows great self-confidence or conceit; his attempt to get to the fallen tree shows courage and determination. In "A Glow in the Dark," Gary Paulsen's decision to run the dogs without a lamp may show either bravery or foolishness; his actions toward his dogs show that he is affectionate and good-natured; and his decision to approach the light shows that he is courageous. Students' preferences for one character over another will vary, but should be supported with reasons.

Difficulty: *Easy*

Objective: *Essay*

17. A fictional narrative tells a story about made-up characters or events. For example, in "Up the Slide," the character of Clay Dilham and the events of his journey are all imaginary. However, the author of a fictional narrative can borrow details from real life, such as the Yukon River and the town of Dawson. A nonfictional narrative, on the other hand, tells *only* about events and people from real life. Nothing in a nonfictional narrative can be made up. For example, the author of "A Glow in the Dark" describes something that actually happened to him. Even though he tells the story in an exciting way that makes it *sound* fictional, every detail in the story is actually true.

Difficulty: *Easy*

Objective: *Essay*

18. Students should point out that both characters face fear. Clay loses his nerve after he falls in the avalanche. He must overcome his terror and climb upward again before he freezes to death. The narrator of "A Glow in the Dark" is terrified of what he imagines is a ghost He only gets over his fear when the dogs show him it is a stump. Students may note that both characters overcome their fear by facing it directly.

Difficulty: *Average*

Objective: *Essay*

Selection Test B, p. 115

Critical Reading

1. ANS: A   DIF: Average   OBJ: Interpretation
2. ANS: D   DIF: Challenging   OBJ: Comprehension
3. ANS: C   DIF: Average   OBJ: Interpretation
4. ANS: D   DIF: Average   OBJ: Literary Analysis

5. ANS: B   DIF: Average   OBJ: Comprehension
6. ANS: A   DIF: Challenging   OBJ: Literary Analysis
7. ANS: C   DIF: Challenging   OBJ: Comprehension
8. ANS: B   DIF: Average   OBJ: Interpretation
9. ANS: D   DIF: Average   OBJ: Comprehension
10. ANS: A   DIF: Challenging   OBJ: Literary Analysis
11. ANS: C   DIF: Challenging   OBJ: Literary Analysis
12. ANS: D   DIF: Challenging   OBJ: Interpretation
13. ANS: D   DIF: Average   OBJ: Literary Analysis
14. ANS: C   DIF: Average   OBJ: Literary Analysis
15. ANS: A   DIF: Average   OBJ: Literary Analysis

Vocabulary

16. ANS: A   DIF: Average   OBJ: Vocabulary
17. ANS: B   DIF: Average   OBJ: Vocabulary
18. ANS: C   DIF: Challenging   OBJ: Vocabulary
19. ANS: A   DIF: Average   OBJ: Vocabulary

Essay

20. Students should note that the details of each story reveal a great deal about each character. In "Up the Slide," Clay's expedition shows that he loves a challenge; his reaction to each problem along the way shows intelligence and determination; and his underestimation of the time required for the outing and its risks shows his great self-confidence or his recklessness and youth. In "A Glow in the Dark," Gary Paulsen's choice to run the dogs without a light may show either his bravery or his foolishness; his reactions to his dogs show that he is affectionate and good-natured; his reaction to the light shows that he has an active imagination; and his investigation of the light shows his courage and curiosity.

Difficulty: *Average*

Objective: *Essay*

21. Students should define *narrative* as any type of writing that tells a story; they may mention that most narratives are told in chronological order. "Up the Slide" is a fictional narrative. Its characters and events are invented, although it borrows some details (such as the Yukon River and Moosehead Mountain) from real life. "A Glow in the Dark" is a nonfictional narrative. Everything in the story actually exists or occurred in real life. Some of the details that Paulsen includes, though, give the story the excitement of fiction. For example, his slow approach to the strange glow adds drama and suspense to the narrative.

Difficulty: *Average*

Objective: *Essay*

22. Students should point out that both characters face fear. Clay loses his nerve after he falls in the avalanche and must overcome his terror and climb upward again before he freezes. The narrator of "A Glow in the Dark" is terrified of what he imagines is a ghost and only gets over his fear when the dogs show him it is a stump. Students

thoughts and situations or that it forces readers to make too many inferences about the reality of the situation because Charlie himself often does not understand it.

Difficulty: *Average*

Objective: *Essay*

18. Students should recognize that the title underscores the attachment Charlie developed for Algernon, the white mouse used in a laboratory experiment. They should understand that what happens to Algernon eventually happens to Charlie and that seeing Algernon's deteriorating behavior is sad and disappointing for Charlie, but shows Charlie's persistent humanity.

Difficulty: *Average*

Objective: *Essay*

19. Students should explain that the wedge is the tension, or hatred, that results when his co-workers see the change in his intelligence. The tension is so strong that almost everyone signs a petition to have him fired; ultimately, Charlie quits his job because of it. Students may suggest that Charlie did not mean to cause trouble and could not have avoided it. Students should also explain that some of Charlie's co-workers accept him again when his mental state deteriorates, but that resolution of the problem is a tragedy for Charlie.

Difficulty: *Average*

Objective: *Essay*

"Charles" by Shirley Jackson

Vocabulary Warm-up Exercises, p. 146

A. 1. kindergarten
2. identified
3. warily
4. toughness
5. privileges
6. enormously
7. influence
8. respectfully

B. Sample Answers

1. F; *Passionately* and *prayerfully* suggest that a person is very involved.
2. F; A *haggard* person looks just the opposite—tired and worn out.
3. F; A person acting *scornfully* is one who acts without respect for someone or something.
4. F; I was born long after the *era*, or period, when cars came into wide use.
5. T; Fancy things are designed *elaborately*, with great care and detail.
6. T; *Corduroy* is a casual fabric, not appropriate for suits and other clothing worn to formal events.
7. F; A family *institution* occurs regularly.

Reading Warm-up A, p. 147

Sample Answers

1. child's garden; One thing I did in *kindergarten* was learn to count to ten.
2. (because they didn't see how playing could lead to learning); If you act *warily*, you are being cautious.
3. special; Two *privileges* I have are staying up until midnight on weekends and going to the movies on Saturday if I've done all my chores.
4. Froebel *identified* three ways of using the gifts.
5. (were opening in many countries); I am *enormously* fond of listening to music.
6. rein in, unruly; *Toughness* is very useful when trying to reach a difficult goal.
7. (the teacher and . . . one another); If I'm acting *respectfully*, I'm being polite because I think something or someone is important.
8. the idea that young children should be educated; My older brother has had a strong *influence* on me because he taught me about taking responsibility.

Reading Warm-up B, p. 148

Sample Answers

1. detailed; My sister planned her wedding *elaborately*, and it turned out perfect.
2. (dismissed them); We treated the players *scornfully* by booing at them.
3. We all felt so *passionately* about recycling that we organized a town clean-up committee.
4. tired; When I returned from a twenty-mile hike, my mom said I looked *haggard*.
5. (Tending to the tree); An *institution* at our house is playing touch football on Thanksgiving morning.
6. The *era* of the "adopt a tree" program was the school year. During the Revolutionary War *era*, our country won its freedom from Britain.
7. (overalls); The couch we used to have in our television room was covered with green *corduroy* material.
8. He mumbled *prayerfully* because he was really hoping that the tree was not Phyllis. When I passed the car accident, I said *prayerfully*, "I hope no one was hurt."

Writing About the Big Question, p. 149

A. 1. insecurity
2. interact
3. reaction
4. irritate

B. Sample Answers

1. I had to interact with a small group to prepare an oral presentation. One member of the group began to irritate me because she never did any work.
2. I asked why she wasn't participating. She said she didn't know what to do, so I showed her.

C. Sample Answer

Adjusting to new situations is always a challenge. Keep in mind that a new situation is a learning experience. If you did not have any new situations, life would be boring. Welcome the new experiences, and learn from them.

Reading: Notice Details to Make Inferences, p. 150

Sample Answers

1. Laurie does not behave as well as he did before starting school. Laurie is acting out because he is nervous about starting school.
2. Charles behaves badly in school. The narrator accepts Laurie's reports about Charles at face value.
3. Charles continues to behave badly. When the story took place, some teachers still washed children's mouths out with soap.

Literary Analysis: Point of View, p. 151

A. Sample Answers

1. The narrator, Laurie's mother, is somewhat upset to see her baby boy go off to school. A part of her seems to regret that he is getting older.
2. Most students will agree that the narrator has a sense of humor because of the details she chooses to report, including Laurie's rude poems, and the observations she makes. They may recognize that the story pokes fun at her and her husband for being fooled by the stories about Charles.
3. Because she is a devoted and unsuspecting parent, she does not recognize that Laurie is the real class troublemaker, in spite of many clues (such as the rude poems).

B. Students' responses should show an awareness of the other character's point of view.

Vocabulary Builder, p. 152

Sample Answers

A. 1. No, parents go <u>simultaneously</u> to meet with teachers.
2. She reports that Laurie has mostly <u>renounced</u> his bad behavior.
3. According to Laurie, Charles is <u>deprived</u> of his blackboard privileges because he threw chalk.
4. Laurie's mother expects Charles's mother to look <u>haggard</u> because of Laurie's reports concerning Charles's behavior.
5. When Laurie's father hears that Charles has been behaving well, he responds <u>cynically</u> because he assumes Charles is plotting further mischief.
6. To show that Charles is behaving <u>insolently</u> toward the teacher, Laurie says that Charles hit her.

B. 1. During a game, a sports announcer would be delivering messages about the plays, the players, and the stats.

2. People might denounce their political leaders for poor economic policies, lack of support for schools, and raising taxes.
3. When your pronunciation of a foreign language is excellent, you convey the message that you respect the other culture enough to take time to learn the language.

Enrichment: Child Development, p. 153

2. Laurie's behavior is immature for a five-year-old, who should be able to use the grammar he hears around him. Given his mother's reports, he hears standard English at home. It is likely his nonstandard speech is intentional and part of his misbehavior.
3. It is normal for Laurie, at five, to enjoy rhymes, though the rhymes he uses are somewhat rude.
4. It is normal for a five-year-old to tell stories and enjoy imaginative play.

"Flowers for Algernon" by Daniel Keyes
"Charles" by Shirley Jackson

Integrated Language Skills: Grammar, p. 154

The Present, Past, and Future Tenses

A. 1. present; The scientists used mice in their experiments; The scientists will use mice in their experiments.
2. future; Some children behave badly on the first day of school; Some children behaved badly on the first day of school.
3. past; He visits a psychologist twice a week; He will visit a psychologist twice a week.

B. Students should write one sentence in the past tense, one in the present tense, and one in the future tense, as well as underline the verbs and correctly identify each tense.

Open-Book Test, p. 157

Short Answer

1. The story is told from the first-person point of view by Laurie's mother. The point of view is clear from the first sentence, which begins "The day my son Laurie started kindergarten."

   Difficulty: *Easy* **Objective:** *Literary Analysis*
2. Laurie feels grown-up, bold, and rebellious. He has "renounced corduroy overalls with bibs" in favor of blue jeans. He swaggers and does not offer a good-bye wave.

   Difficulty: *Easy* **Objective:** *Reading*
3. Readers learn about Charles through Laurie's reports to his parents. Because the narrator knows only what Laurie tells her, the point of view is limited—that is, the narrator does not have full knowledge of all the details.

   Difficulty: *Average* **Objective:** *Literary Analysis*
4. Laurie's mother infers that Laurie stayed after school with the other children in the class to "watch" Charles, who has been given detention. Readers may infer that

Laurie's story is not true and that Laurie himself may have had to stay after class.

Difficulty: *Challenging* **Objective:** *Reading*

5. To "do a Charles" is to misbehave. The narrator gives a few examples: the baby's crying all afternoon, Laurie's pulling a mud-filled wagon through the kitchen, the husband's incident with the telephone cord. Any one of Charles's misbehaviors in class—throwing chalk, hitting the teacher, and so on—also qualifies.

Difficulty: *Easy* **Objective:** *Interpretation*

6. The father is doubtful that Charles's improved behavior is sincere or that it will last. He may base his belief that it "may mean he's only plotting" on his experience with his own children.

Difficulty: *Average* **Objective:** *Vocabulary*

7. *During the first Friday,* Charles throws chalk.

During the next Tuesday, Charles kicks the teacher's friend.

During the third and fourth weeks, Charles helps the teacher.

During the day of the second PTA meeting, Charles says a bad word and throws chalk. Charles may miss the attention he received when he was bad.

Difficulty: *Average* **Objective:** *Interpretation*

8. Laurie's parents are eager to see what a mother with such a wild child is like. At the meeting the narrator says she is looking for the person "who hid[es] the secret of Charles," but it seems likely that Laurie's parents are eager to find out if Charles's mother is flawed or weak.

Difficulty: *Challenging* **Objective:** *Interpretation*

9. The narrator realizes that Laurie has been talking about himself. Her realization is an inference because the information is not stated; she figures it out by putting the teacher's comment together with clues about Laurie's interest in reporting Charles's behavior.

Difficulty: *Average* **Objective:** *Reading*

10. The teacher would miss the element of Laurie's creation of Charles. It is clear from her closing comment that she has known nothing about Charles. On the other hand, her close contact with the children would allow her to add thoughtful insights about Laurie and humorous details about teaching a class of kindergarten children.

Difficulty: *Challenging* **Objective:** *Literary Analysis*

Essay

11. Students should understand that Laurie's mother will probably be shocked and upset when she realizes that Laurie is Charles—that all of Charles's misbehaviors are Laurie's. Students may predict that she will tell her husband and that together they will punish Charles. Students may also predict that the parents will feel foolish and may be concerned that they had not seen through Laurie's stories. Some students may predict that the parents will privately be impressed with Laurie's creativity in inventing the character of Charles.

Difficulty: *Easy* **Objective:** *Essay*

12. Students should recognize that Laurie misbehaves in school and lies about it at home. Some students may think that his misbehavior is a result of his being scared or upset by the big change that starting school represents, as is true of many children his age. Others may suggest that Laurie is overactive or has trouble socializing and that he enjoys the attention that his misbehavior attracts. Students might also point out that his parents are not especially aware of Laurie's feelings and are letting him get away with misbehavior at home, and those factors have made Laurie poorly prepared for the transition from the relatively free environment at home to the structured environment of the classroom.

Difficulty: *Average* **Objective:** *Essay*

13. Students should recognize that parents often fail to see negative traits in their beloved children. Students may point out that the mother is very attached to her son and thinks of him as a "sweet-voiced nursery-school tot," but she overlooks all the clues to the contrary, beginning with the "swaggering character who forgot to stop at the corner and wave good-bye." His parents do not comment when he slams the front door, shouts raucously, speaks insolently, and spills the baby's milk. Laurie's father does not react when Laurie tricks him and says "Gee, you're dumb" or calls him "y'old dust mop." When Laurie tells his father the "bad word" that Charles told the girl to say, his father reacts "respectfully." Although the mother might be busy with the baby, there is no evidence that that is the problem. Laurie's parents are intrigued and amused by Charles, and they are so caught up in his story that they do not stop to wonder why their son is focusing on him so intently.

Difficulty: *Challenging* **Objective:** *Essay*

14. Students should explain that Laurie's first day in kindergarten is marked by conflict with his teacher (he is fresh), the situation worsens (with Laurie hitting the teacher, throwing chalk, yelling, hitting a visitor, punching a classmate, and so on), improves briefly (with Laurie helping the teacher), and then worsens again (with Laurie saying a bad word and throwing chalk again). From the teacher's comments at the second PTA meeting (especially that he is "a fine little helper. With occasional lapses"), students may feel that the conflict has lessened somewhat but has not been resolved.

Difficulty: *Average* **Objective:** *Essay*

Oral Response

15. Oral responses should be clear, well organized, and well supported by appropriate examples from the selection.

Difficulty: *Average* **Objective:** *Oral Interpretation*

"Charles" by Shirley Jackson

Selection Test A, p. 160

Critical Reading

1. ANS: A	DIF: Easy	OBJ: Comprehension
2. ANS: C	DIF: Easy	OBJ: Interpretation
3. ANS: B	DIF: Easy	OBJ: Literary Analysis
4. ANS: B	DIF: Easy	OBJ: Reading
5. ANS: D	DIF: Easy	OBJ: Interpretation
6. ANS: C	DIF: Easy	OBJ: Interpretation
7. ANS: B	DIF: Easy	OBJ: Reading
8. ANS: C	DIF: Easy	OBJ: Comprehension
9. ANS: B	DIF: Easy	OBJ: Comprehension
10. ANS: D	DIF: Easy	OBJ: Reading
11. ANS: A	DIF: Easy	OBJ: Literary Analysis

Vocabulary and Grammar

12. ANS: D	DIF: Easy	OBJ: Vocabulary
13. ANS: A	DIF: Easy	OBJ: Vocabulary
14. ANS: C	DIF: Easy	OBJ: Grammar
15. ANS: C	DIF: Easy	OBJ: Grammar

Essay

16. Students should summarize Laurie's accounts of his new experiences at kindergarten, in which a boy named Charles misbehaves badly and is often punished by the teacher. His parents and the readers trust Laurie's statements. Students should then indicate what Laurie's mother learns when she meets with the teacher: There is no boy named Charles in the class. Laurie is the boy who was misbehaving.

    Difficulty: *Easy*

    Objective: *Essay*

17. Students should recognize that Laurie's mother will probably be shocked and upset by her discovery. Some students may predict that she will also be angry and will punish Laurie for his dishonesty as well as his other bad behavior. Other students may feel that the mother will feel very foolish and perhaps will even worry about her skills as a mother, since she did not recognize the truth about Laurie. Students should accurately cite story details in explaining their predictions.

    Difficulty: *Easy*

    Objective: *Essay*

18. Students might note that in his first day in kindergarten, Laurie has a conflict with his teacher (he is fresh). The situation gets worse (Laurie hits the teacher, throws chalk, yells, hits a visitor, punches a classmate, and so on). Things improve briefly (Laurie helps the teacher), and then get worse again (Laurie says a bad word and throws chalk again). From the teacher's comments at the second PTA meeting (especially that he is "a fine

little helper. With occasional lapses"), students may feel that the conflict has lessened a bit but has not been resolved.

Difficulty: *Average*

Objective: *Essay*

Selection Test B, p. 163

Critical Reading

1. ANS: B	DIF: Average	OBJ: Literary Analysis
2. ANS: A	DIF: Average	OBJ: Reading
3. ANS: A	DIF: Average	OBJ: Reading
4. ANS: B	DIF: Average	OBJ: Literary Analysis
5. ANS: D	DIF: Average	OBJ: Interpretation
6. ANS: D	DIF: Challenging	OBJ: Interpretation
7. ANS: B	DIF: Challenging	OBJ: Reading
8. ANS: C	DIF: Average	OBJ: Comprehension
9. ANS: D	DIF: Average	OBJ: Interpretation
10. ANS: A	DIF: Challenging	OBJ: Literary Analysis
11. ANS: C	DIF: Average	OBJ: Reading
12. ANS: D	DIF: Average	OBJ: Interpretation
13. ANS: C	DIF: Challenging	OBJ: Reading

Vocabulary and Grammar

14. ANS: D	DIF: Challenging	OBJ: Vocabulary
15. ANS: D	DIF: Average	OBJ: Vocabulary
16. ANS: C	DIF: Average	OBJ: Grammar
17. ANS: D	DIF: Average	OBJ: Grammar

Essay

18. Students should recognize that Laurie misbehaves in school and lies about it at home. Some are likely to feel that his misbehavior comes from being scared or upset by the big change created by starting school. Others may suggest that Laurie is an overactive child or that he has trouble socializing.

    Difficulty: *Average*

    Objective: *Essay*

19. Students should recognize that parents often fail to see negatives in beloved children. Students may mention that the mother is very attached to her son and thought him sweet until he went off to school. They may also suggest that Laurie's going to school was a new experience for the parents as well as for Laurie, and that before then they had no idea their son could behave as he does.

    Difficulty: *Average*

    Objective: *Essay*

20. Students should explain that Laurie's first day in kindergarten is marked by conflict with his teacher (he is fresh), the situation worsens (with Laurie hitting the teacher, throwing chalk, yelling, hitting a visitor, punching a

classmate, and so on), improves briefly (with Laurie help-ing the teacher), and then worsens again (with Laurie saying a bad word and throwing chalk again). From the teacher's comments at the second PTA meeting (espe-cially that he is "a fine little helper. With occasional lapses"), students may feel that the conflict has lessened somewhat but has not been resolved.

Difficulty: *Average*

Objective: *Essay*

"Thank You, M'am" by Langston Hughes

Vocabulary Warm-up Exercises, p. 167

A. 1. contact
2. blondes
3. frail
4. switched
5. cocoa
6. combined
7. release
8. permit

B. Sample Answers
1. The coach yells "go," *whereupon* the runners in a race charge out of the starting blocks.
2. In any beauty salon, you can find *brunettes* looking for lighter hair and *redheads* seeking curls.
3. I would say *good-night* to my best friend when she sleeps over at my house or right before getting off the phone late at night.
4. A cute but *devilish* puppy might jump on furniture and people, chew up things, and even make a puddle on the floor.
5. The strangest *pocketbook* I ever saw was made of clear plastic so that you could see everything inside.
6. I would always keep butter, cheese, and juice in an *icebox.*
7. A neat person would want a towel hung up properly on a rack, not *slung* over a chair.

Reading Warm-up A, p. 168

Sample Answers
1. cooking, cleaning, and managing helpers; When I was a babysitter, I used the *combined* skills of teaching and cooking.
2. Frail elderly people, traveling salesmen, workers from the town, Fair-skinned young blondes, dark-haired ladies; *Contact* means "communication or meeting."
3. *Frail blondes* might be tall, thin girls who have fair hair and look weak.
4. (televisions); Air conditioners could not be *switched* on to cool off the stuffy bedrooms.
5. hot drink; I like the creamy chocolate taste of *cocoa* when it has marshmallows on top.

6. (couples to hold hands); My parents will not *permit* me to go on dates alone; we have to go in groups.
7. (fingers entwined); *Release* means "let go" or "stop hold-ing something."

Reading Warm-up B, p. 169

Sample Answers
1. for ice to apply to their sore feet; Five things usually found in an *icebox* are milk, butter, cheese, lettuce, and ice cream.
2. The word *devilish* means that something is very bad, and shoes that hurt your feet are very bad indeed!
3. (to bed); After saying *good-night* to my family, I usually snuggle under my covers and read for about fifteen min-utes before turning off the light.
4. I finished my homework, *whereupon* I could talk to my friend on the phone.
5. (shoes); The best type of *pocketbook* is small and can be easily carried over your shoulder.
6. another pair; *Slung* means "hung or thrown loosely over something."
7. (on fashion show runways); I love my sister, who is a *brunette*, and my favorite *redhead* is the character Annie in the play about Little Orphan Annie.

Writing About the Big Question, p. 170

A. 1. violence
2. argument
3. compromise or negotiate, solution
4. viewpoint

B. Sample Answers
1. I trust my best friend completely. She has always been on my side and has never hurt me.
2. One solution would be to have a long talk with the person. Maybe we could work out some kind of com-promise that would help.

C. Sample Answer

The best way to earn trust is to consistently do what you say you'll do. One time, I earned the trust of a younger student I was tutoring. His previous tutor would often fail to show up for lessons. I was there every time, and he soon knew he could count on me.

Reading: Identify the Connections to Make Inferences, p. 171

Sample Answers
1. Mrs. Jones is a lot stronger than Roger thought.
2. Mrs. Jones will take Roger home and make him clean up.
3. Roger is a materialistic child who has been poorly disci-plined at home.
4. Treated with kindness, Roger begins to show signs of a conscience.

Literary Analysis: Theme, p. 172

Accept all reasonable details on word webs. For example, for Roger, students may say that he is poor, materialistic, initially thoughtless, and not well supervised or disciplined at home; for Mrs. Jones, that she is bossy, strong, poor but generous, lonely, and sympathetic to Roger's offense because of her values and her own past.

Sample Answers

1. crime, poverty, rehabilitating potential criminals, supervising teenagers, putting yourself in other people's shoes.
2. Instead of simply punishing youngsters when they start going wrong, we should treat them with understanding and try to show them the error of their ways. Those considering committing crimes should instead recognize that their targets are human beings and should give up the error of their ways.

Vocabulary Builder, p. 173

A. Sample Answers

1. Yes, they comb their hair in order to look <u>presentable</u>.
2. Yes, the frozen sheet of ice near the South Pole is a <u>barren</u> part of the world.
3. If you and your friends have e-mail, you can use it to stay in <u>contact</u> with friends who move away.
4. Weather that changed from cool to warm would prompt me to take off my jacket and wear it just <u>slung</u> over my shoulder.
5. If I <u>mistrusted</u> a strange dog, I would ask its owner before attempting to pet it.
6. A person with <u>frail</u> muscles could improve his or her strength through weight-lifting exercises.

B. 1. An ad might mislead a potential customer by falsely claiming that the product will make the user's hair smooth, shiny, and silky.
2. A politician might misrepresent himself or herself to voters by claiming to be in favor of an issue that he or she secretly opposes.
3. A beginner might misuse headphones by turning the volume up too high.

Enrichment: Inflation, p. 174

2. $1.89 price increase; 945% inflation.
3. $1.83 price increase; 704% inflation
4. $16,890 price increase; 647% inflation
5. $163,325 price increase; 1,289% inflation

Open-Book Test, p. 175

Short Answer

1. The woman is old (from the boy's perspective); more important, she is alone, and she has a large purse. He is probably sorry because he loses his balance, and she grabs hold of him.

   Difficulty: *Easy*   **Objective:** *Interpretation*

2. The statement indicates that Mrs. Jones is strong-minded. Based on her courage in fighting off an attacker and her boldness in lecturing him, readers can infer that she has inner strength and determination. Her use of her full name is further evidence of her determination.

   Difficulty: *Challenging*   **Objective:** *Reading*

3. When Mrs. Jones says "You thought I was going to say, *but I didn't snatch people's pocketbooks.* Well, I wasn't going to say that," she implies that, like Roger, she has wanted things she could not afford and has also committed crimes or at least acted in unethical ways.

   Difficulty: *Average*   **Objective:** *Interpretation*

4. *Mrs. Jones does not* . . . watch Roger or her purse.
   Roger does . . . sit where Mrs. Jones can see him.
   Roger does not . . . take money from the purse or run away.

   Students should note that Mrs. Jones is showing Roger that he can be trustworthy if he chooses to be, or they should note that Roger wants to be worthy of Mrs. Jones's trust.

   Difficulty: *Average*   **Objective:** *Reading*

5. Roger wants Mrs. Jones to trust him, and he wants to show her that she can. By sitting where she can see him—and far from her purse—he shows that she can trust him.

   Difficulty: *Challenging*   **Objective:** *Interpretation*

6. She means that shoes bought with stolen money ("come by devilish like that") will cause Roger to suffer from guilt ("will burn your feet"). Her words relate to the theme of honesty: She is encouraging Roger to be honest, just as they have been honest with each other.

   Difficulty: *Challenging*   **Objective:** *Literary Analysis*

7. The story says that younger people can learn from their elders if they are not preached at. Mrs. Jones knows that Roger will learn from her only if she shows that she understands his experience, trusts him, and treats him with kindness and charity. Roger's gratitude at the end shows that Mrs. Jones's approach has been successful.

   Difficulty: *Average*   **Objective:** *Literary Analysis*

8. The characters have physical contact when Mrs. Jones grabs Roger and "drags" him along with her. They have intellectual contact when they talk. There is emotional contact in that Mrs. Jones's words and example inspire Roger to prove himself trustworthy.

   Difficulty: *Average*   **Objective:** *Vocabulary*

9. Roger wants to say, "Thank you, m'am," but he is unable to say anything. From his silence, readers can infer that Roger is overwhelmed by Mrs. Jones's generosity and compassion.

   Difficulty: *Easy*   **Objective:** *Reading*

10. The story explores the importance of trust, especially the desire to be found trustworthy. It is Mrs. Jones's trust in Roger—by feeding him and giving him money—that encourages him to trust her and want her to trust him.

   Difficulty: *Easy*   **Objective:** *Literary Analysis*

Essay

11. Students should understand that when Roger asks about going to the store, he is inviting Mrs. Jones to trust him—to give him money and expect him to return. It is an important question because it indicates a change in Roger: It shows that Roger is thinking carefully about what Mrs. Jones has said and that he wants to be trusted.

    Difficulty: *Easy* **Objective:** *Essay*

12. Students should discuss any two of the following points: Mrs. Jones's having done dishonest things when she was young helps her understand that young people can make mistakes and learn from them; her mention of God suggests that her faith helps her forgive people who have wronged her; her work in a beauty parlor may have shown her that people are not always what they appear to be. Students may conclude that those experiences helped Mrs. Jones look past Roger's scruffy appearance and even his behavior and see a boy in need of her care.

    Difficulty: *Average* **Objective:** *Essay*

13. Students should recognize that the title effectively underscores the gift of kindness and goodwill that Mrs. Jones gives the troubled boy. Students should also point out that the title is unusual because it is a statement that is never actually uttered in the story (although it is intended). They may argue that it makes a good title for the reason that it says for Roger the words that he has trouble saying.

    Difficulty: *Challenging* **Objective:** *Essay*

14. Students should explain that the immediate conflict, between Roger and Mrs. Jones, has been resolved: She lets him leave freely, and he is grateful to her, not resentful. It remains to be seen, however, whether Roger will continue to prove himself trustworthy. He seems to be genuinely moved by Mrs. Jones's kindness and wisdom, but he may disregard the entire experience if he wants something badly enough to consider stealing it.

    Difficulty: *Average* **Objective:** *Essay*

Oral Response

15. Oral responses should be clear, well organized, and well supported by appropriate examples from the selection.

    Difficulty: *Average* **Objective:** *Oral Interpretation*

Selection Test A, p. 178
Critical Reading

1. ANS: C   DIF: Easy   OBJ: Comprehension
2. ANS: C   DIF: Easy   OBJ: Reading
3. ANS: B   DIF: Easy   OBJ: Reading
4. ANS: D   DIF: Easy   OBJ: Reading
5. ANS: A   DIF: Easy   OBJ: Comprehension
6. ANS: D   DIF: Easy   OBJ: Interpretation
7. ANS: C   DIF: Easy   OBJ: Comprehension
8. ANS: C   DIF: Easy   OBJ: Interpretation

9. ANS: A   DIF: Easy   OBJ: Literary Analysis
10. ANS: B   DIF: Easy   OBJ: Literary Analysis

Vocabulary and Grammar

11. ANS: B   DIF: Easy   OBJ: Vocabulary
12. ANS: D   DIF: Easy   OBJ: Vocabulary
13. ANS: B   DIF: Easy   OBJ: Grammar

Essay

14. Students should recognize that Roger is neglected at home, wants more material possessions, and is at first somewhat unable to distinguish right from wrong. Among the evidence they should cite are his dirty face, his remarks about his home life, and his readiness to steal, not for a necessity but for cool shoes. Some students may point out that Roger does seem to have a conscience once Mrs. Jones touches him; they may say that he is a changed person who will heed her advice. Others may feel that the changes in Roger will not be long lasting once he leaves Mrs. Jones's company.

    Difficulty: *Easy*
    Objective: *Essay*

15. Some students will think that letting someone get away with a crime is never justified and that Mrs. Jones should call the police and turn in Roger immediately. Others may argue that Mrs. Jones's decision is the right one: Roger is still young and able to change; and by showing him understanding and compassion, Mrs. Jones may help break the mold of mistrust and neglect that has led him to street crime in the first place. Mrs. Jones helps him understand the power of trust and love.

    Difficulty: *Easy*
    Objective: *Essay*

16. Students might note that the conflict between Roger and Mrs. Jones has been resolved: She lets him leave freely, and he is grateful to her, not resentful. We do not know however, whether Roger will remain worthy of trust. He seems to be genuinely moved by Mrs. Jones's kindness and wisdom, but he may forget the experience if he wants something badly enough to consider stealing it.

    Difficulty: *Average*
    Objective: *Essay*

Selection Test B, p. 181
Critical Reading

1. ANS: C   DIF: Average   OBJ: Comprehension
2. ANS: C   DIF: Average   OBJ: Interpretation
3. ANS: A   DIF: Average   OBJ: Comprehension
4. ANS: B   DIF: Average   OBJ: Reading
5. ANS: D   DIF: Average   OBJ: Comprehension
6. ANS: C   DIF: Challenging   OBJ: Reading
7. ANS: D   DIF: Average   OBJ: Comprehension
8. ANS: C   DIF: Average   OBJ: Reading

9. ANS: C	DIF: Challenging	OBJ: Literary Analysis
10. ANS: C	DIF: Average	OBJ: Interpretation
11. ANS: D	DIF: Average	OBJ: Interpretation
12. ANS: A	DIF: Challenging	OBJ: Reading
13. ANS: B	DIF: Average	OBJ: Literary Analysis

Vocabulary and Grammar

14. ANS: B	DIF: Average	OBJ: Vocabulary
15. ANS: D	DIF: Average	OBJ: Vocabulary
16. ANS: B	DIF: Challenging	OBJ: Grammar
17. ANS: D	DIF: Average	OBJ: Grammar

Essay

18. Students should recognize that Mrs. Jones, after initial anger, shows herself as a kind, confident, somewhat bossy person who wants to do good by Roger and help him mend his ways. They may feel that this desire is part of her religious faith, evidenced by her remarks about the devil and about God, or they may explain the sympathy she feels for Roger is related to her own bad behavior in her younger days. Some students also may feel that Mrs. Jones is lonely and therefore more tolerant of Roger in spite of his bad behavior. Students should cite Mrs. Jones's own remarks and behavior to support their suppositions about her.

Difficulty: *Average*

Objective: *Essay*

19. Students should recognize that the title underscores the gift of kindness and goodwill that Mrs. Jones gives the troubled boy, Roger. They may argue that Roger's thinking of the phrase is significant even if he cannot give voice to it. Students should cite details from the story to support their ideas.

Difficulty: *Average*

Objective: *Essay*

20. Students should explain that the immediate conflict, between Roger and Mrs. Jones, has been resolved: She lets him leave freely, and he is grateful to her, not resentful. It remains to be seen, however, whether Roger will continue to prove himself trustworthy. He seems to be genuinely moved by Mrs. Jones's kindness and wisdom, but he may forget the experience if he wants something badly enough to consider stealing it.

Difficulty: *Average*

Objective: *Essay*

"The Story-Teller" by Saki

Vocabulary Warm-up Exercises, p. 185

A. 1. conduct
2. unspeakable
3. horribly
4. utterly
5. retort

6. promptly
7. momentarily
8. approval

B. Sample Answers
1. No, a person who seeks perfection would probably want to hear that his work is better than *satisfactory*.
2. A shy person would find it hard to speak to a new student, much less *assail* that person with questions.
3. Something *inevitable* is likely to happen.
4. An *extraordinarily* large house cat would weigh more than twenty pounds and be the size of a spaniel.
5. Because early peoples' lives often revolved around the ability to make and keep a fire, having a matchbook would be quite a *novelty* that would change their lives.
6. Since an alarm is supposed to warn you or wake you, it certainly must be *audible*.
7. Usually, *repetition* through practice is the only way to learn a new skill.
8. Since a flowing stream always has water moving through it, its sound is *persistent*.

Reading Warm-up A, p. 186

Sample Answers

1. watching a best friend lie motionless in bed, hardly seeming to be alive; I think it is *horribly* sad to see young children who are very hungry.
2. (coma); *Unspeakable* means "so bad that you can't describe it."
3. Parents are very concerned about their children's *conduct* and look on them with *approval* when they behave well in public places.
4. to see my friend; *Utterly* means "completely."
5. (choked up); *Momentarily* means "for a short time."
6. I looked more closely at Sam's face; The author might have *promptly* moved to sit beside Sam's bed.
7. (some story detail I had managed to mess up); If Sam could give a *retort*, it would mean that he had come out of the coma and could talk.

Reading Warm-up B, p. 187

Sample Answers

1. stories on all kinds of topics; *Audible* means "loud enough to be heard."
2. (Feelings of being connected to history, people, and culture); My feelings *assail* me when I visit my grandfather in the nursing home.
3. A person telling an *extraordinarily* well-told story would use lots of expression in his or her voice and might include sound effects and different voices for the characters.
4. *Repetition* of stories, or telling them over and over, is what will help people remember the stories so that they can pass them on.
5. its success over the years and the increased interest in storytelling worldwide; *Novelty* means "something new and different."

6. When you are *persistent* about something, you say it often and firmly so that people know it's important.

7. I know that it's *inevitable* that my younger brother will lose his baby teeth.

8. For me, a *satisfactory* relationship involves respect for one another, trust, and the ability to laugh together.

Writing About the Big Question, p. 188

A. 1. victorious
2. reaction
3. argument, violence
4. interact

B. Sample Answers

1. In "Jack and the Beanstalk," one conflict is between a boy and his mother. She is angry because he has traded their cow for a few beans.

2. A parent might have the viewpoint that violence on TV is very harmful to a child's development. It frightens children and gives them a sense of insecurity.

C. Sample Answer

The endings of fairy tales are usually very predictable. The conflict in the story usually involves a powerful evil-doer who does terrible things to the hero or heroine. The poor victim endures the abuse for a while, but then fights back somehow. The hero or heroine always wins and gets amazing rewards.

Reading: Identify Connections to Make Inferences, p. 189

Sample Answers

1. The aunt wants to distract him and make him stop misbehaving.
2. Cyril is an active, curious, mischievous boy with a vivid imagination.
3. The bachelor is annoyed and wants the aunt to get the children to behave, otherwise he may call the train staff and complain to them.
4. The children are delighted by a story that strays from the usual wholesome themes and seems a little outrageous.

Literary Analysis: Theme, p. 190

Accept all reasonable details on word webs. For example, for Bertha, students may say that she is polite, punctual, obedient, and horribly good. For the Prince's park, they may say it is filled with pigs, has no sheep, has no flowers, has ponds with fish, has trees with parrots, and is delightful.

Sample Answers

1. He wants them to think about good behavior and whether it is possible to be too good.
2. Being too good sometimes causes a person's downfall. Being perfect sometimes causes resentment that can lead to one's downfall. Being too wholesome can be very boring.

Vocabulary Builder, p. 191

A. Sample Answers

1. You should speak about it with <u>conviction</u>.

2. If I am <u>persistent</u> in saving half my allowance for a year, the result will be that I'll have a few hundred dollars.

3. If my young cousin were to <u>assail</u> me with story demands, I'd prepare myself by reading lots of stories that I could retell.

4. A school event that is <u>inevitable</u> is a vocabulary test on Friday.

5. One accomplishment that makes me feel <u>immensely</u> proud is that I painted my room by myself.

6. I <u>suppressed</u> my laughter during a wedding ceremony when the groom's expression struck me as very humorous.

B. 1. These plants are <u>perennials</u>, so they will bloom again year after year.

2. The color red is easily <u>perceptible</u> against a yellow background.

3. Charlotte's <u>perfect</u> performance had no mistakes.

Enrichment: Parks, p. 192

Students' descriptions should include details about the landscape, natural inhabitants, and facilities as well as the students' activities and feelings.

"Thank You, M'am" by Langston Hughes
"The Story-Teller" by Saki

Integrated Language Skills: Grammar, p. 193
The Perfect Tenses and the Subjunctive Mood

A. 1. has collected
2. had assigned
3. will have reviewed
4. were

B. Students should write one sentence in the past perfect tense, one in the present perfect tense, one in the future perfect tense, and one using the subjunctive mood. They should show some understanding of when each is used. They should underline each verb and correctly identify the tense or mood.

Open-Book Test, p. 196
Short Answer

1. Most of the aunt's remarks begin with "Don't"; most of the children's remarks begin with "Why?" Clearly, the children are challenging their aunt. The comparison of the children to a persistent housefly also suggests a lack of control.

Difficulty: *Easy*   **Objective:** *Reading*

2. The children may be persistent because they sincerely want to know about the countryside, or they may be

persistent because they know that their behavior bothers their aunt.

Difficulty: *Average*   **Objective:** *Vocabulary*

3. Their boredom and discomfort (in the "sultry" railroad car) may be so great that they can make themselves feel better only by misbehaving. Students might also point out that the children are traveling in a group of four and the bachelor is traveling alone; they may feel emboldened because they are in the majority.

Difficulty: *Easy*   **Objective:** *Interpretation*

4. The girl seems to think that the theme of her aunt's story is that misbehaving children will not be rescued when they are in danger. Her question is based on the conclusion: The good girl was rescued by people "who admired her moral character."

Difficulty: *Average*   **Objective:** *Literary Analysis*

5. The children understand that Bertha is so good that people find her a little awful. The children are enthusiastic because the description reflects the way things are in real life.

Difficulty: *Average*   **Objective:** *Interpretation*

6. *The bachelor observes:* The children are bored by their aunt's story; *The bachelor thinks or knows:* The aunt is a poor story-teller.
   The bachelor observes: The children are fascinated by his story. *The bachelor thinks or knows:* Children enjoy stories that are a little twisted.
   The bachelor is not comfortable around children, but he understands them.

Difficulty: *Average*   **Objective:** *Reading*

7. Readers might infer that the children are naturally inquisitive or that they are testing to see how the bachelor will respond to their pestering. The bachelor responds quickly and patiently, offering new details that hold the children's interest. Readers can infer that he is imaginative and better than the aunt at interacting with children.

Difficulty: *Challenging*   **Objective:** *Reading*

8. Based on the outcome of the story—that "horribly good" Bertha is eaten by a wolf—it would seem that one theme is that good behavior is not always rewarded or that it is fun to make fun of behavior that is "too" good.

Difficulty: *Easy*   **Objective:** *Literary Analysis*

9. Both stories are about little girls who are exceptionally well behaved and whose lives are threatened by an animal. The children prefer the bachelor's story because it twists their expectations: No one rescues "horribly good" Bertha, and she dies a gruesome death.

Difficulty: *Challenging*   **Objective:** *Interpretation*

10. If "The Story-Teller" had ended before the bachelor spoke up, the theme probably would have been that some children are uncontrollable or that some adults know little about taking care of children. The bachelor's story shows that children can be controlled by adults who know how to appeal to their imagination and sense of fun (and occasional rebelliousness).

Difficulty: *Challenging*   **Objective:** *Literary Analysis*

Essay

11. Students should recognize that the aunt's judgment shows that she disapproves of making fun of moral behavior. Students may point out that most of the aunt's remarks at the beginning of the story began with "Don't," an indication that she has a strong sense of what she sees as right and wrong and that she expects to be obeyed. Her "deplorably uninteresting story" about a girl whose "moral character" saves her life also reflects her devotion to good behavior.

Difficulty: *Easy*   **Objective:** *Essay*

12. Students should recognize the importance of arousing the listener's curiosity. They might also point to the bachelor's ability to gauge his listeners' interest, his ability to adapt the story to hold their interest, and his ability to improvise in response to their questions. Students should support their definition and explanation with examples from the bachelor's story and the children's reaction to it (for example, their enthusiasm for the description of Bertha as "horribly good" and their approval of the prince's choice of pigs instead of flowers).

Difficulty: *Average*   **Objective:** *Essay*

13. The message of the aunt's story is that good behavior will be rewarded, whereas the message of the bachelor's story is just the opposite. The message of the overall story is that acceptable behavior can be encouraged through an understanding of people's needs and an appeal to their imagination. The theme of the aunt's story was shown by the older girl to be flawed, and the theme of the bachelor's story amuses the children but is clearly not intended to be taken seriously. Only the theme of the overall story is a broad, useful message.

Difficulty: *Challenging*   **Objective:** *Essay*

14. Students should recognize that the bachelor succeeds where the aunt does not because he understands children's interests, knows how to appeal to their curiosity, and is willing to have fun with them. Students may suggest that even if the aunt recognizes his skill, she is unlikely to follow his example because she sees the children only as beings needing control and because she disapproves of anything that she considers "improper."

Difficulty: *Average*   **Objective:** *Essay*

Oral Response

15. Students should give oral explanations in response to the questions they choose or that are assigned to them.

Difficulty: *Average*   **Objective:** *Oral Interpretation*

"The Story-Teller" by Saki

Selection Test A, p. 199

Critical Reading

1. **ANS:** A	**DIF:** Easy	**OBJ:** Comprehension
2. **ANS:** D	**DIF:** Easy	**OBJ:** Comprehension
3. **ANS:** D	**DIF:** Easy	**OBJ:** Reading

4. ANS: D	DIF: Easy	OBJ: Interpretation
5. ANS: C	DIF: Easy	OBJ: Reading
6. ANS: C	DIF: Easy	OBJ: Interpretation
7. ANS: A	DIF: Easy	OBJ: Interpretation
8. ANS: D	DIF: Easy	OBJ: Interpretation
9. ANS: B	DIF: Easy	OBJ: Comprehension
10. ANS: C	DIF: Easy	OBJ: Literary Analysis
11. ANS: D	DIF: Easy	OBJ: Interpretation
12. ANS: C	DIF: Easy	OBJ: Literary Analysis

Vocabulary and Grammar

13. ANS: B	DIF: Easy	OBJ: Vocabulary
14. ANS: B	DIF: Easy	OBJ: Vocabulary
15. ANS: B	DIF: Easy	OBJ: Grammar

Essay

16. Students should recognize that the children are bright and curious but that they also behave restlessly in the railway carriage. Students should explain that the hot carriage and the long way until the next stop may contribute to the children's restless behavior.

Difficulty: *Easy*

Objective: *Essay*

17. Students should recognize that the children like the imaginative details in the bachelor's story and also the fact that it is a little improper. They should recognize that the children find the aunt's story boring because they have heard so many stories like it before. They find it stupid because it does not reflect the behavior of real children.

Difficulty: *Easy*

Objective: *Essay*

18. Students should recognize that the bachelor succeeds where the aunt does not because he understands children's interests and is willing to have fun with them. Students may suggest that even if the aunt recognizes his skill, she is unlikely to follow his example because she is interested only in controlling the children and disapproves of anything that she considers "improper."

Difficulty: *Average*

Objective: *Essay*

Selection Test B, p. 202

Critical Reading

1. ANS: A	DIF: Average	OBJ: Comprehension
2. ANS: D	DIF: Average	OBJ: Comprehension
3. ANS: D	DIF: Average	OBJ: Reading
4. ANS: A	DIF: Average	OBJ: Reading
5. ANS: C	DIF: Challenging	OBJ: Reading
6. ANS: D	DIF: Average	OBJ: Interpretation

7. ANS: C	DIF: Average	OBJ: Interpretation
8. ANS: C	DIF: Average	OBJ: Reading
9. ANS: D	DIF: Average	OBJ: Reading
10. ANS: D	DIF: Average	OBJ: Literary Analysis
11. ANS: A	DIF: Challenging	OBJ: Literary Analysis
12. ANS: C	DIF: Average	OBJ: Literary Analysis
13. ANS: B	DIF: Average	OBJ: Interpretation

Vocabulary and Grammar

14. ANS: C	DIF: Average	OBJ: Vocabulary
15. ANS: B	DIF: Average	OBJ: Vocabulary
16. ANS: B	DIF: Average	OBJ: Grammar
17. ANS: D	DIF: Average	OBJ: Grammar

Essay

18. Students may state a theme that focuses on the best way to deal with children, on the value of imagination and curiosity, or on the tendency of children or people in general to grow restless and rebellious when given too much worthy advice. They should support the theme with details from the story.

Difficulty: *Average*

Objective: *Essay*

19. Students should recognize the role of curiosity and imagination in good storytelling. They should cite examples from the bachelor's story and the children's reaction to it to support their definition and explanation.

Difficulty: *Average*

Objective: *Essay*

20. Students should recognize that the bachelor succeeds where the aunt does not because he understands children's interests, knows how to appeal to their curiosity, and is willing to have fun with them. Students may suggest that even if the aunt recognizes his skill, she is unlikely to follow his example because she sees the children only as beings needing control and disapproves of anything that she considers "improper."

Difficulty: *Average*

Objective: *Essay*

"The White Umbrella" by Gish Jen
"The Medicine Bag"
by Virginia Driving Hawk Sneve

Vocabulary Warm-up Exercises, p. 206

A. 1. assigned
2. filthy
3. despair
4. fatigue
5. reluctantly

6. consideration
7. sacred
8. wrung

B. **Sample Answers**

1. Because she wanted a fancy look, she chose a *fringed* scarf.

2. Since it was beautiful weather outside, Franco took the *convertible* and put down the top.

3. Being able to travel to new places and meet exciting people are two *glamorous* things about some jobs.

4. Young people need *guidance* from their elders.

5. I could tell from her red face that she felt a great deal of *embarrassment*.

6. The tall trees made the long brick driveway look *stately*.

7. Many famous scientists had refused to approve the report because of its *unreliable* nature.

8. Her face was *radiant* as she handed the new mother a rose.

Reading Warm-up A, p. 207

Sample Answers

1. jobs; I have been *assigned* the chore of loading and unloading the dishwasher.

2. (losing their land and way of life); *Despair* means "a feeling of no hope."

3. Officials had little regard for the Plains Indians' needs. If the officials had had *consideration* for the Plains Indians, they might not have forced them onto reservations.

4. disease; *Fatigue* can cause your body to ache and react slowly, and can make your mind less quick as well.

5. (the Great Spirit); *Sacred* means "holy, or deserving great respect."

6. (dust storms); *Filthy* means "very dirty."

7. gave up their weapons; The Plains Indians would have *reluctantly* agreed to live in the small spaces of reservations.

8. Wet clothes can be *wrung*.

Reading Warm-up B, p. 208

Sample Answers

1. admiration; My *embarrassment* at dropping the ball was overcome by my little brother's *admiration* of my skills.

2. (complete with band music, honored speakers, and plenty of pomp); When something is *stately*, it is very impressive because of its size or because of the way it's done.

3. The girl's *glamorous* outfit might have been a simple black dress worn with high heels and pearls.

4. (shawl); I once saw a beautiful leather vest, *fringed* all along the shoulders.

5. I think Robin's father would drive a bright red *convertible* with only two seats.

6. picking Robin up, attending important events, or remembering her birthday; I think the worst thing that Robin's father does to be *unreliable* is forgetting her birthday, since that is a big event that only happens once a year.

7. My friend looked *radiant* the day she won the science award.

8. Eighth graders like to receive *guidance* from their parents on important things, like going to college and not using drugs, rather than being talked to daily about every little thing.

Writing About the Big Question, p. 209

A. 1. irritate
2. reaction
3. mislead
4. violence

B. **Sample Answers**

1. One time, I had to negotiate with my brother about baby-sitting duties.

   Another time, I had to negotiate with my mom about summer vacation activities.

2. With my mom, the conflict was that I wanted to learn how to water-ski. She was opposed to it because of the possibility of injury.

C. **Sample Answers**

   People are most likely to react with embarrassment when they feel that they have done something stupid. One way of resolving feeling embarrassed is to realize that people do stupid things all of the time.

Literary Analysis: Comparing Symbols, p. 210

Sample Answers

1. The narrator first sees the umbrella while waiting for Eugenie to finish a piano lesson.

2. The narrator thinks the umbrella is beautiful, and she longs to have one like it. She wants to ask for one for Christmas, but she believes her mother will say no.

3. The umbrella comes to represent the narrator's desire to be a part of American culture as well as her embarrassment over her mother's working.

4. The bag belongs to Martin's grandfather, to whom it had been passed by earlier generations. Martin is embarrassed because his grandfather does not look like the Indians in the movies; he is poor and scraggly.

5. At first, Martin does not want to wear the medicine bag. He describes it as a "dirty leather pouch" and fears his friends will make fun of him if he wears it. He is embarrassed by it.

6. In the story, the medicine bag represents the family's Sioux heritage. The boy's initial embarrassment over his grandfather parallels the boy's initial embarrassment over the medicine bag. Later, the boy's pride in his grandfather parallels his pride in receiving the medicine bag.

Vocabulary Builder, p. 211

A. Sample Answers

1. Lying would hurt your <u>credibility</u>.
2. At a funeral, there is often a <u>procession</u> of cars going to the cemetery.
3. I could make the <u>revelation</u> that I am a straight-A student.
4. I own an <u>authentic</u> diamond ring.
5. It used to be <u>unseemly</u> for girls to show their ankles.
6. You should be <u>discreet</u> when someone trusts you with a secret.

B. 1. B; 2. A; 3. D; 4. B

Open-Book Test, p. 213

Short Answer

1. It reveals that she is a bad driver.
   Difficulty: *Easy* **Objective:** *Interpretation*

2. She is afraid that Miss Crosman will realize that their mother is late because she is working and will think poorly of the family because the mother must help support them.
   Difficulty: *Challenging* **Objective:** *Interpretation*

3. Students should recognize that Miss Crosman gives the narrator the umbrella because she feels motherly toward her, because she feels sorry for her, and/or because she wants to indulge her with a gift.
   Difficulty: *Average* **Objective:** *Literary Analysis*

4. The narrator fears that his friends will laugh at the picture because Grandpa does not look like the Indians they see on television.
   Difficulty: *Easy* **Objective:** *Interpretation*

5. It is a bad thing; that is, it is inappropriate.
   Difficulty: *Average* **Objective:** *Vocabulary*

6. Martin learns that he had misjudged his friends.
   Difficulty: *Average* **Objective:** *Interpretation*

7. Sample answer:
   White umbrella: the narrator's desire for a typical American life; *Medicine bag:* the narrator's new appreciation for his heritage.
   These symbols are similar in that they represent something the narrator values.
   Difficulty: *Average* **Objective:** *Literary Analysis*

8. Both adults symbolize the narrators' culture of origin and his or her embarrassment at being different from neighbors, friends, and classmates.
   Difficulty: *Easy* **Objective:** *Literary Analysis*

9. Both actions symbolize the narrator's acceptance of his or her identity, his or her elders, and his or her cultural heritage.
   Difficulty: *Challenging* **Objective:** *Literary Analysis*

10. The narrator of "The White Umbrella" realizes that her mother might die; Martin understands that Grandpa will die very soon.
    Difficulty: *Challenging* **Objective:** *Literary Analysis*

Essay

11. Students writing about "The White Umbrella" should note that the narrator feels embarrassed because her mother has taken a job outside the home. Evidence includes her not asking her mother about the job, her envy of Eugenie Roberts's mother, and her not telling Miss Crosman why her mother is late. Students writing about "The Medicine Bag" should respond that Martin is embarrassed by Grandpa's appearance. Evidence includes his not showing Grandpa's photograph to his friends and his not wanting his friends to meet Grandpa.
    Difficulty: *Easy* **Objective:** *Essay*

12. The narrator of "The White Umbrella" feels embarrassed by her mother; the narrator of "The Medicine Bag" feels embarrassed by Grandpa. The narrator of "The White Umbrella" wishes her mother were more typically American; Martin wishes Grandpa were more stereotypically Indian. The narrator of "The White Umbrella" wants the white umbrella because for her it symbolizes American culture; Martin does not want the medicine bag because for him it symbolizes the unpleasant aspects of American Indian culture. In the end, both characters embrace their cultural heritage, one by throwing away the symbol of American culture and the other by accepting the symbol of Indian culture. Students might also note that the narrators' attitudes toward the central symbols change when they come to see their relatives as human beings rather than objects that they are embarrassed by.
    Difficulty: *Average* **Objective:** *Essay*

13. Students should identify the central symbols as the white umbrella and the medicine bag and should offer valid explanations of each symbol's meaning and the way in which each narrator's attitude toward the symbol changes over the course of the story. Students should also identify secondarily symbolic objects or actions—for example, the convertible, Miss Crosman's blanket, or the narrator's hiding of the umbrella in "The White Umbrella" and Grandpa's journey, the narrator's dream, and the narrator's gathering of the sacred sage in "The Medicine Bag."
    Difficulty: *Challenging* **Objective:** *Essay*

14. Students are likely to argue that the conflicts are resolved. Some students may respond that although the narrators have come to a new appreciation of their heritage, there are likely to be moments in the future when they will struggle with the competing needs to both fit in and embrace their cultural identity.
    Difficulty: *Average* **Objective:** *Essay*

Oral Response

15. Oral responses should be clear, well organized, and well supported by appropriate examples from the stories.
    Difficulty: *Average* **Objective:** *Oral Interpretation*

Selection Test A, p. 216

Critical Reading

1. ANS: C   DIF: Easy   OBJ: Interpretation
2. ANS: A   DIF: Easy   OBJ: Literary Analysis
3. ANS: A   DIF: Easy   OBJ: Literary Analysis
4. ANS: B   DIF: Easy   OBJ: Comprehension
5. ANS: A   DIF: Easy   OBJ: Comprehension
6. ANS: C   DIF: Easy   OBJ: Interpretation
7. ANS: B   DIF: Easy   OBJ: Comprehension
8. ANS: A   DIF: Easy   OBJ: Interpretation
9. ANS: D   DIF: Easy   OBJ: Literary Analysis
10. ANS: D   DIF: Easy   OBJ: Literary Analysis

Vocabulary

11. ANS: C   DIF: Easy   OBJ: Vocabulary
12. ANS: A   DIF: Easy   OBJ: Vocabulary

Essay

13. The narrator of "The White Umbrella" is at first ashamed of her mother and her Chinese heritage. Then, she realizes how attached she is to her mother and feels guilty for her earlier feelings. At the beginning of "The Medicine Bag," Martin is proud of his grandfather but at the same time embarrassed by him. Later, he feels proud of his grandfather. Each narrator develops a greater appreciation of the person who embarrassed her or him.

    Difficulty: *Easy*
    Objective: *Essay*

14. The symbolic item in "The White Umbrella" is the white umbrella. The narrator desperately wants the umbrella because it represents American culture and would make her similar to American girls. At the end, the narrator throws away the umbrella because it comes to represent the embarrassment she felt about her mother and the guilt she felt for saying she wished Miss Crosman were her mother. The symbolic item in "The Medicine Bag" is the medicine bag. At first, Martin feels ashamed that he will have to wear the medicine bag and plans to accept it only because he feels he must. The medicine bag represents Martin's grandfather, and Martin is embarrassed by Grandpa and earlier generations. So, by extension, Martin is embarrassed about the medicine bag. Martin's feelings change when his grandfather impresses Martin's friends and when Martin learns more about his family heritage from his grandfather. The bag changes from an embarrassment to something Martin is proud of. The bag comes to represent Martin's grandfather and his heritage.

    Difficulty: *Easy*
    Objective: *Essay*

15. Students are likely to argue that the conflicts are resolved. Some students may respond that although the

narrators have realized the value of their heritage, there are likely to be moments in the future when they will still have to work out the best way to both fit in and embrace their cultural identity.

Difficulty: *Average*

Objective: *Essay*

Selection Test B, p. 219

Critical Reading

1. ANS: B   DIF: Average   OBJ: Comprehension
2. ANS: D   DIF: Challenging   OBJ: Interpretation
3. ANS: B   DIF: Average   OBJ: Interpretation
4. ANS: D   DIF: Average   OBJ: Literary Analysis
5. ANS: B   DIF: Average   OBJ: Comprehension
6. ANS: C   DIF: Average   OBJ: Interpretation
7. ANS: B   DIF: Average   OBJ: Comprehension
8. ANS: D   DIF: Challenging   OBJ: Literary Analysis
9. ANS: B   DIF: Average   OBJ: Literary Analysis
10. ANS: B   DIF: Average   OBJ: Literary Analysis
11. ANS: C   DIF: Average   OBJ: Literary Analysis
12. ANS: D   DIF: Challenging   OBJ: Literary Analysis
13. ANS: A   DIF: Challenging   OBJ: Literary Analysis

Vocabulary

14. ANS: A   DIF: Average   OBJ: Vocabulary
15. ANS: C   DIF: Average   OBJ: Vocabulary
16. ANS: B   DIF: Average   OBJ: Vocabulary
17. ANS: D   DIF: Average   OBJ: Vocabulary

Essay

18. The narrator of "The White Umbrella" at first desperately wants the umbrella because it represents American culture and would make her similar to the American girls. Martin in "The Medicine Bag" at first feels ashamed to wear the medicine bag because it represents his grandfather, who embarrasses him. Both symbols have a cultural meaning—the white umbrella represents the American culture that the narrator wants to be a part of, and the medicine bag represents the Sioux culture that Martin has conflicting feelings about. At the end of "The White Umbrella," the narrator throws away the umbrella because it comes to represent the embarrassment she felt about her mother and the guilty feelings her thoughts caused. In "The Medicine Bag," the bag changes from being an embarrassment to being an object of pride.

    Difficulty: *Average*
    Objective: *Essay*

19. The narrator of "The White Umbrella" feels both ashamed of her mother and her Chinese heritage and guilty for

being ashamed. Her feelings are what cause the umbrella to become so important to her. To her, the umbrella would make her similar to American girls. You can infer that the narrator is very insecure and concerned about what others think of her and her family. Her feelings are resolved when she feels so guilty about being embarrassed of her mother and fears that her mother has died. At that point, she throws away the umbrella. Martin is at once proud of Grandpa and terribly embarrassed by him in "The Medicine Bag." Martin is mostly sensitive and kind, and he enjoys his visits to Grandpa, but he is also highly sensitive to the opinions of his peers and afraid that his friends will find Grandpa ridiculous. Only when Martin comes to see that his friends respect Grandpa and learns more about the medicine bag is he ready to accept it without reservation.

Difficulty: *Average*

Objective: *Essay*

20. Students are likely to argue that the conflicts are resolved. Some students may respond that although the narrators have come to a new appreciation of their heritage, there are likely to be moments in the future when they will struggle with the competing needs to both fit in and embrace their cultural identity.

Difficulty: *Average*

Objective: *Essay*

Writing Workshop

Short Story: Integrated Grammar Skills, p. 223

A. 1. act; 2. goes; 3. is awarded; 4. wear

B. 1. My favorite artist does vivid oil paintings.
2. Kayla and Nichole prefer watercolors.
3. When I grow up, I want to study to be an architect.
4. Here are three good paintings by Picasso.

Vocabulary Workshop—1, p. 224

Sample Answers

1. progress
2. subscribe
3. traction
4. subscript
5. digress
6. portfolio
7. transcend
8. transport

Vocabulary Workshop—2, p. 225

1. D
2. B
3. C
4. A

I am most like the bibliophile because I read every chance I get.

Benchmark Test 4, p. 227

MULTIPLE CHOICE

1. ANS: A
2. ANS: B
3. ANS: A
4. ANS: C
5. ANS: D
6. ANS: A
7. ANS: C
8. ANS: D
9. ANS: A
10. ANS: B
11. ANS: D
12. ANS: B
13. ANS: C
14. ANS: D
15. ANS: D
16. ANS: D
17. ANS: A
18. ANS: B
19. ANS: C
20. ANS: D
21. ANS: A
22. ANS: B
23. ANS: C
24. ANS: C
25. ANS: A
26. ANS: B
27. ANS: D
28. ANS: A
29. ANS: D
30. ANS: B
31. ANS: A
32. ANS: D

WRITING

33. Students' dialogues should use words and behavior that seem natural and realistic. They should include details from which a reader can infer the characters' unspoken feelings about the subject of the conversation or about each other. Students should present their dialogues in correct format.

34. Students should identify the work under consideration and clearly state the theme or life lesson that they drew from the work. They should then explain how the theme or lesson applies to one or more real-life situations drawn from their own experience.

35. Students should state the theme they wish to convey. They should also indicate the characters in their story, the setting in which the story unfolds, the plot events centering around a conflict that a main character faces, and the outcome of that conflict. They may also include dialogue and thoughts of particular characters.

Vocabulary in Context 2, p. 232

MULTIPLE CHOICE

1. ANS: C
2. ANS: A
3. ANS: B
4. ANS: D
5. ANS: B
6. ANS: B
7. ANS: D
8. ANS: B
9. ANS: C
10. ANS: A
11. ANS: D
12. ANS: D
13. ANS: A
14. ANS: B
15. ANS: C
16. ANS: D
17. ANS: A
18. ANS: D
19. ANS: C
20. ANS: B